MATRIARCH II

Journey to Purpose

A Novel

MATRIARCH II

Journey to Purpose

A Novel

Wajeedah Mohammad

WM Publishing
Newark, New Jersey

MATRIARCH II
Journey to Purpose
Published by WM Publishing
Tel: 484-649-1743
w7mohammad@rcn.com

Wajeedah Mohammad, Publisher/Editorial Director
Yvonne Rose/Quality Press, Production Coordinator
The Printed Page, Interior Design & Cover Layout
Cover Illustration by Jerry Booker and David Alsieux

DEDICATION

Dedication to my great supporters: Brenda Horne, Wakeelah Muhammad, Lillian Furqan, Quadyrah Muhammad, Cecil Berry, Baseemah Muhammad, Linda Nelson, Kareemah Muhammad, Sakinah Sabur, Shira Oglesby, Lavania Robinson, Basimah Abdus-Salaam, Lucille Roberts, Mary Barr-James, Roberta Morton, Brenda Hayes, Matina Ismeal, Sandy Wright-Nelson, Daphne Benyard, Zaidah Bilal--Shareefah--lawyees sisiter--Sabrina Harris, Micheal McDougald, Hassana Shaw, Sutanah Witfield, Gloria Valentine, Amina Bey, Aminah Bilal, Zaritha Mateen, Elizabeth Nasari, Andrienne Terry, Vera Marshall, Sandy Daily, Debra Duhart-Ball, Evelyn Lee, Trisha Edwards, Latifah Hamid, Aishah Abdul-Hakim, Tara Williams, Aminah Walker, Rasheedah Zaid, Sandy Daily, Deish Williams, Carol Griffith, Rasheedah Ziyad, Qadriyyah Saku, Allie Davis, Junita Moore, Salima Rasul, Bennedette Lamb (Quadriyyah)Latifah Hamid, Baheerah Salaam, Naimah Damatra Wallace

Salahuddin K. Muhammad, Roy Crawford, Richard Boyd, Labeeb Malik Abdullah, James Daids, Abdul-rahman Muhammad, George Sabir, Rasul Ansari, A. Akbar Muhammad, Rajahn, Nassiruddin, Bilal Muhammad, Thomas James, Darriel Collier

Dr. Trevor Atherley, M.D., P.A.; Dr. Gaylln Faust- Rukus, DO, FACOOG Mayor Cory Booker; Mayor Wayne Smith

Imams: K. Abdul Kreem, Wyudeen Shareef, Craig Drinkard, Mustafah El-Amin, Aqueel Mateen, Akbar Muhammad, Siraj Wahhaj
In loving memory: Irene Horne, Annie Mantion, Mary (Dee) Barr, Grandmnother, Rosa Cooper, Ora Moore

ACKOWLEDGEMENTS

I'm grateful to Allah (G'd) who gave me the health and strength to endure the trials and tribulations of accomplishing this novel.

In loving memory I dedicate this book to my beloved grandmother, Rosa Cooper; My mom, Ruth Fleming the number one Matriarch of my life.

To my beloved friend Debra Lee who is very special. She devoted her time, always lending her ears to me, never giving up on me and sharing my dreams.

To Mrs. Yvonne Rose, Director of the # 1 African American Self-Publishing Book House/Quality Press. Meeting her as an editor was a blessing. She heard my concerns and consulted with me; she delivered kindness, opportunity and a willingness that gave me hope.

In loving memory of Clara Muhammad. I dedicate this book to the Matriarch, Mother Clara Muhammad, the First Lady of the NOI. She was married to the Honorable Elijah Muhammad. She helped establish the University of Islam and Muslim Girls Training schools providing education to the Nation of Islam. Clara and Elijah Muhammad carved a space in American history –she was The Mother of Education and he was the foundation of Islam in America- and opened up the very first Islamic School in the nation;

thus changing the face of freedom and education in America forever.

In 1975 her son Warith Deen Mohammed, who assumed leadership of the Nation Of Islam, renamed the University of Islam schools the Sister Clara Muhammad Schools in her honor. There are roughly 75 Clara Muhammad schools across the country.

To the movement of the beautiful spirit of the women all over the world, taking a stand and listening to their hearts, telling them to listen to the troubles of family and the world, taking on the challenge, just like a "*Matriarch*".

TABLE OF CONTENTS

PROLOGUE

There's a "Hell" traveling on the road, searching for purpose. On one side of the coin, there are many hidden dangers of deception. There is a risk factor, for not knowing what lies ahead of the unseen, for any of them. Love, convictions, lies, and hatred, challenges the emotions like a pendulum... not knowing how deep it will cut, or how close it will bring Matri to the bridge, between life and death. Being confronted with the characters of a snake and a live snake... awaits her.

There's a "Heaven" traveling on the road, searching for purpose. On the flip side of the coin, there are many rewards upon, discovering the need to find purpose. There is a reward for convictions, faith, trust, and love, that patiently challenges, what lies ahead of the unseen. There is a satisfaction that is gained, and a hidden sweetness of finding out, that love is a many splendid thing. "True Love," is like going down into the bottom of the ocean, finding a pearl.

CHAPTER 1
THE MOSQUE AND THE LIVES OF MEN

*S*unday... *the doorbell is ringing.*
Osmon's jaws move rapidly. He rubs the sweat off his forehead and thinks, *I know Claudia did not stand me up now.*

"Osmon, Osmon." Claudia yells, looking down from the top of the stairs. Claudia's boys are looking down at Osmon. "Up here," says Paul.

Under his breath, Roy calls Osmon, "A knucklehead."

Osmon looks up the stairs at Claudia. "Well, what are you doing up there? I thought you were going with me to the Mosque?"

Claudia gazes at Osmon. "I am."

"If that's the case, why are you just standing there looking at me?" asks Osmon.

"Maybe cause, ya' look real good in that FOI uniform. I 'member ya' tole me, it waz' called a 'Fruit of Islam' uniform. Ya' face have a nice glow in it," she stares at him.

He blushes, standing up like a soldier. He says firmly, "Thank you Claudia."

"Well, If ya' feel that way, just gimme a minute. Go on, in the car. I'll be right out in one minute," says Claudia

"Ah.. okay," says Osmon.

Matri, Taresa and Claudia are all wearing pretty scarves, with long skirts. Osmon and Anthony stand proudly, with the door open, waiting for them.

Ruth's standing in the door, watching them walk downstairs, just like ladies. Taresa walks down the stairs, holding her stomach, with her slender hands. Claudia thinks. "I got some of Matri in me now; I'm a lady."

Osmon wonders, *Who is the pregnant woman with Claudia?*

Anthony's mesmerized by Matri. He asks, "Who's that other beautiful looking Queen, with Claudia?" Matri, Claudia and Taresa walk with their heads held high, just like beautiful peacocks.

Osmon couldn't take his eyes off of them. "Umm, that's Claudia's sister... Matri."

"Matri... ummm," says Anthony. His flawless skin is glowing. Standing tall like a soldier, dressed immaculately in his blue FOI uniform. Anthony walks with militancy, escorting the ladies to the car, like a gentleman. Ruth stands at the door with the children, watching attentively.

They're all impressed with the way Brother Anthony escorts them to the car. He reaches out to their hands, putting them into the back seat. Matri gets in first, thinking, *Well now, I 'clare. This is fit for a lady. Anthony makes you feel special, like a lady should... just like a beautiful flower.*

Claudia gets in next, smiling at Osmon. She glances at Matri, and looks up, as Osmon watches her in the mirror. Osmon thinks, *Now what is more beautiful than seeing this in the wilderness of North America?*

Anthony bows to Taresa, extending his hand very gently to her. She holds onto his hand like Cinderella, who has just met her prince. She acknowledges Osmon and says, "Peace brother."

Osmon glances from the side. "Peace be unto you, my Queen," says Osmon. Taresa slightly holds her head down, blushing. "Queen?" Taresa says to herself.

Claudia looks at Osmon thinking, smiling, *Told cha' I would do some fishin'. Caught two mermaids.*

Osmon, reading Claudia's mind, looks through the mirror, chuckling and nodding at her. Thinking, *You sure did.*

As they ride along slowly, Taresa thinks to herself, with teary eyes, *He called me a 'Queen.' Ain't never been called no 'Queen b'fore. Do he know what he sayin'? Hate to think, of what I was called b'fore.*

"Here we are sisters," says Anthony. "I'll let you, right out." Anthony reaches for Taresa's hand, helping her out of the car.

Taresa thinks, "*Oh he's reachin' for my hand to let me out of the car? Well, I ain't never had nobody reach for my hand, to let me out of no car before. Who he think I am? I 'clare."*

"Oops", says Anthony. "Watch your step, sister," he says politely.

He so gentle with me and this here stomach, Taresa's eyes widen. *It makes me feel like a Miss America pageant person, and I know I ain't no Miss America. I ain't that foolish.*

Anthony reaches for Claudia's hand. Claudia mumbles, "Now Lorraine alwaze say ta' move the right leg first." Claudia swings her right leg and Osmon looks at her hard. She starts walking straight ahead, like a lady.

Matri gets out of the car, walking like royalty. Anthony is taken by her beauty and elegance. Osmon elbows him to get it together.

"Brother!" he yells…"Oh—yes! " Osmon wants to laugh. Anthony straightens himself up.

Everyone watches Matri as she walks gracefully across the floor. "Go to the right, sisters. The sisters are going to check you. It's a formality. Don't take it personal," says Anthony.

A very pleasant lady dressed in white says, "Come on over here, sisters." They all look at her with astonishment.

Matri says, "These women are friendly and graceful."

Taresa glances at the men, talking to herself and says, These sure is some good lookin' men. Ain't never seen nothin' like it, in my life. If I wasn't pregnant, I'd sure work hard on gettin' me one. We're bein' escorted by the sisters to our seats. This sure is alotta escortin', though."

"Sit here my sisters," the woman says pleasantly.

Claudia thinks, The men and women sit on opposite sides of the room. "Guess they look so good, they have ta' separate 'em.

A tall stout man, caramel complexion, enters the room. His eyes protrudes, as he looks through his glasses... very innocently. He silences the audience, holding on to the microphone at the podium. He's very militant looking, wearing a beige FOI suit. He also, has flawless skin and pearly white teeth. Everyone's very attentive. Taresa thinks, glancing around the room. *Well now, these women look so beautiful. Don't know what kindda' chance I would have with these men. I wonder what these women are doin' for their skin, to look so pure?*

Claudia elbows Matri, whispering. "Matri, there goes Freddie."

Martri glances, "I see."

"As-salaamu 'alaykum, my brothers and sisters," a deep voice echoes into the room.

"That voice," Taresa says to herself.

Vociferously, the man spoke with great compassion, pushing his glasses up on his nose. He glances around, holding the posture of a dignitary. "Brothers and sisters, I'm here to give you 'The Message to The Black Man'. The message is this:

Elijah Muhammad says,
"One of the gravest handicaps among the so-called Negroes is that there is no love for self, nor love for his or her own kind. This not having love for self is the root cause of hate, dislike, disunity, disagreement, quarreling, betraying, stool pigeons and fighting and killing one another. The duty of the civilized man is to teach civilization to the uncivilized, the arts and sciences of civilized people and countries of advanced civilization.

A Divine Messenger of Allah raised among His people with a Divine Message, is held responsible for its delivery. His message teaches spiritual civilization, which is important to the success of a nation and society. According to history, the people who refuse to accept Divine Guidance or His Message sent by His Messengers are classified as uncivilized or savages. A well-educated, cultured and courteous people make a beautiful society, when it is spiritual. Good manners come from the civilized man who does not fail to perform his duty.

"Allah wants us to clean ourselves up." He bends slightly, shaking his head pleading, asking, " How can you be loved, if you have no love for self? Elijah Muhammad says, 'America is going to fall. It has to reap what it has sown.'

"That's right!" shout the brothers and sisters.

He stands erect, "We must do for self. We must have our own businesses, before the fall takes place. He said the man that feeds you controls you. "He takes out a handkerchief wiping the sweat off of his forehead, grinding his teeth. "We must become gallant men. Our beloved brother Malcolm X says, "Allah has given Elijah Muhammad some sharp truth. It is like a two-edged sword. It cuts into you. It causes you great pain, but if you can take the truth, it will cure you and save you from a certain death."

An hour later:

In closing, the speaker pleads humbly, with love in his eyes, "Brothers and sisters, bring someone when you come back, because I know you're coming back." He nods his head. " Bring some friends to share this uplifting message to the Black man." With exaltation, he says, "Let us help Elijah Muhammad get our brothers and sisters out of the mud." He pauses suddenly, and then hits the podium, " We've been in the mud too long!" The speaker then wipes the sweat from his face, with his handkerchief, staring off.

Ten days later- The Death of a Prince:

Marvin Gaye sings,
"There will come a time. When the world won't be singing. Flowers won't grow... no. Bells won't be ringing...
Who really cares? Who is willing to try? To save a world,
that is destined to die. When I look at the world, it fills
me with sorrow. Little children today really gonna suffer
tomorrow. Oh what a shame, such a bad way to live. Who
is to blame, when we can't stop livin.' Save the children,
save the baby. If you wanna love, you got love. Save the
baby."

"Hello, Matri..."
"Just a minute, let me put Civil down, Thaddeus. Civil please don't
get jealous, I have to put you down for a minute. Okay, Thaddeus."
"Matri, did you hear what happened?" His voice trembles.
Matri shivers. "What happened?"
"Go and turn your TV on. El-Hajj Malik got assassinated!"
Matri drops the phone, placing her hands on her heart.
"Matri, Matri...
Matri is silenced. "Oh my God! Thaddeus I'm sorry, you
scared me."
"Just go and turn on the news, it's on all the news stations."
Matri runs into the living room, and sits down on the floor.
Hypnotized by the talk on El-Hajj Malik, she becomes frantic. "Oh
no! Brother Malcolm."
"Matri, Matri," Thaddeus yells to remind her he's on the phone.
She notices the phone is off the hook and picks it up. "Oh
Thaddeus, this is horrible... oh my God. You see how they killed
him."
Ruth and Claudia comes running out of the room. Ruth asks,
"What's goin' on in here?"

"Oh ma God, somebody kill Malcolm," says Claudia.

"Oh Lawd, no Jesus come by here," says Ruth.

"Claudia, go and get Dawn. Go upstairs and see if Taresa's home," says Matri.

"Somebody's knockin' on the door," says Claudia.

"What is goin' on? I heard you upstairs. Lasett left my door open," says Taresa.

Claudia's upset. "Just look!" she says.

Taresa focuses on the tv. She falls on the couch and starts crying. Everybody started crying, except Matri.

"Thaddeus... this is really very shocking news," says Matri.

Hurtful, he says, "Yeah, everything seems like it stopped moving... like, time doesn't exist for now," says Thaddeus.

"Are you going to the funeral?" Matri asks.

Sounding dispirited, "The only being that could stop me is God, and why would he stop me from going to such a man's funeral?"

There seems to be a cloud of darkness over the earth, carrying emotions of sadness, tears, and anger, that pervades the world. There is no expression for the moment. It's silenced by the blanket of shock, and the pain of agony, of not knowing why or who. We are left with the memory of a Prince, engraved in our minds, with a smile that touched our very souls. Leaving us with his energy that's like electricity. It will never die. Has anyone ever heard of electricity dying? It's always around... no one sees it, but it's always there, waiting to ignite with its magnetic force of a beautiful Prince. We think of them as dead, but nay, they are but alive.
As-salaamu'alaykum.

El-Hajj-Malik Shabazz said, "The Muslims of "white" complexions who had changed my opinions were men who had showed me that they practiced genuine brotherhood. And I knew that any American white man with a genuine brotherhood for a black man was hard to find, no matter how much he grinned... I hope that my trip to Hajj has established our Muslim Mosque's authentic religious affiliation with 750 million Muslims of the Orthodox Islamic world.

My pilgrimage broadened my scope. I shared true brotherly love, with many white-complexioned Muslims, who never gave a single thought to race, or to the complexion of another Muslim. I saw what I never had seen in thirty-nine years here in America. I saw all races, all colors, blue-eyed blonds to black-skinned Africans in true brotherhood... In unity. Living as one. Worshipping as one. No segregationists, no liberals. They would not have known how to interpret the meaning of those words.

In the past, yes, I have made sweeping indictments of all white people. I never will be guilty of that again, as I know some white people are truly sincere, that some truly are capable of being brotherly toward a Black man.

The assassination of El-Hajj Malik will go down in history as the greatest blow the American integrationist movement has suffered since the shocking assassinations of Medgar Evers, Dr. Martin Luther King, John F. Kennedy, John Brown and Patrice Lumumba - who martyred on freedom's cause."

Ossie Davis did the eulogy of El-Hajj Malik Shabazz. Davis said, "And if you knew him, you would know why we must honor him. When we honor him, we honor the best in ourselves... and we will know him then, for what he was and is – a Prince, our black shining Prince. He did not hesitate to die, because he loved us so."

CHAPTER 2

BRING THE BOYS HOME

Looking like an ant, moving between the mountains. The wind blows like one big giant fan, across Isiah's face, as he drives a light green convertible Cadillac. He's making the car rock back and forth. "Ya' kno' it's a hot day, but it's a different type of heat with the wind blowin'. This convertible is doin' his job man," says Isiah.

Robert pops the beer top. "Dig it. Here man," giving the beer to Isiah.

Scratching his face, Hezikiah says, "Yeah it seems the weather is welcomin' us home."

Robert, very smooth, cocoa complexion. He takes a sip of his beer with a half moon smile. Smiles with a slender face. Places his slender lips on the can of beer, taking a sip of beer.. His Chinaman eyes, closing up mischievously, looking at Hezikiah. "Hey man, I really didn't know you were poetic," says Robert.

Jerking his head back. "Po...what?" asks Hezikiah.

Robert pauses, continuing to stare at Hezikiah. He drinks from his beer and chuckles, like something is scratching his throat. Bends over with his chest sunken in, and his slender shoulders jumping up and down, as he laughs.

Hezikiah is persistent. "I'll say it again… po… what?"

Robert laughs and goes into his intellectual act. Eyes half closed, jesting with his hands, he says, "Okay man, it's like this. Poetic means, displaying the imaginative qualities, rhythmically."

With thick eyebrows and lashes, hisfeyes frowns up, "What—I think ya' better try that again," Says Hezikiah.

Robert stares seriously at Hezikiah. He takes a sip from his beer, slants his mouth and slurs his words, saying, " Well… the imagination can speak for the beauty that it senses, sees, and observes. What you see and feel, you have just expressed in a very beautiful way, baby."

Isiah turns the radio on, bobbing his head. "Man listen, Oooh!" He yells, "Marvin Gaye, baby." He starts singing, turning it up. Hezikiah and Robert listen attentively, swaying their heads.

Marvin sings,
Mother, mother, there's too many of you crying. Brother, brother, brother there's too many of you dying. You know we've got to find a way, to bring some lovin' here today. Hey baby what you know good. I'm just gettin' back, but you knew I would. War is hell, when will it end. When will people start gettin' together again? Are things really gettin', better like the newspaper said? What else is new, my friend, b'sides what I read? Can't find no work, can't find no job, my friend. Money is tighter than it's ever been. Say man I just don't understand what's going on across the land. Ah—what's—happening Bro. What's happening?

Isiah yells, "Man that cat is bad! Wooo, sing it baby," says Isiah.

Robert sips his beer, "Know what man, that cat is saying a lot… I just hope that's not our plight man," says Robert, staring off.

"What chu' mean man?" asks Hezikiah's huge hands, holds onto the beer can ightly.

"I mean, it would be a nightmare, if we fought for Uncle Sam... came home... and old Sam didn't help us survive," says Robert.

"I hate ta' think of it man... especially after they don' mess me up like this. No job, no work... and can't have no woman," says Hezikiah.

"Dig it man, you right. 'Nam waz' a nightmare in hell, don' kno' if I'll ever git' over it man," says Isiah.

Being provoked, Robert's slanty eyes try to widen. "It ain't no getting over it. You have to just deal with it, just like in the service," Robert says angrily, eyes shrinking.

Isiah empathizes and says, "I hope this is just a song, man."

Two hours later, at home:

Ruth says, "Matri please git' that phone will ya'?"

"Hello."

"It's Ramone," he says romantically.

Her cheeks redden, "I recognize your voice, Ramone."

"What's been happening baby?"

"I've been busy with work and school."

"Well... we have to do, what we have to do... that's for sure," he says.

"Always, Ramone," she blushes.

Testing her, he asks, "How's your love life?"

"Well, I could say, that's all good because there are a lot of things and people to love."

"Hmmm, I see. Hey Matri, did you say that you had a brother in 'Nam?"

"Oh yeah, as a matter of fact, he should be home late tonight... sometime."

"Matri, are you going anywhere today?"

"I didn't have any plans."

"Actually, I didn't want to wait until night. I wanted to show you something."

Anxiously she asks, "Do you mind me asking, you what it is?"

"Here's the thing, Matri…I would like to surprise you."

Smiling from ear to ear, she says, "Okay, I'm too excited to ask."

"It's 12:00 now… let's say 2:00 sharp."

"I'll be ready," she jumps up, smiling..

Right on time, Matri runs down the stairs. Ramone's in the back seat. Luther stands with the door opened for Matri, smiling. Matri stares into his eyes, this time. She thinks, *There's something?....*"Hi Ramone."

"Hi baby, you thirsty?" asks Ramone

Jovially, Matri answers. "As a matter of fact, I'll take some Seven Up on the rocks." Luther has an unsettling stare at Matri through the mirror. Matri glances, catching him, but pretends she doesn't notice. "So, Ramone where were you? You come and you disappear."

He stares at Matri, taking a quick view of her entire body. "Matri we're going to take a ride." Abruptly he says, "Luther... do you know where I'm going?"

Jokingly he says, "Yessah boss." Ramone laughs.

Approaching the mountains, Matri becomes very curious. "I 'clare, look at that sierra," Matri points.

Ramone looks out of the window at the mountains, "Yes, this scene is awesome."

"Oooh," Matri presses down on her ears. "My ears feel clogged up."

"I know baby, it'll stop in a minute, baby."

Matri notices Luther staring at her again. With his right eye fluttering, straining to see out of it. She turns towards Ramone.

Smiling, he asks, "Are you okay, baby?"

"Oh, Yes," says Matri.

Luther rode through the sierra slowly, passing beautiful homes. "I 'clare Ramone, these are some beautiful homes."

"That they are, Matri."

Matri looks at one particular house sitting at the edge of a cliff. "Ramone is that house going to fall, sitting on that cliff like that?"

Ramone turns towards the house. "I think it's possible, over a period of time, from heavy rainfall."

Matri looks at the houses like a kid in a candy store. "These houses are breathtaking, I 'clare."

Ramone is entranced by her behavior. He thinks, *Matri, you're something like out of a novel—a best-seller, of course. You're a woman, for sure… but yet, H*e pauses, turning towards Matri, almost saying what's on his mind. Matri is preoccupied, looking at the houses. Continuing to think…*Yes indeed, I have to have her. I'm going to do everything in my power.*

"We're here," says Luther.

Matri thinks, *He does have a southern voice….* "Here…?" she looks at Ramone.

"Yup, this is part of the surprise." Luther comes to the door to let Matri out.

Matri gets out like a lady. "Thank you."

Luther reaches his arms out for Matri. She takes hold of Ramone's arm, continuing to walk like a lady.

Ramone looks at her with admiration. "Yes indeed, you are a lady, Matri."

Matri blushes.

"Ramone, come on in here. Who is the lady you're with?" asks a very friendly, casually dressed woman. Emerging from the beautiful house, made of beige, white and brown colored rocks. She's medium height, very fair-skinned, with curly red hair like Ramone's. Her keen features also resemble Ramone's.

"Shawn, this is Matri. Matri… my sister, Shawn."

Shawn hugs Matri. "Hello Matri."

Matri is very coy. "Nice meeting you, Shawn."

"Come right on in my home, Matri. Have a seat. Now... is there anything I could get for you? Water, tea, beer, ice cream," she smiles.

"Just water, please," Matri responds.

"Ramone?" She questions.

"Water." says Ramone.

"I 'clare, you two look so much alike," says Matri. They both smile.

"It's funny you should say that, because everyone always thought we were some sort of twins... but I would tell them, he's just a little too old to be my twin," says Shawn.

"Ramone, is this your only sister?" asks Matri.

Ramone and Shawn's eyes meet.

Shawn smiles, her eyes express anxiousness, "Let me tell her Ramone, please."

"Alright, be my guest, little sister."

"Matri, I don't know whether or not Ramone told you what happened," Looking at Ramone, Shawn's face shines brightly. Very tenderly she says, "Well, my beloved brother, delivered me, during the worst winter storm in history."

Affectionately, "Yes, Shawn... he did share that experience with me," says Matri.

"When he told me the story of how he delivered me, I've been endeared to him for that. I love my brother very much. I just wish that he could've..." Ramone coughs interrupting her from continuing on. Matri took wind of it.

Ramone says, "You know Shawn, we didn't come to stay. I have something I'd love to show Matri. I just wanted Matri to meet my better half."

Shawn's eyes spells loneliness. "Ohh no. Matri, I thought you could stay and have dinner with me. My husband's away for two weeks again."

Ramone gets up and hugs her, kissing her on the forehead. "I'll come back tomorrow evening and have dinner with you, I promise."

"I 'clare, it's been nice meeting you," says Matri.

Shawn imitates Matri. "Well, I 'clare, it's been wonderful meeting you too." Turning towards Ramone, "Ramone you have to bring Matri back, now."

"Okay, let's go Matri."

"Luther, take us to our destiny, please."

"Destiny?" asks Matri.

"Oh, your surprise Matri. Speed up a little, will you Luther. Matri's brother is coming home from 'Nam, and I know she needs to be there."

Luther puts his thumbs up in the air. "Yup."

"We're not too far from there, actually," says Ramone.

Driving a mile up. "Here we go boss," says Luther.

Ramone gazes at Matri, marveling at her beauty. "Here we are," says Ramone.

Matri gets out of the car, in awe of Ramone's huge brick stone home. "I 'clare, this is absolutely beautiful."

Smiling at her, he says holding his hands out to her from the door. "Step in, this is my world, within a world." Ramone flips the lights on.

Excitingly Matri says, "This carpet… I have to take my shoes off."

"Thank you Matri. I tell people they must take their shoes off. Slippers, are accommodated."

Matri notices a huge portrait, of an exceptionally pretty, fair-skinned woman. Curly red hair hanging down to her shoulders. "Now, Ramone—is this…?"

Glimpsing at Matri, while looking at the portrait, he slightly looks away. "Yes, this is what I work so hard to keep." He exhales, staring at his mother's portrait. "That beautiful, fiery woman there, is my mother. In her beauty, she reminds me of the lovely Lena Horne. With the exception of her red hair… from her Irish decent." Seeming a little perturbed, he drifts as he watches his mother.

Matri gazes at the picture, then twirls around, fascinated over the décor of the place. There is plush eggshell carpet, and on top of the carpet are two brown throw-rugs. At each side of the fireplace, stands two tall statues of tigers. Adjacent to the fireplace is a dining room set.

"Oh Ramone, this eggshell dining room set, with gold trimming is breathtaking…what kind?"

"It's imported from China. I go there for business," says Ramone.

Matri is impressed, looking around at the living room. "China?"

He takes her hands gently. "One day I would like to invite you to dinner. My maid…"

"Your maid…?"

"Matri, people think it's a big deal to have a maid. But really, they're very affordable. I only need her four times a month."

Matri is silent, as her eyes roam uncontrollably, by such an elaborate house. "Matri let me show you around. I have three bedrooms upstairs."

Matri is awestricken by the elegance of the guest room. "Th… three rooms?"

"Yes, just in case I have houseguests, or after-party guests," answers Ramone.

Matri exhales. "I 'clare."

Ramone imitates Matri. "Well… I 'clare," They both laugh. "Matri we have to get out of here, I have to get you home."

⟩⊹ ⊹⟨

At 12:30 a.m. Ruth says, "Matri, somebody is ringin' the bell."

Claudia, with her voice sounding parched, not wanting to get up, says "Matri… Matri somebody's ringin' the bell."

"The bell?… ohhh!" Matri jumps up, looking out of the window, shaking excitedly. "Claudia, it's Isiah! Civil, it's Isiah." Matri runs to Ruth's room. "Get up Mama, it's Isiah." Matri runs down the stairs, jumping up on Isiah, with her legs wrapped around his hips, hugging him and kissing his face.

"Matri, ma' Matri," says Isiah, looking into Matri's eyes.

Very gently, Matri says, "Oh Isiah, I love you very much, too."

Claudia and the children stand at the top of the stairs. Isiah takes a glimpse of them, at the top of the stairs, staring down at him.

Yawning, Claudia says, "Matri let the man come on upstairs now, we wanna hug em' too."

"Here, Matri take this bag upstairs fa' me. I'll bring the rest of ma' thangs in the mornin'," says Isiah, as he walks up the stairs. Ruth, Claudia and the kids start backing up, giving him room to come in the door. Ruth, biting down on her lips, is silenced with tears of joy.

Claudia jumps up on Isiah. "Oh, Isiah I miss ya' too much. I 'clare."

Isiah turns towards Mama, who is speechless. He raises his voice while laughing, with tears in his eyes, scolding her. "Mama now don't chu' stand back there actin' like ya' can't say nothin'. Now, I didn't drive all this long way, fa' ya' ta' freeze up on me now. I 'clare, ya' better give me some love." He hugs Ruth gently, with tears running down his face. Paul and Roy hold onto his legs. Claudia pulls them away, kissing them.

Ruth is overwhelmed. She gulps. "Oh ma' Lawd, Isiah... the Lawd answers prayers." She starts crying, rubbing his face, staring at him and kissing him all over his forehead. "Yes, yes, thank ya' Jesus."

His picture perfect set of teeth glistens, like a mouthful of white pearls. Isiah's feeling joy in his heart. Eyes flapping, says with fervor, "Oh Mama ... I told chu', ya' didn't have ta' worry 'bout me now. Here I am Mama." He wipes her tears. "Thank God now, I ain't no fool. I kno', didn't nobody bring me back from that hell I waz' in but Him." He rubs her hair gently away from her face. "Yes Mama," he whispers. "Ya' right Mama, there is a God."

They all move towards the sofa, slowly sitting down. He starts shaking his head. Ruth and Claudia starts crying. Matri sits on the floor, at Ruth's feet. Claudia's little boy Paul, grabs Isiah around the legs, sniffing.

"Paul is so sensa-tize, he don't even kno' why he cryin,' just cause he see us cryin'," says Claudia.

Isiah gives Claudia advice. "Don't say that Claudia, he got feelins' too. A man can cry too now... don't raise 'em thinkin' he can't. It's good he cries, cause now if he don't... he'll keep everythang bottled up inside of 'em, and a woman won't never get through ta' 'em."

"Matri, you and Claudia better go ta' bed, we ain't got too much longer ta' sleep no how. Cause we got a lotta' cookin' ta' do ta' 'morrow," says Ruth.

"Isiah where is Hezikiah?" asks Matri.

"I took him and Robert ta' his uncle's house."

"Tomorrow, you have to go and get them. We' having a big dinner tomorrow.," says Matri.

"Matri, how is Thaddeus?" Isiah asks.

"He'll be here tomorrow for the dinner, then he's going back to Philly. He's on a job assignment," says Matri.

"Isiah you could sleep in the room near the kitchen, for now. I put some fresh sheets on the bed fa' ya'. I kno' how ya' like your sheets. I ironed them fa' ya'," says Ruth proudly.

He hugs Ruth. "Now, Mama…."

"Don't—say—it now, I do thangs with love, now goodnight," says Ruth.

═╬ ╬═

The next day, Matri's eyes sparkle.

"Claudia, Mama really set this table... it's pretty," says Matri.

Zestfully, Claudia says, "Yeah, I guess she put love inta' it."

Matri looks at the plates. "Wait a minute, she forgot one thing..."
Claudia's eyes widen. "What's that?"

"I better ask Mama... Mama what forks are we going to use?"

Ruth yells from the bathroom. "Wait a minute child." Ruth comes out of the bathroom in a towel, looking like a mummy with mayonnaise all over her face, wearing a towel on her head. Matri and Claudia chuckles..

"Mama ya' look so funny." Claudia giggles.

Matri frowns. "And what's that on your face?"

Ruth puts her hands on her hips. "Child, ain't got ta age ugly, I'm tryin' ta' age gracefully. Sister at the chuch, tell me 'bout mayonnaise treatment fa' the face."

Matri's eyes protrude. "You 'clare?"

"She say, it ain't nothin' wrong with lookin' in the mirror, and likin' what chu' see. No matter what age." Ruth's eyes bulges out, as she nods her head.

Matri and Claudia both laugh, saying, "You 'clare!"

The bell rings, louder than ever. "Oh ma' Lawd!" Matri and Claudia chuckles at Ruth's expression. Only seeing her eyes, because of the mayonnaise on her face.

Ruth pants. "Claudia look on ma' bed and bring ma' dress in the bathroom." Ruth runs back in the bathroom. Claudia notices her sons standing in the kitchen with their faces shining. They have nice haircuts, wearing white shirts with little bow ties. "Oh, ya' two look very nice t'day," she says, while smiling. kisses them on the forehead.

Ring... ring... ring. "Okay!... comin', I 'clare", says Claudia. Isiah is standing at the door with Robert and Hezikiah. Hugging both of them, she says, "Hi! Robert, Hezikiah!"

"I kno' Mama's gon' be surprised ta' see ya' Hezikiah," says Isiah.

Matri screams! "Hezikiah, Robert this is a great day for us all."

Claudia says, pointing to the chair, "Y'all, sit down. 'Cause we ain't lettin' ya' go, no time soon."

Matri calls Claudia's little boys to meet them. "Paul and Roy, come on and speak to Hezikiah and Robert. Children need to know, that they are special and important also," says Matri.

Ruth comes out of the room dressed in a blue dress. Everybody looks at her beauty; pearl earrings and necklace. Her hair, is gorgeous, hanging midway down her back. Teary-eyed, she says, "Oh Hezikiah, the Lawd' don' bring ya' back ta' me, too."

"Mama! Look—a—here, look—a—here, ya' sho' look just as pretty as ya' ever did." He hugs her. "Yes Mama the Lawd' did bring me back, and I ain't no fool, says Hezikiah

Ruth turns towards Robert. "Ya' come on here too, Robert. I feel like ya' all ma' sons," she pauses. "The Lawd wouldn't let me keep Claf," she smiles. "But he replaces thangs."

Robert rubs his eyes, with his handkerchief, hugging Ruth. "I love ya', Mama."

Someone knocks. Everyone freezes, looking at the door. Isiah opens the door. When he opens the door, Dawn stands there in a multi-colored dashiki, with a matching head-piece; and big round earrings, looking sensuous. Isiah stares, observing her high cheekbones and full lips. Everyone's waiting for Isiah to let the person in. Bending her head back to look at him, Dawn is stilled by Isiah's handsomeness. His height and stocky masculine structure, makes her blush.

"Isiah," says Claudia," Who is it?"

Isiah steps back letting Dawn walk in like a Queen. He swerves around speechless, continuing to look at Dawn. Robert and Hezikiah chuckles

. "Dawn," says Matri, "Let me introduce you to Robert, Hezikiah, and my brother Isiah."

Gracefully she says, "Pleased to meet you all."

"Dawn I 'clare, it's ma' pleasure ta' meet chu, that's fa' sure," says Isiah.

Dawn smiles and nods, "Sure, it's my pleasure too."

Knock, knock… Everyone looks at the door again. "Let me git' it this time," says Claudia. "Look at ya' two. Lasett, ya' dress is so pretty and ya' wearin' a scarf?" asks Claudia.

Taresa and Lasette are wearing Muslim attire. Reginald is wearing a suit with a bowtie. "Now, this is just too much, you look wonderful," says Matri.

Taresa nudges them. "What do you say Lasette and Reginald?"

"Thank you Miss Matri", says Lasett.

"Thank you Miss Matri," says Reginald.

Isiah looks at Reginald shaking his hands and chuckling, "Man, ya' kno' ya' sharp?"

Robert and Hezikiah chuckles, agreeing and shaking Reginald's hands.

"Ya' gotta make a man feel important now," says Isiah.

Ruth is ecstatic, standing in the middle of the floor, saying, "Ya' boys sho' look good with them army uniforms on. Now ya' all, ma' chirrin'. I got somethin' special fa' ya' t'day." She exhales, starry-eyed. "I 'clare I'm just too happy. Sit down and git ta' kno' each other, while I fix the food."

"Does anybody want any coffee or tea?" asks Matri.

"I'll have some coffee," says Robert.

"Me too," says Hezikiah.

"Taresa, I'm gonna let the kids play in their room, 'til Mama call us fa' dinner," says Claudia.

Matri says, "So Robert… tell us what your plans are, now that you're home."

He starts squinting up his eyes and twisting his mouth, looking perplexed. "You know Matri, I haven't given it much thought at all."

"You haven't?" she asks.

Rolling his eyes in a very sneaky manner. "I can't say what I wanna say," he pauses, and facetiously says, "Hell, I might not ever do anything." His chest and stomach sinks in, as he laughs. "I swear, Uncle Sam took a lot out of me."

"What about you Hezikiah?" asks Matri.

He crosses his leg, shaking his foot. "I have ta' settle a score with Uncle Sam. Once I do that, I'll just take life as it comes."

"Isiah... Isiah?" Matri notices he's staring at Dawn.

"I might just find me a pretty woman. Settle down and give Mama a couple grandchildren... that's if she don' mind havin' at least two," says Isiah.

"Yeah man, I was an only child... or should I say brat," Robert says, placing his hands on his chest, laughing.

"Matri what chu doin, now?" asks Isiah.

Matri answers, "I work for a law firm in New York. My boss is sending me to school to study law."

"I'm proud of ya', sis," says Isiah.

"Taresa," says Matri.

Taresa speaks very shyly. "Oh y'all don' really need ta' kno' my stuff."

Robert leans forward putting his index finger on his cheek, squinting his eyes, "Hey come on, we all have... some stuff ta' tell, and it's important because..." He imitates her... "It's our stuff." Everyone patiently waits for her comment.

"Well, right now I have a baby, but I won't work until the baby is at least two years old." Exhaling, "But I'm engaged now to be married," she blushes.

"What!" says Matri and Claudia simultaneously.

"Brother George proposed to me last month." Teary- eyed she says, "He said he wanted ta' save me and the children from the fall of America." She shows her star and crescent ring.

Robert continues to keep his finger on his cheek, "Hmmm, that's a pretty interesting statement... honorary of course. Star and crescent—that's definitely unique, lady," says Robert.

"He loves ya'," says Hezikiah.

Happily, Matri says, "That's a wonderful thing."

Dawn coughs. "Well okay, I'm an artist."

Isiah is very attentive to Dawn. "Well now, that's a good thang. As a matter of fact, I alwaze wanted somebody ta' paint a big family picture. "

"A portrait," she says.

Isiah snaps his fingers. "Yeah, that must be what it is, a portrait."

Dawn smiles bashfully. Isiah looks at Dawn and smiles also. He cannot stop looking at her.

The bell rings. "Who is it this time?" asks Claudia, running down the stairs.

"Oh child, I forgot all bout' chu'. Where ya' been fa' the last month?"

"I been workin' at somethin'," says Sadie.

"Come on upstairs, I got a big surprise fa' ya'," Claudia says.

Sadie walks in the door flabbergasted. "Lawd! Now when y'all come?" asks Sadie.

"Now, ya' just don't start all that talkin', b'fore we git' these hugs over with," says Isiah.

"That's right," says Hezikiah.

"Robert, ya' don' kno' Sadie," says Isiah.

"That ain't got nothin' to do with gettin' a hug. Anyway I could get to know 'er." He blinks his eyes, nodding his head convincingly.

Sadie stays in one spot, looking at him with a big smile, squinting up her big eyes. "Since ya' feel that way, give me a hug and it's nice meetin' ya," says Sadie.

Robert places his hands on his chest, chuckling. "Same here baby, same here."

"Matri, y'all been sittin' in the livin' room long enuff' now. It's 5:00. Let's come ta' the table," says Ruth.

Matri gets up. "Okay, let the men go first."

"I like that Matri," says Robert.

Ruth sits at the head of the table, proudly. The table is set for a feast. "Y'all come on in now, make ya' self comftable."

Everyone inhales the good smells from fried chicken, smoked turkey, candied yams, buttered corn and collard greens. The peach cobbler is drenched in sweet syrup and almost leaves no room for apple and sweet potato pie. Isiah notices the picture of Dr. King and a beautiful big picture of assorted flowers hanging on the wall. A huge Bible is opened on top of a small table. Thick, long curtains with a mixture of brown and pink are hanging down to the floor. There's a pink tablecloth. Robert starts shaking his legs underneath the table. With laughter he says, "I'm glad mama and daddy gave me a good set of teeth, because I can't wait to sink my teeth in this food, like a tiger." He roars like a tiger. Ruth laughs.

"Mama, ya' gon' sit the kids in the kitchen?" asks Claudia.

"Oh, yeah I fa' got bout ma' babies. I set the table up fa' them. Just take a look at it now," says Ruth. The plates were neatly fixed, with small dishes of food and children's decorations on the table."

"Okay come on children, put the toys away. Mama want us ta' eat." She pauses, smiling. "Y'all look so nice t'day."

"Thank you ma'am," says Lasette.

Reginald holds his head down. Smiling bashfully, he says "Thank you."

"Mama," says Isiah, watching her closely.

"What is it Isiah?" Ruth asks. "Mama you are one pretty woman...y'all look at ma' mama." He turns around, looking at Dawn. "Umm, Dawn do ya' think ya' could draw ma' Mama lookin' just like that?"

Dawn looks at Ruth and smiles. "Isiah that's what art is all about. Capturing the beauty of a person or object. There is so much beauty, to capture in Mama."

Ruth blushes. "I guess that mayonnaise is workin'," says Ruth.

Isiah, Hezikiah, and Robert seem baffled by Ruth's comment. "Oh it's just a woman's thing," says Matri.

Ruth gets very quiet, bringing stillness to everybody, like a judge in a courtroom.

"I'd like to say ta' ya' all, that it ain't by no chance that I sit here at the head of this table. The Lawd don' call Jessie, but I had ta' be the head, and carry on... and when I leave, somebody will have ta' be the head and carry on. 'Cause ev'rythang have ta' have a head... gots it set time ta' end." Ruth pauses and places her hands on her heart.

"Are you okay?" Matri asks.

"Mama...?" says Isiah.

She shakes her head and waves her hand up in the air. "Oh this here somin' I been dealin' with fa' some time, don't worry." Ruth buckles her mouth in. "I'm so happy. If ya'll could just see what the Lawd' is blessin' me ta' see, as I sit here watchin' ya' all. I see a lovin' family, and family is what it'z all 'bout... 'family. You here boys, made it back ta' join the family."

Ruth looks over at the photo of Dr. King and says in a whisper, "Yes Lawd, want ma' chirrin' ta' kno' that, when I would hear talk of Dr. Martin Luther King, I begin ta' listen. Dr. King kno'd nothin' waz wrong with dreamin' and everybody should have one. I had a dream that I would be sittin' at a table just like this, lookin' at ma Isiah, Hezikiah, and Robert. Yes, I prayed and cried too. The Lawd don't mind it. Never be free, without a dream. Ain't nothin' wrong with dreamin'. I betcha they can't take that away from ya."

Robert chuckles, "Now that's what I call, real poetic truth, Mama." He gets up and kisses her on the forehead.

Isiah says, "Mama, I will attest ta' that, 'cause that's how I made it back from that horrible war. I don' wish it on ma' worst enemy. I first give the credit ta' God, Mama... like ya' teach me. He starts staring away. " Ya' kno', it seem like I kept dreamin', I waz' fallen'... and in the dream, I waz' so scared. I felt like, I waz' goin' ta' die, had I fall. So in the dream, God couldn't show himself to save me." He turns towards Mama with sparkling eyes. " He showed me you Mama, to keep me from fallin'. It's strange that I'm sittin' right next ta' a artist who could do a picture, or a por...

Dawn leans forward and says, " A portrait."

"Love can carry us over troubled waters, Mama," says Isiah.

Hezikiah quietly says, "Wait a minute, I need ta' say this. Mama, I need cha' ta' kno' that I experienced the longest, coldest day of ma' life in 'Nam, but t'day Mama, I experienced the warmest day of ma' life," his eyes sparkles staring at Ruth.

Ruth smiles warmly, holding her head down. "Let us pray over the food. Thank ya' Lawd' fa' this food. We want chu' ta' bless this food fa' us Lawd. We all kno' that we wouldn't have this here food, if ya' didn't have a hand in it. We all thank ya', Amen." Everyone says, "Amen."

CHAPTER 3

THE WEDDING

Isiah sees Dawn going up the steps, dressed in a beautiful red dashiki with a red headwrap. "Wow! Bring the boys home," says Isiah.

"Well, I ain't trying to bring no boys home baby," she says adamantly. "Anyway, I can't do anything with no boy, under any circumstances." She waves her hands up in the air.

Isiah laughs. Eyes fluttering. "Is that right?" He pretends to be timid. "Well ma'am... could I ask ya' somethin'?"

Staring at Isiah, she puts her hands in a akimbo position.

Isiah continues to act timid. He says politely, "Ma'am?"

Dawn exhales, feeling relaxed. "Well since you put it that way—sure."

Isiah stands like a statue, staring at her and smiling.

Acting sassy, she says, "Well go ahead... you telling me something by smiling?"

Isiah is hesitant to inquire about her head wrap. "Okay... why do ya' wear your head wrapped up like that... and why ya' wearin' those long skirts? Ya' look beautiful... it's different."

Nodding her head, she says, "Ah-ha."

He gulps, talking quickly. "Ya' sure nuff, catch a man's eyes. Ya' make a man think fa' a change. He... he don' kno' why, but it catch his attention," he stares. "'Cause he's so use ta' somethin' else," he stares at her, sizing her up, " Ya' leave a whole lot ta' a man's thinkin'," says Isiah.

Dawn stands tall, holding her head up in the air, blushing. Isiah blushes too. "Well, that's what he needs to do... think."

He quickly nods his head. "Yes ma'am, ya' right." He continues to gaze at her.

Abruptly she says, "Oh Isiah, maybe Matri didn't get a chance to tell you. Taresa is getting married in two weeks, on a Saturday, at the Mosque. We're all going."

Isiah thinks. "Did cha' say ta' the Mosque?"

"Do you have a problem with that?" Dawn asks.

"No, no, I'd take pleasure in that," he convinces her.

"Then we're going to New York to the Savoy Club. Hajj Malik used to go there. Lena Horne is going to be singing at the Savoy."

Isiah is smitten by Dawn. "Savoy?" He asks.

"Don't worry about it, you guys will love the place. It's one of the best spots in New York." She looks at Isiah smiling. "Best entertaining place, to bring the boys home to."

He looks at his watch. "Okay, I better get upstairs, need ta' read this here paper. Have ta' get a job. The money I have from the service won't last forever."

Dawn nods her head, walking into the house, like a queen on a throne.

Isiah feels a rush, watching her as she walks into the house. "Well, well, well," he thinks.

⊷⊶

It's Saturday, Taresa is watching herself in the mirror on the floor... reminiscing. "You children, get back in that living room and sit down. Wait... turn around, let me look at chu, Lasette—Reginald." She gazes at both of them, proudly. "Okay, you look very nice, both of you," she smiles.

"Tank you mommy," says Reginald.

"Reginald," says Taresa. "Say th... th, not tank you."

He holds his head up, looking at her smiling, "Th... th.. th... tank you."

"Thank you mommy, says Lasette."

Taresa's big eyes, turns back towards the mirror... smiling like a shining star. "I can't believe this is me, dressed in all this white," she says with exhilaration. "I said I would get me one of them men in that Mosque. But, I didn't think, I would get one while I was pregnant. Knock, knock. "Come in Matri." Matri opens the door slowly. "Come on in Matri," says Taresa.

Matri says jovially, kissing the baby in the crib. "Now how did you know it was me?"

Slowly, she turns towards Matri. "Matri, I grew to feel your spirit."

Raising her eyebrows, "Oh?" Matri teases her.

"It's something about you..." Taresa pauses, turning towards Matri. "Matri, there is something about you... that I don't think, you fully know about yourself."

They grab and hug each other. Tear jerkingly, Taresa says, "Matri, I have never in my whole life been so happy, like I am to-day. That first day going to the Mosque, I said I was going to get me one of them men. I, I never thought I really could, especially being pregnant and all. You gave me a spirit that I never had b'fore... the spirit of dreamin'. When I went to the Mosque, and the way they treated us Matri..." Teary-eyed, she says," I realized somethin' awful had happened to me." She steps away from Matri, walking around prancing proudly. "I began to see something different in me. I realized, that I had to see another me to change... and the Muslims showed me another me. I also needed new words to do that, because they showed me that, words forms the mind..." her eyes swells up with tears. She gulps, "I started dreamin', Matri. I said one day, I'm gonna be a new person in my life... " eyes, looking afar, "I had to look over the mountain top of my life."

Matri wipes the tears from Taresa's face. "Now I can't give you a bath this time, to stop these tears." They both laughed.

Taresa twiddles her thumbs. "Matri... here comes this man in my life and he didn't care what kinda condition I was in. Pregnant, or not." Tears travel down Taresa's cheeks. "Matri, he stayed with me throughout the delivery, and told me not to worry about the one who laid the seed. Think about the one who nourishes and takes care of the seed."

Matri outlines Taresa's small face, huge eyes, and pointy nose... features that resembles Diana Ross. She listens carefully to Taresa.

"This man saw something in me... that I didn't see in myself. Matri, Brother George told me that the Honorable Elijah Muhammad explained, what George had within himself. He stuck by me, fed me, took care of my children, and called me his beautiful cream of the crop. Matri, I 'clare... I am that beautiful rose flower. I'm a lady now, and Mama say, you know when you got real love, cause that is what real love do for ya."

Matri looks into her eyes. "I told you in your apartment that day. Taresa, now you've got love."

Someone knocks, "Y'all come on now. It'z time. Everybody's waitin' downstairs.

Matri picks the baby up. "Come on children, I'll take little Elijah," says Matri.

"Thank you Matri," says Taresa.

"Taresa don't worry, you look just like a Queen," says Matri.

Half an hour later:

Tthe Muslim Brothers escorts, the men to sit on the opposite side of the women. "Hey man, is these some kindda soldiers?" asks Isiah.

"These cats is spit clean man. Uncle Sam ain't got nothin' on 'em," says Hezikiah.

"Man, I've never seen a group of people, so healthy looking," says Robert.

Isiah keeps peeping over at Dawn. "Isiah…." Robert chuckles. "You're going to have to keep your head straight, like everybody else man."

The minister stands before them, making the ceremony very short and sweet. Hezikiah, notices that there was no throwing of the bouquet. "Looks like it's over now."

The brothers and sisters start yelling, "Allahu Akbar, Allahu Akbar."

A brother yells over the microphone, "Brothers and sisters go upstairs and someone will escort you to the room for the reception."

"Hezikiah, my father made a true statement about a man," says Robert.

"What's that?" he asked.

"My father said, "When a man wants a woman, he will walk through fire with gasoline underwear on to get her. That's why he better be careful who he picks."

"Yo' father must be right, 'cause Brother George, took the mother, the children and the newborn baby," says Hezikiah.

Robert walks over to Brother George, shaking his hands, while flashing a big smile.

"Hey man, I mean brother. Jjust want you to know, you're a heck of a man." He chuckles, with his shoulders jumping. "You got my vote."

Brother George, medium height. Brown skin, with light brown eyes; holds little Elijah. Reginald has on a bowtie and suit.

"Brother George, hugs Robert and says, "Thank you… love you my brother."

Hezikiah walks over. "Hey, congratulations, ma' brother."

Isiah keeps his eyes on Dawn, smiling from ear to ear. He thinks to himself, "I 'clare. I'd like ta' make this woman ma' Queen."

Dawn catches Isiah watching her. "I ain't doin' nothin', he whispers to Dawn." Dawn smiles slightly.

Osmon compliments everyone, "Mama, Claudia, Matri, Sadie, and Dawn. You all look mighty nice today."

They all smile, thanking him. Osmon continues to look at Claudia, starry-eyed, with a big smile.

"Captain," a brother gets Osmon's attention.

"Excuse me," Osmon starts bowing himself away. "Claudia", he says.

"That man Osmon sure reminds me of Jessie, with all that smilin'," says Ruth. Claudia watches Osmon as he walks away.

"Claudia, he's a good man," says Matri.

Matri notices Anthony watching her. "Ooops, here he comes," Matri says to herself.

He walks, giving the appearance of a giant, tall and focused. "May peace be upon you my Queen."

Matri was hypnotized by the deepness of his voice. "Peace be unto you, too," says Matri.

"Are you enjoying our way of life?" asks Anthony.

Admirably, Matri says, "Of course, I am. The way you treat your women is commendable."

Matri is suddenly focused more on the sound of his voice. He continues to talk, "We have to respect and honor our women, because if we don't, nobody will respect us. Elijah Muhammad says, where you find no decent women, you'll find no decent men."

"I'm assuming it works both ways," says Matri.

Someone yells, "Brothers and sisters have a seat. We're going to serve the food."

After dinner, Ruth talks to the sisters. "We had a wonderful time, but it's time ta' go now. I must say, people tell me 'bout ma' cookin,' but I have ta' say…" She shakes her head. "Lawd' ya' sistas could cook, I'm tellin' ya.''

"Ya' right 'bout that Mama. Them bean pies and bean soups, and I have ta' say, ya' steak and take… great day in the monin'. I could eat two at one time," says Claudia.

"Matri," asks Anthony, "Can I escort you to dinner sometime?"

She shrugs. "I date… don't have any commitments at this time."

He bows to her. "Okay, my sister."

CHAPTER 4

THE UNEXPECTED GOOD
AND BAD

A week later:
"Hello," says Charlotte.

"Charlotte, please ask Matri if she's ready for lunch?"

"Sure, Thaddeus."

"Hello Mrs. Washington, I'll type out your deposition today. Mr. will review it on Monday morning," says Charlotte.

" Hello, no he stepped out. Mr. Tucker, Mr. made an appointment for Tuesday, is that okay? Charlotte asks.

"Ohh...Okay," Charlotte's eyes, stares over at Matri

"Hello Charlotte, tell Matri I'm wafting for her response to my invitation. Did you get around to telling her, or did you forget?"

She begs, "Mrs. Watenburg, hold please." Charlotte, eases the phone down. "I swear sometimes this job is almost unbearable. These clients can be burdensome." Charlotte walks over to Matri's desk. "Matri girl, Thaddeus asks, are you ready for lunch? And please, calm Mrs. Watenburg and tell her if you accept her invitation."

Matri pauses, "Tell Thaddeus, I'll meet him there in twenty minutes. Tell Mrs. Watenburg, yes I accept."

Charlotte exhales. "Okay."

While having Lunch, Matri confesses to Thaddeus. "Matri, can I give you a little history about where we're headed tonight?"

Sticking her fingers in Thaddeus' French fries… "Ah-ha, let me taste your French fries."

He looks at her, "Oh sure, go ahead," says Thaddeus.

"You said we're hanging out in Harlem tonight?" Matri asks.

"Umm, hmm. You know Matri, Harlem hasn't always been a community of Negroes. As a matter of fact, you're going to an area where, El Hajj Malik used to hang out at. But first, allow me to do a little history."

"Thaddeus I need to tell you something first," she pauses. "I've been dating someone else, besides you. It's about friendship and meeting new people."

He, is stunned. "Well, Matri, I adore you beloved. But what can I say, really. I'm hardly ever here. Besides, we're taking our time to get to know one another. Before I ask you to mar…" he pauses. "Just be careful… promise me." He kisses her on the forehead.

She's startled by his response. "Sure, I promise." Matri kisses Thaddeus right back on the forehead.

"Now, Harlem at first was a Dutch settlement. Then came the massive waves of poor and half-starved, ragged immigrants from Europe. They arrived with everything they owned in the world, tucked in bags and sacks on their backs. Then the Germans came. The Dutch edged away from them, and Harlem became all German. Then the Irish from the potato famine, took over Harlem. The Germans left and the Italians came; the Irish ran from them. The Jews came later and the Italians left.

Today, all these same immigrants' descendants are running as hard as they can to escape the descendants of the Negroes who helped to unload the immigrant ships. Then, in 1910, a Negro real estate man somehow got two or three Negro families into one Jewish Harlem apartment house. The Jews flew from that house, then from that block, and more Negroes came to fill their apartments. Whole blocks of Jews ran, and still more Negroes came uptown. Until in a short time, Harlem was like it still is today, virtually all black.

Then, early in the 1920's, music and entertainment sprang up an industry in Harlem, supported by downtown whites who poured uptown every night. It all started about the time a tough young New Orleans man, named Louis "Satchmo" Armstrong, climbed off a train in New York, wearing clodhopper policemen's shoes. He started playing music with Fletcher Henderson. In 1925 Small's Paradise had opened with crowds all across Seventh Avenue. In1926, the great Cotton Club is where Duke Ellington's band, would play for five years. In 1926 the Savoy Ballroom opened with a whole block front on Lenox Avenue. A two-hundred-foot dance floor, under spotlights before two bandstands and a disappearing rear stage. Negroes danced like they never have, anywhere before or since", said Thaddeus.

"So you're going to take us to this historical place, the Savoy?" asks Matri.

"I figured it would be a really good place to go, along with its great historical past and entertainment. Even though it's not quite the same, but knowing its reputation, we would just enjoy being there. Listening to the beautiful Lena Horne would be a great treat." Thaddeus fantasizes about the Savoy.

Matri acts bubbly, "Hmmm, I'm excited."

"Okay, I guess I'll see you guys tonight at 8:00 sharp," says Thaddeus.

⇥⇤

Robert, Hezikiah, and Isiah walks into the Savoy with their army uniforms, getting everyone's attention. Isiah steps aside from the door. "Ladies before gentlemen," he says.

"You ladies smell good tonight," says Robert.

Hezikiah looks around the room, "Hey man, this place is hip."

Giving a slanty smile, "Yeah man, dig it." says Robert.

"It sho' is more relaxin', than where Lorraine takes me, that's fa' sure," says Claudia.

"Lorraine," says Matri? "Let's say, more class."

"This place used to be a swinging place," says Dawn.

"Thaddeus told me." Matri agrees.

"Harlem is where El-Hajj Malik did his partying back in his heyday," says Thaddeus.

"What waz' his name b'fore Malcolm, man?" asks Isiah...

"In his heyday, they called him Red, because of his hair color. He was a street hustler then. He played the game. Later in his life, he showed that anybody could change if you want to," says Thaddeus.

"That's true," says Isiah.

"Here comes the waiter," says Thaddeus.

"I'll have white wine, on the rocks please," says Dawn.

Isiah imitates Dawn, in a low tone. She catches him. "You're so funny," says Dawn.

"Give me King Arthur on the rocks," says Sadie.

Everyone frowns. The waiter looks baffled. Abruptly, Claudia says, "She means Kijafa on the rocks."

Claudia's mouth waters, "Scotch and orange juice on the rocks."

"I'll take a ginger ale on the rocks," says Matri.

Robert says, "I ain't trying to lie, I'm a drinker. You just give me scotch on the rocks, double baby."

"A little bourbon on the rocks," says Hezikiah.

"White wine," says Thaddeus. "Same thing," says Isiah.

Isiah yells out, "Ohhh nooo... hey baby, Marvin!" Everybody gazes at Isiah. "Is it alright ta' dance in here, Thaddeus?"

"You kidding! This is where brother Malcolm X use to throw down, man. Do your thing," says Thaddeus

"Dawn?" Isiah reaches out to her.

Robert winks his eyes at Sadie. "Come on Sadie, let's do this, baby."

"Claudia?" Hezikiah asks.

"Yeah, what chu' think I come here fa'?" Claudia puts on her street walk to the dance floor.

Isiah smiles at Dawn. "Hey look at chu, dancin' real smooth."

Dawn smiles, dancing to the beat of the music, closing her eyes. "That's the way of a Queen baby," says Dawn.

"Alright," Isiah sings "Oh make me wanna holler, baby." Grabbing Dawn's hands, swinging her around and humming, "Da, da, Da, da."

Dawn sings to herself. "Hang ups, let down, set backs… make me wanna holler, throw up both my hands." She throws up her hands, singing aloud. "This ain't livin, no this ain't livin," says Dawn.

"Dig it baby, go baby!" says Robert to Sadie.

"Now what chu' say baby?" asks Sadie.

"Oh! Make me wanna holler, baby…ow!" Robert chuckles.

"He sho' right 'bout' that… bad breaks, set backs," sings Sadie.

"You know something Sadie?" Robert primps.

Sadie squints her eyes up, and boldly asks, "Now, what's that?"

"I think you are a very interesting person," he says.

"Now, how come?" she rolls her eyes.

Robert is amused by Sadie. He chuckles. "Now, don't kill me because I said it. Actually it's a compliment," says Robert.

Sadie's very stern, "Now I ain't gon' kill ya, but I say like Marvin Gaye say, he' tired of bad breaks and so am I," nose widens.

"Do you like poetry baby?" Robert tries to be a little more subdued.

Sadie squints up, her eyes. "Now I ain't never heard—nothin' bout' no po—try."

Robert chuckles. "Hey, don't worry about it, I'll teach you."

She looks at him boldly. "Well that's what chu gon' have ta' do, then," says Sadie.

Hezikiah gazes at Claudia's curvaceous body. Claudia sways her legs from left to right, displaying her body, showing off the gifts God gave her.

"Dig it baby, make me wanna holler," says Hezikiah.

Claudia continues to model while she dances. She notices the other men, sitting at the bar fixated on her.

Dawn and Isiah started holding their hands up in the air, as they sing. They all started holding their hands up in the air singing, "Bad breaks, set backs, make me wanna holler." People joined in with them dancing, waving their hands up in the air.

"I'm going to give Claudia a beating when she comes back here, for dancing like that. I don't know who told her it was alright to dress like that either. You see all those men looking at her?" Matri asks Thaddeus. He tries to control his laughter.

"You know my poor sister started changing since she started going out with that Lorraine thing."

"Lorraine?" He thinks.

"Some girl she works with. Osmon doesn't like her. He told me to keep an eye on her and Lorraine. I'm beginning to see the affect she has on Claudia."

"Be careful with that. You'll push her right into her arms. Don't be so conspicuous. Watch with one eye open." Thaddeus warns.

Matri stares at him. "She doesn't call Osmon, or she won't speak to him sometimes when he calls, but he says Lorraine won't win. He talks about going to Allah for Claudia. He says he didn't make the seed, but he's going to take care of it. Said he, knows that Claudia is a very special kind of woman, and he is not giving up on her." Matri looks up and sees Ramone with two women. One white, one black. He sees her and he's very surprised. He comes over to the table.

"Matri, what a pleasant surprise... oh, pardon my manners. Thaddeus man, I haven't seen you in years. You know Matri?" he asks.

"Do I? Why we're from the same place," Thaddeus explains, proudly.

Stunned by his remark, he asks, "Is that right?"

Thaddeus frowns. "Yeah man, where have you, disappeared to?"

"Well, it's quite a long story, but perhaps at some other point and time we'll talk for old times' sake." He turns around, introducing the two girls by bowing to them. "As you see, I'm here with my friends." They look across the room smiling at Thaddeus and Matri. He exhales, "Well, I'm not going to be rude," bowing to Matri and Thaddeus, as he leaves.

Everybody comes back to the table huffin' and puffin'. "Ah man, that Marvin Gaye. I just love that cat. Ya' kno' he sings 'bout what's happenin' now?" says Isiah.

"You can say that again," says Sadie.

"Oh, this is my drink," says Claudia, with a big smile.

"Hey you cats, I'll be right back," says Robert. Everybody looks at him.

Abruptly, Isiah asks, "You'll be right back?"

Robert guzzles his drink down, and stands up, winking his eyes smiling. "Hey look, I'll give you all a penny for your thoughts, dig it?" He walks away.

A very poised, tall thin man, with dreamy eyes; caramel complexion; processed hair with a part in the middle of his head; wearing glasses, dressed in a suit and tie, comes on stage and says, "Ladies and gentlemen, we have here a dancer, actress, and singer. She's one of the most popular performers of her time... greatest there is … right here at the Savoy. So we want that great history to continue by surprising you with the treat of your life, and also giving new talents a chance. We're going to do something very unusual tonight. We're going to have people imitating other stars tonight, doing their thing. Let's say this is a night of discovery. Who knows where it may take you?"

A beautiful, deep dimpled fair skinned elegant woman, walks towards the mic. He announces, in a poised manner, "For the record, this is certainly no imitation. I'd like to present the one and only, Lena Horne. Let's give this beautiful lady a round of applause. "*Stormy Weather,*" " *Out of Nowhere*" and "*All I Desire,*" by the one and only beautiful... Ms. Lena Horne," he smiles slightly, bowing.

Everyone, stands up applauding her. "This is great," says Thaddeus. Matri notices Ramone applauding her, dazzled by her distinct beauty of deep sunken dimples; eyes nestled deeply into the socket; drawing you in and capturing your attention. She smiles graciously.

"Sounds like Lena Horne," says Thaddeus.

An hour later:

After Lena Horne sings, the applause gets louder and louder. "Ladies and gentlemen," he enchanted by her, "Uunfortunately she cannot stick around tonight. She has another engagement," he smiles, engratiating himself, " You're leaving us elated by your performance. It's been a pleasure. Thank you, thank you. Miss Lena Horne," slightly bows.

Robert comes back with flowers for Sadie. "Here you go young lady."

Sadie and everyone else stare at Robert. He looks up at everybody and says, "Ah...well, better me than someone else. I always say, you have to beat the other guy to the punch." Sadie stares at Robert, smiling from ear to ear. Matri's face brightens, watching Sadie's reaction to Robert.

"Ladies and gentlemen, are we ready? Once again we're going to give you a surprise with a man that's known as a giant in a sea of gems. His delivery is eclectic and sincere, as a soul artist could possibly get. Give Mr. Donny Hathaway a round of applause, singing "*Someday We'll All Be Free*" and "*I'll Love You More Than You'll Ever Know.*" By the way, when I heard his first song, I literally cried when I sat and listened to it "

A dark brown-skinned man, with an oval shaped face; big oval shaped eyes, wearing an apple hat... sits at the piano. He sings, "Someday We'll All Be Free."

Hang on to the world as it spins around, Just don't let the spin get you down. Things are moving fast. Keep your self-respect.... Keep you're self-respect... your manly pride... Get yourself in gear... Keep your stride.... Never mind your fears.... Brighter days will soon be here... Take it from me... Someday We'll All Be Free... Keep on walking tall... Hold your head up high. Play your dreams right up to the sky... Sing your greatest song... and you'll keep going on. Take it from me... Hey just wait and see ... We'll All Be Free. Now, I'll Love You More. ...

"Let's give another round of applause for Mr. Hathaway."

"Man that cat touches my soul," says Robert.

"Dig it man, we need to be free, before we could do anything," says Thaddeus.

Sadie continues to stare at Robert. He winks and she blushes. Robert purposely lets Sadie see him whispering to Hezikiah. "I like to see a woman blush. That's how I know she likes me, man."

"Ladies and gentlemen, he's going to do one more song, "*I'll Love You More Than You'll Ever Know.*"

"Man this cat is awesome," says Robert.

Isiah and Hezikiah say, "Dig it baby."

"A round of applause for Mr. Hathaway... but he too has other engagements tonight."

He smiles saying, "Thank you, it's my pleasure being here with you tonight, for this short time, but I really wanted to share these songs with you... thank you."

"Now, is there anyone in the audience that would like to sing a song, tell a joke... anything... imitate someone. Come right on up."

Dawn jumps up. Everybody is surprised. She continues to walk like a Queen... without looking back.

"Okay, what do we have here? What would you like to sing Miss African Queen?" Dawn blushes, taking the mic, she looks back at the table, smiling. She notices that they're all dazed by her. She could see Isiah's eyes glued onto her.

Looking at the man, she says, "I'd like to sing *"Wishing On A Star"*, by Rolls Royce."

He turns around looking at the band. "Do you think you could do this one? I know it's unrehearsed." They all nod their heads. "Okay, it's all yours."

Dawn sings, *"Wishing On A Star."*

I'm wishing on a star... to follow where you are... I'm wishing on a dream... to follow what it mean... I'm wishing on a star... to follow where you are... I'm wishing on a dream to follow what it means.

The audience was in awe of her voice. Everyone at the table is speechless by Dawn's voice. Her voice echoes like an angel from heaven. Folks in the audience are teary- eyed.

Dawn looks straight at the audience, focusing on everyone's eyes.

And I wish that all the rainbows that I see... I wish that all the people who really dream... And I wish that all tomorrow bring... And I wish that all the love in me never die... Looking afar, she continues to sing. *I never thought I'd never see...* Looks at Isiah, *The time that you would be so far away from home... so far away from me.*

"Please, please, let's give this wonderful woman a round of ap-plause. Let's give them all a round of applause. Everybody stands up, applauding, whistling and clapping.

As Dawn walks to the table, everyone's eyes are fixated on her. Excitedly Matri says, "Dawn, I 'clare. I didn't know you could sing like that."

"I know Matri, I just never got around to telling you," she blushes.

Isiah spoke very softly, "Dawn, that was beautiful, and ya' could sing ta' me any tame." Everybody stares at Isiah. "What… what?" Isiah acts clueless.

"Hey Dawn, where did you get a voice like that?" Robert asks.

"Dawn I 'clare, got a voice like Claf," says Claudia.

"You the best, "says Hezikiah.

"I 'clare, you could sing to me anytime," Sadie emphasizes.

"This has been a really great night for me," says Matri.

"I have to say something to Robert now," says Sadie. Everyone stops talking abruptly. Sadie says firmly, "Robert, I just want ta' say that.. well I could barely say what I want ta' say." Looking at Robert smiling, "'Cause I don't have the words," she pauses. "Thank ya' fa' the flowers. Now, ya' really touched ma' heart t'night."

Robert imitates her, by looking at Isiah and Hezikiah, blushing. "You welcome, and Sadie don't worry about words so much… sometimes there are no better words than what the heart will give you. The heart speaks for you too, Sadie."

"Now this cat need ta' go up there on stage his'self, for poetic charm. He's good, I'll tell ya," says ' Hezikiah..

Robert starts laughing, chest sinking inward. "It's from the heart, man that's poetic. Dig it baby?"

⊱⊰ ⊱⊰

"Matri," says Timothy, "The school is going to close in a minute. It's 8:30."

Matri exhales, "Okay, ten minutes and I'm done."

"I want to walk you to your car," Timothy says caringly.

Matri slams her books closed. "There you go. I'm done."

"By the way, I never got a chance, all this time to tell you, I really like your car. That convertible, is uniquely you," Timothy assures Matri.

"It's okay, you were away, so how could you," says Matri.

"I'm glad I decided to take these classes for the summer. It's going to get me out of school quicker," says Timothy.

"Yeah, me too." Matri agrees.

Timothy walks Matri to her car. "Okay Matri, you be safe, now."

"I'm going to the drive-in movie. I need a little time to myself. I need to do some thinking." Matri' seems a little troubled.

"Hey, it's like that sometimes," says Timothy.

"Yeah, goodnight," says Matri.

⇒⊱ ⊰⇐

Two hours later, Matri sits in her car. "Hmmm, I enjoyed that movie. Maybe I'll tell Isiah about it. Maybe he and Robert might want to double up and see it ." Her stomach growls. *Oooh, I'm starving. I could go to that diner over there and treat myself to a late meal.* "I'm gonna have to park at least three blocks away. Oh, I'm starving."

As she begin to walk, she notices a crowd of people, about three blocks away from the diner. The guys are yelling. "Yeah man, stomp 'em!"

"Man! What chu waitin' on man, you got 'em' down."

"Go 'head man, out his lights. He wouldn't give you no break!"

The crowd cheers the guys on. Yeah finish 'em off. Do it now… do it… do it." A chocolate complexion, medium- framed, muscular guy named Smitty jumps up. Letting the other guy get up, reaching out for his hands. Smitty shakes his hands. "Hey man, it was a fair fight," says Smitty. The other guy is shocked by his decision to let 'em get up.

The guy that he beat, says, "Thank you man—you a better man than me. You beat me twice."

Smitty is puzzled by his comment. The guy turns around looking at the people, saying, "I guess ya' people don't understand what I just said. He beat me twice." Points out one finger." One time for beating me," points out second finger, "And the second time for not having the need not to kill me, and prove his manhood over somethin' that really didn't make no sense."

Matri walks over to the guy and applauds. "I have to say, that you did something very special."

He looks up at her, talking cool and smooth. "It really ain't no—thing baby... but, thank you anyway."

Matri stares at him. "Tell me somthin'," he says.

"What?" asks Matri.

"What's a pretty little Red Robinhood, doin' out this time a night? You ain't scared of these big bad wolves out here?"

"Thank you. I think, for the compliment." He starts looking as if he lost something. "What did you lose?" asks Matri.

"Cinderella, I'm looking for that shoe you lost, 'cause the prince is going with you. A pretty girl like you ain't got no business being out here like this. I'll protect you from the wolves. Elijah Muhammad said protect the Black woman."

Matri laughs.

"I mean if you don't mind... that is," says Smitty.

"How can I refuse protection as a Black woman," she says proudly. Matri's amused by him. "Are you Muslim?"

" Elijah Muhammad says 'We are all Muslims by nature', so I just leave it like that."

He starts walking cool. "Now Matri, when we walk in there, there might be some guys in there that I know." He pauses, "You don't mind me showing you off... do you?"

Matri blushes, and says softly, "No."

"Look—at chu—you blushin'… you make me—blush. Don't no woman make me blush—they make me mad." he stares at her, "You real sweet Matri," says Smitty.

"Well…I," Smitty interrupts her.…

"Come on, there's a table over there near the window." Smitty points to the corner.

Two guys are sitting at the diner, watching Matri… very boldly. The waitresses gazes at Matri. "You see those waitresses watching you? I wanna make them jealous," says Smitty.

Teasing him, Matri says, "Hey now, I didn't come out here to get beat up."

"Oh no, they have to come through me first." He shakes his head. "Believe me, they don't want to do that," He says firmly, "They know me."

"Here she comes," says Matri.

He is smitten by Matri. "Dig here, you just git' what chu want, I'm payin', baby."

"You don't have…"

Smitty sings abruptly. "App… don't—saaay—it."

Matri laughs. "Okay, you could pay."

Smitty says, "I'll have fish, potatoes, and a vegetable with ice tea."

"I'll have candy yams, collard greens, string beans with rice, and ice tea."

He looks up to Matri, "Now my beautiful angel… no meat? I want chu to eat all you could eat," Smitty explains.

Matri looks at Smitty, taking out two Chinese proverb cookies, from a brown paper bag. He throws it, into his mouth. "No, Smitty you don't eat that, there's paper sticking out of it." He turns around to see if anyone is looking, and takes it out of his mouth. They both laugh.

Matri tells him to open the cookie. "Smitty, it looks like you're supposed to open it."

Smitty opens it... he stares at it.

"Well, what does it say Smitty?" asks Matri.

He hesitates to look at her. "Angel, you read it." He's a little disturbed by it.

Matri reads it. "There's always an angel at the end of the road." They both are quiet.

"Here, I'll give you one. Matri read, I'm not gonna' let you git out of it, my angel," he says.

"Alright, let's see. The weight of the future is heavy, only when you don't understand it."

Smitty stares at her. " I'm talking like, I been knowing you for a lifetime. I don't understand it, man. It's kind of crazy," he stares into her eyes, " Dig it."

"Smitty, you seem like a really good guy at heart. What are you doing with your life?" asks Matri.

Acting nonchalant…"It ain't nothin' for me ta' do…"

Matri's not excepting this. "What?" She stares at him.

He looks around the diner…. pauses. He looks around again… ."Matri, I—sell things baby."

Her forehead crinkles."What kind of things... do you have a store?"

He pauses, getting annoyed with her. "You sure ask a lot of questions, baby."

"Mama always said," she pauses.

Abruptly he says annoyingly, "Sometimes it ain't good to ask too many questions." He nods at her, "Didn't Mama tell you that?"

Puckering her lips. "Ummm, for some reason I still wanna know."

Acting agitated, he says. "Okay… okay… I work for a drugstore."

Matri doesn't believe him. "Now I might be green, but you've got to come better than that."

He feels, compelled to tell her. " Baby, look... I sell drugs. You know... dope, cocaine, heroin," looks at her, hunching up his shoulders.

Matri puts her hand on her heart. Sadness in her eyes. "Drugs... why?"

"It's quick and easy. Marvin Gaye sings, *"Make Me Wanna Holler."* "I ain't gotta work all day and give it to the man. I'm my own boss," points finger in his chest.

She imitates him. "Oh cause you ain't—gotta, give it to--the mannnn?"

Smitty looks at her with compassion and love. "Marvin Gaye also mentions, trigger happy policemen," Matri tries to warn him.

He looks around,"Matri, you don't need to be out here in these streets. Little Red Robinhood... where you from?"

She presses against her heart. "I came from South Carolina, two years ago."

"You green ha?" He laughs. "Listen to me girl, and listen to me good. I want this to be the last time I see you, or see you out in these here streets at this time of night." He stares at her, holding her hands.

She grabs his hands gently, asking him. "What's wrong?

He slowly looks up at her. "Listen, I had a beautiful sister. She was a beauty, just like you. Her body was tight, like a grown woman's. She turned a lot of men's head. But I lost her to the streets. She became a prostitute... was young, sort of green, like you. The girl didn't know what she was doing, wanted to be grown. Ran away from home with this older guy. He ended up putting her on the streets as a prostitute. That's all he intended to do in the first place. He was a real charmer," Matri notices the venom in his eyes.

Matri listens as if she has known this man for a lifetime, "Hmmm."

"When I approached him about my sister, I swear he tried to charm me too. I had to let him know that I wasn't no woman, and he couldn't charm me... no sugar in my tank either.

"Sugar in your tank?" asks Matri.

"I ain't no homosexual," says Smitty.

He balls his fist up angrily. "Mama tried to stop 'er. Mama suffered so much. My mama almost lost 'er mind behind it."

"How old was she?" asks Matri.

He became furious. "She was sixteen at the time. Mama and daddy tried, everybody tried to get 'er away from him."

Matri's saddened. "Oh I'm so sorry," lookin into his eyes, shaking her head.

He starts shaking his head. "Finally we gave up." He banged on the table. "It was like he had a spell on 'er. "Mama said, they were just two of a kind, and that people have things in 'em, that are alike... but 'chu just can't see it."

With dismay, she asks, "Well, what are you doing out here then?"

Mischievously he says, "It was like the hunter gets captured by the game. Never intended on this way. But I, was gonna rescue my sister. I got caught out here, like that and messin' with drugs too."

Matri thinks to herself. My heart, this is painful. Matri grabs his hands. "Let me help you." Looking into his eyes, "I believe I can."

Smitty smiles and kisses her hands. "My beautiful angel. Remember this, just like I couldn't help my sister... you can't help me. There are some people you just can't save. Sometimes it's destiny." He pauses, looking into her eyes, "Just like now. Maybe, I did meet an angel at the end of my road. I'm probably dreaming, because it's too late. There are some people lookin' for me now."

Matri commiserates over his pain. "What people... why?"

He grabs Matri's hands, holding them tightly, looking into her eyes again, "It was good to have this time, to talk with you. I don't know where you... why we came together, but listen my angel, I want you to get away from me... now." He looks out of the window. "It ain't even safe for you to be 'round me, not even for a second... really."

A voice yells, "Smitty get down!" Smitty looks towards the window. Bullets start firing through the window. People are screaming and running scared. Smitty took a dive over Matri to protect her from the bullets. Glass and blood cover the diner. The gunmen pulled off fearlessly down the street.

⇥ ⇤

Hours later, someone says in a very friendly tone, "Hello ma'am, can you speak?" The nurse asks Matri.

Matri opens her eyes. Oblivious to her surroundings, she tries to get up, and falls back. "Ouch, my head. I feel dizzy," says Matri

Very friendly face, caucasian nurse says, "Ma'am, you'll be okay. You have a few scratches from the impact of the glass. You're dizzy because, you must've hit your head on something. Fortunately, it's just a mild concussion," says the nurse.

"Oooh," Matri grabs her head.

Observing her, she says, "You were out when you got here."

Struggling to speak, "What happened to me? I need to call my family," she says.

Smiling, she says, "I did that for you. Got the number out of your phonebook. Told your family to come in about noon."

Matri stares at her round face and black hair; combed back in a bun." What? asks Matri, noticing the mole on her lip.

"You're going to need, just a little more rest, to remember anything much."

Six hours later, a nurse comes into the room with a detective. "Matri, I see you ate your food...good," says the nurse.

"I don't feel so dizzy now," says Matri

"You needed that time to sleep it off," the nurse said.

Matri feels the white cloth around her head.

The nurse winds the bed up into a sitting position, checking Matri's temperature. "Are you up to answering a few questions?"

"I am," Matri responds.

"Your family, will be here in about an hour."

"Good," says Matri.

The detective stands outside the door. "Matri, there's someone that would like to talk to you, for a minute."

"Sure," she says.

A tall, very soberly-looking Caucasian man, with black hair and huge feet, steps into the room. Lookin over his glasses, "Hello Matri, my name is Detective Goe. I'm only gonna ask you a few questions," he says.

"Okay."

"Do you know Mr.....ah," He looks at his notes.... "Mr. Smitty?"

Matri pauses…"Yes, he's my brother."

"In a few words, could you tell me what happened?" He asks.

Matri exhales, Okay, let me think. We were in the diner eating... sitting at the window. I just happened to look out of the window, and…" She started panting. "I noticed some men had guns, aiming towards the window, pointed towards Smitty. But Smitty kept smiling at me. By the time he figured out what I was saying... and looked, it was too late. Then someone yelled out, "Get down!" Matri becomes rigid. "I remember Smitty was diving towards me. He was trying to take the bullets to protect me,"

"This is a very precarious situation. Now, do you have any idea what it was about?"

Matri is baffled. She shakes her head. "It's…enigma …" Matri grabs her head. "Ooooh, that's what… I need to know…why?" She grabs her head again.

The nurse says, "Mr. Goe, I think that better be all, right now."

He agrees. "Yes, yes, of course. Matri I'll need you to come downtown for a report of this, when you're better."

Matri seems out of breath. "Sure."

Matri's clock watching, as she lays in the bed, perturbed over what had happened. Everyone comes in the door.

"Matri, are you alright?" asks Dawn, teary eyed.

"What happened ma' sister?" asks Claudia.

"Claudia, don't start, I know how you are. I'm fine. Just look at me Claudia," says Matri.

"Ya' okay?" She nods. "We didn't want to worry Mama. We told Mama, ya' fine."

The nurse comes in. "She'll be out of here tomorrow. Had a mild concussion. We have to keep her for observation."

"Matri, ya' don' have ta' tell us everythang right now," says Isiah.

"Claudia, call Charlotte and tell her I had an accident. I'll be out for a few days," says Matri.

The nurse comes back. "I'm sorry, everybody. I have to make the visit short. She has to get as much rest as she possibly can, so that she can leave tomorrow."

"Okay Matri," says Dawn, kissing her on the forehead.

Git' some rest," says Isiah.

"I'll tell Mama you'll be home t'morrow," says Claudia

"Oh wait a minute Isiah," says Matri. "Here take my keys and pick my car up. It's on Warren Street, three blocks from the Fishboat.

"Okay, we'll go there now, b'fore someone tries ta' steal it," says Isiah.

"You can pick her up at noon," the nurse says, smiling.

"Wait," says Matri, "I have to see Smitty first."

"Smitty?" asks, Isiah.

"He's the guy involved in this too," says Matri.

Everybody stares at her, with no comment.

The next day, a different nurse comes in. Short stubby, nurse, with red shoulder length hair. "Oh, there you are. I came in a few minutes ago, you were in the bathroom."

Matri asks, "What happened to the other nurse?"

Putting her finger underneath her chin, she thinks for a minute. "Ohh, you're talking about the one you had yesterday? She's off today. People are always asking for her, she's very well-liked by the patients."

Matri says, "I feel so much better now. No dizziness."

"Good," the nurse says, as she strips the bed. "Matri, you're brother needs to see you, in the intensive care unit. Your mom and dad are down there waiting for you."

Matri thinks, "My mom and dad?"

"Do you want me to push you to the ICU?" The nurse insists.

"No, no, I honestly feel good enough to walk."

The nurse takes Matri to the ICU unit. "We have to take this elevator, then make a left turn."

Matri thinks, Oh my God, how am I going to explain to them, why I'm posing as his sister?

The nurse slightly smiles to Smitty's parents. "Here you go Matri. It wasn't too far now, was it?" she smiles pleasantly.

Thinking, Oh boy, Smitty's parents are looking at me, from head to toe. I can't say that I blame them.

"Try to make yourselves comfortable. If you need anything, the nurses at the desk will help you," says the nurse.

A stocky, blond haired caucasian doctor, comes out with a very stern face. "Hello," bowing his head to Smitty's parents. "Now, I need you to come inside... to talk to him as long as you can," very firm, he says, "We've done everything we could do," his lips puckers, " He was shot eight times. He was shot several places on the body. There are two bullets in his head, and one in the back and spinal area, that's causing him excruciating pain." Smitty's mother steps back, losing strength. Her husband holds onto her tightly. The doctor pauses, for a minute, "If we tried to remove them, it would cause massive hemorraging. We had to give him very strong doses of medicine for pain through the IV," the doctor 's eyes expresses deep concern for the family. He gives them time to digest this terrible situation.

Smitty's mother leans her head on her husband's shoulder. Matri walks over to Smitty's parents. Her mouth is almost too dry to talk. She's afraid to speak. "I… I…was with him when it happened," she says timidly. Smitty's mother just looks at Matri, too full of pain to talk. She shakes her head, giving her the okay.

The doctor says, very jently, "Please step this way."

Walking towards the ICU, Matri thinks to herself.… *I remember when Claf…* She freezes. *No–I don't need to think.*" In her mind, she's reliving that tragic experience of Claf's death, before she stepped into the ambulance. Having to experience the unknown of what was behind the door. She's visualizing, the door to the ambulance. She thinks, "The coldest day of my life. The walk to the ICU seems far... but in reality, it isn't.

Mr. Smith opens the door to the intensive care room. Matri sees Smitty, laying in the bed, bandaged from head to toe… just like Claf. Her head is pounding, and she's having flashbacks of Claf before he died. "Ohhh!" Eyes weary... very gently, she whispers to herself. "Claf… is—that—Claf?... oh—no!...." She stares, heart beating rapidly, vision blurred, "He… he—looks like Claf!" She starts wiping the sweat from her forehead, and tries to camouflage herself by smiling. Mrs. Smith sadly watches her. Matri tries to compose herself. She gulps, "I'm okay... I had a mild concussion… that's all."

Matri thinks, *We stand around Smitty's bed, nervously waiting... giving him the courtesy of speaking first. Understanding the precious seconds of his life… for truly, time is of the essence for him.*"

"Ohhh!" says Mrs. Smith, exhaling, wiping the tears from her eyes.

Matri continues to think. *As we watch, all of our eyes are in a world of hope… not realizing, Smitty lays still… he has stilled us… waiting for just one move… a flutter of the eye… a twitch from his painful body. Mama says, there comes a time when God says, 'Be still and know, that I am God.' And when you're patient… he never leaves you… I must say this to them.* "Let us be patient please."

Looking at Mrs. Smith, Matri continues… "We need God here."

"Ohhh, he's moving!" whispers Mrs. Smith.

Mr. Smith thinks, *Oh son, I really don't see you surviving this; but they say, God can bring back the dead to life… so who am I to give up?*

Matri thinks, We all move tightly together, towards Smitty; to catch every breath that he breathes… taking it as a sign of life and hope.

" Maaama." Smitty struggles to speak.

"Yes baby," She kisses him on the forehead.

"Maaama," he says again.

Matri thinks, We tryin' to move even closer, but there is no more space.

Mrs. Smith says, "Yes, my baby, I love you and will always love you. Your sister… no matter what… will always be with you."

Mr. Smith realizes that he better say his last words. His big oval shaped eyes, widens, "Hey man, " with husiness in his voice, "you know we had something special going on. You got that mule-head stubbornness, like your father. From man to man, I had to let you do what a man felt he had to do… even with failure. I knew what you were trying to do," he pauses, shaking hs head, "You loved your sister," buckles in his lips, " I love you… my son."

"Mr. and Mrs. Smith left me to talk to you alone. For some rea- son it's hard for me to get words out right now." Matri stills herself.

She gulps, smiling, "Hey, Smitty… ha-huh. You know, even though we knew each other for a very short period of time. I, I don't know why this happened. My mama tells me, that we can't always understand things right away; sometimes they come when we are long gone. Truth comes on its own time."

Smitty stares at Matri, and smiles peacefully… then suddenly, looks up at the ceiling, as if he sees something. He becomes dys- pneic, barely able to breath; then he slowly closes his eyes.

At Smitty's funeral, Matri looks around at everyone. Isiah and Dawn are present. When the coffin drops, Matri thinks about the purpose, of life and death. " Is this all an illusion, and is death the reality of our total existence?"

⇒⊹⊹⇐

King says, 'We've got to get over being afraid of death.' ' When the coffin is lowered, this affects me the most.... makes me think, of my own death.'

Mrs. Smith is squeezing my hands. I guess she feels close to me. She wanted me to ride in the funeral car with the family. Wait—a—minute. Matri pauses, looking adjacent to her. There is someone, staring at me. She or he... looks... incognito? Matri looks at the person dressed in all black... not too clean. Wearing a big black cap; dark shades, a coat that's really too big. The person keeps staring. Mrs. Smith squeezes Matri's hands again.

The minister speaks, "Everyone please throw the dirt now." Matri throws the dirt with Mrs. Smith.

Waiting for the person with the black cap on, to throw dirt. She wants to see who this person is... man or woman? Matri's looking around, but the person never comes to throw dirt on the coffin. They disappear. Matri looks all across the cemetery. "Was that person an illusion?"

Standing behind a tree. The person watches from afar, whining like a child..."Unnn... unnn... unnn. My brother, ohhh, my brother. They killed him.... my brother. Oh my brother, oh my brother... unnnn... unnnn." The person takes off, whining and running. "Uunnn...unnn."

⇒⊹⊹⇐

Matri is sitting at the dining room table with Civil, reading a letter from Lasette. "Civil, do you want me to read this to you, too? Oh

Mama this is so heartwarming. Come here Mama and listen to this."

"Matri, I ain't got time ta' fool with ya' this mornin', got rehearsal. Don' kno' why ya' and Claudia won't come ta' chuch with me sometime." Ruth is clearly, frustrated.

Matri turns around, facing Mama. "Mama... I 'clare now, if it means that much to you, you know I'll come. As a matter a fact, today is Saturday... I'll go tomorrow."

"Where is Claudia anyway?" Ruth wonders.

"Mama, we have to talk about Claudia. She went out with Lorraine last night and she didn't get back yet." Mama starts looking around for the children. "Claudia took the boys to Sadie's last night."

Ruth chews down on her lips. "Matri, I been watchin' Claudia 'with that old Lorraine girl. I don' have good spirits 'bout that child, no how. Claudia needs a good old fashion whippin'... that's all. She kno' I didn't raise her like this, and she gon' git' it in a minute," nods her head, "Let 'er just keep on playin' with me, I 'clare."

Matri didn't want to laugh, but couldn't help it. Looks at Ruth's expression on her face.

"Now let me see this here letter... I need some chewin' tobacco," says Ruth.

"Okay Mama... now, can I read it to you please, Mama?" Ruth sits down patiently folding her arms up, biting down on her lips.

It says:

Dear Auntie Matri, I miss you all. Mommy say, you are our angel. She say, you say we suppose to dream about what we want and I dream to be just like you, when I grow up. Mommy say it's okay, because I love her too. Thank you and Mama for giving us lots of love, when we needed it. My mommy helped me with this letter. But these are my own words to you.

- As-salaamu'alaykum, Lasette

"Now that's a sweet child," says Ruth.

"Yes, she is," says Matri.

"One day Matri, you'll be married and have ya' own," says Mama.

Matri is still smiling, looking at the letter, thinking about Thaddeus and Ramone. "Oh, what did you say Mama?"

I say, "One day you'll have your own chirrin."

Matri stares at Mama. "Yeah Mama, I sure will. Just have to figure out... who?"

Ruth leans back. "Who?" asks Ruth.

Quietly she says, "Yeah, Thaddeus or Ramone."

Ruth stares at Matri. "When the time come, you'll kno', but I'll bet on Thaddeus," says Ruth.

Teases Ruth, she says, "Ohhh?" eyes buldging.

Isiah comes in the door. He kisses Ruth and Matri on the cheek. "Well, I gotta go ta' chuch now."

"Mama ya' want me ta' take ya'?" asks Isiah.

"No, ma' girlfriend is on her way, I'll just wait downstairs."

"Okay Mama," says Isiah.

Isiah sits at the table with the newspaper. "Matri ya' see this?" He hits the paper with his hand. "Now I'm home for, eight months, lookin' and lookin' for a job. Why can't a man like me find a job? I just served Uncle Sam.... that's my credential. Ya' kno' somethin' Matri? The construction work could help me out real good, but they keep layin' us off."

"You mean Robert and Hezikiah too?" Matri is confused.

"Hezikiah went first, three weeks ago. They claim he missed his turn 'cause he had too many appointments, and with me and Robert, it waz' last hired, first ta' lay off." Isiah appears disgruntled.

"Appointments?" Matri is confused.

"Yeah, he had t ta' go see his lawyer and a psychiatrist, alot in the beginnin'," answers Isiah.

"A psychiatrist?" Matri frowns.

Isiah pauses. "Well Matri, it's a long story, but ain't nothin' wrong with his head now. He just pre-tendin'.'" He shrugs, feelin' dubious about it. "At least, so he say."

Matri chuckles, "Ummm."

" But anyway, they give us a few jobs. But whenever we try ta' git inta' the Union, they lay us off, " he says angrily. " "But mind ya', the white cats is in the Union. That's how they keep the jump on the jobs. It don't mean a damn thang ta' nobody, whether or not we served this country. Don't nobody respect it!" Isiah is furious.

Isiah continues to read the paper. His forehead crinkles. "Listen ta' this Matri. The Urban League reports that, since 1960, unemployment rates for Blacks have been doubled more than for whites," his eyes flutter. "Now would somebody please tell me why, Matri!"

"Absolutely, that is the question." Matri is perplexed by this.

Isiah gets louder; eyes flapping. "Ya' kno' Matri, I begin ta' feel like…"

Matri interrupts abruptly "Feel like El-Hajj Malik says, 'You've been had… you've been bamboozled… you been took," says Matri.

His eyes get moist. "Figured what I been through, in 'Nam… I'd come back ta' the land of opportunity… and possibilities would be just waitin' for me." Isiah shakes his head, tears fall down his face. "It ain't been easy fightin' for old Sam—Matri." He slams his hands on the table, staring at Matri. " I'll never, be the same again!"

Matri feels like running away from Isiah. She starts to feel, a deep sense of pain and hurt, in her heart again. It's taking all she could do to continue to listen. She turns around reaching for Civil, taking the bird out of the cage. "You see this bird Isiah?" With tenderness, she says, "Dear Heart, this bird and his name is like the omen to the future. Mama and me, we don't know where this big white bird came from. Didn't know this bird's name would have a very significant meaning to our movement today."

Matri almost screams out, "It's about civil rights, human rights." Compassionately, looking at Civil, she says softly, "Now I 'clare, isn't that right, Civil?"

"You know Isiah, there are a lot of Black movements that was fought, and are still fighting for the grave injustice being done to our people. There are people like: Marcus Garvey, Dr. King, El-Hajj Malik and Angela Davis, that are still fighting for our causes; not in a harmful way, but civil; fighting with the intellect," says Matri.

"It hurts me, Matri." Isiah puts the paper down. "Ya' kno' Matri, I ain't never told nobody this b'fore, not even Mama." He flattens his hands, scratching on his chest. "Some-tames I feel like I'm hur-tin' real bad inside... like the war hurt me real bad, Matri. I' seen so much... too much, and did thangs, I would've never done in ma' life. I never even dreamed 'bout it; killin' old people, women, and I seen men with heads cut off, hanging on fences. That waz used as a scare tactic, Matri." Like a broken dam, his tears burst through. Matri gets up and sits on his lap, leaning her head against his. Trying not to explode, she whispers, looking into his eyes... wiping the tears. "We all, just have to hold on to one another, like bricks on a wall; with this pain, we carry around in our hearts... from the injustice that causes us to do terrible things," wearily, she gathers strength, " We have to hang on to hope, and believe... we will find the cure, to a broken heart."

The door slams. Claudia comes in from a hard night of party-ing. "Come on Paul and Roy. Let's get dressed so I can take ya' ta' the movies t'day."

Isiah and Matri stares at Claudia. "The movies? You sure don't look like you could take yourself to the movies, let alone anybody else," says Matri.

Angrily, Claudia says, holding her head, "Okay, okay Matri, ya' just watch me."

Isiah says, "Claudia, the brother name Osmon been callin' ya'."

She feels detached, "Who... yeah, what else is new?"

"You know Claudia, I just don't understand you, lately." Matri looks at the bird. "Do you Civil? Do you understand her?"

Stops in her track, "Matri, just leave me ta' ma'self, okay?" advises Claudia.

"Claudia, it's just that Lorraine isn't, the best company you should be keeping. After all, you have children," stares at her frowning, swaying her hands out.

Claudia's eyes widen. "And what is that supposed ta' mean? I take good care of ma' children."

"Yes, you do," Matri says gently, "But you've been a little short-tempered with them lately, because you've been drinking and hanging out too much."

The boys come running to her, grabbing onto her legs. "Mama hurry up! Let's go to the movies now," says Paul. "Right now!" says Roy.

Claudia snatches them from around her legs, stumbling back; falling against the wall. "Now turn me aloose! Damnit!" She yells. The boys starts crying. Matri and Isiah watches her.

"Claudia let me help you with them. Just go and get ready to take them to the movies." Matri gives them both an apple.

Isiah helps. "Hey, come here man. I'm not gonna have these tears now." Claudia runs into the bathroom, crying silently.

Matri says, "Let Uncle Isiah and me, see your homework. Now I know, you've got some school work?" They both ran into the room, getting their papers.

Smiling and acting surprised, "Oh, man ya' did this?" asks Isiah.

Paul says cheerfully, nodding his head, "Yeah."

Jovially, Matri asks, "Oh my, Roy did you do this?"

Pretending to be excited, Claudia comes out of the room. "Well boys, lets go. Kiss Uncle Isiah and Auntie Matri."

The phone rings, Claudia gets it. "Hello."

"What's wrong, my Queen?"

"Ain't nothing wrong, just tired."

"Tired, it's early in the day."

"I—been—out, last night."

"Where did you go?"

"I went to the city."

"Claudia, you better stay out of the city now. You don't know enough to be in no, city."

"I went with Lorraine."

"That's even worse. The city and Lorraine?"

"Osmon what chu' cawl' me fa?"

"Where you goin'?"

"I'm takin' ma' boys to the movie."

"Can I take you?"

"Ummm... if you want to. I thought we ain't suppose ta' be alone?"

"We wouldn't be alone. Your boys would be there right, and b'sides Anthony will drop us off."

"Okay, Osmon."

Claudia looks very tired. Speaking slowly, she says, "That waz' Osmon, he gon' come and take us."

"That's a great idea Claudia," says Matri.

Isiah chuckles, "That Osmon, I like that guy. He's a strong, good man Claudia."

Matri looks at Claudia. "Let me make you some coffee before he comes, maybe it'll wake you up, some."

Isiah thinks, "Ya' kno' Matri, Robert found this place called, 'The Hideaway'. He said it's like a little cave, but it's a bar in a basement. Robert says, it's peaceful, and that I need ta' check it out soon."

Matri thinks about her secret cache. "A cave... ummm, go into your cave, Isiah."

CHAPTER 5

THE BASEMENT PEOPLE

Isiah, Robert and Hezikiah meet up at the basement bar. It's a small bar, that seems off from the world; reminding you of a cave; the walls are clay-colored brick. It has very dim lights and a very peaceful cozy scene.

"Hey Robert, this is a nice... little cozy, peaceful bar," says Isiah.

Wryly he says, with a smile, "Yeah, I just stumbled up on it—wait a minute, I have to be careful what I say around you cats. You seem to think, I love booze. I wasn't drunk, I just happened to run across it," says Robert, chuckling.

"I could understand why they call it 'The Hideaway'", says Isiah.

"You want another hit?" asks Rufus the bartender. Rufus was a short; stout man; big round, baldheaded with big eyes. He was constantly rubbing the counter and cleaning.

"Yeah man, give me another white Saturn on the rocks," says Isiah. The bartender continues to rub the counter.

"Man, you gon' rub the paint off the counter," says Robert.

The bartender laughs. "I guess I'm a clean freak."

Robert says, "Well don't freak out on me, baby?" They both laugh.

He says, "Hey man, I give my hat to both of you… that 'Nam war ain't no joke. Just don't how you did it, with bullets flying at you all the time." He starts sweating. "I couldn't go, 'cause I had asthma real bad," says Rufus.

Robert says, with piercing eyes. "Well man, I tell ya… it goes like this." Looking stern, he puts his finger under his chin, thinking; then points to his head…. "It's psychological man, really. If you think you can't do it, then you won't."

"Oh," says the bartender.

"Listen, it goes like this now." Adamantly he says, "I had a talk with the Lord, telling him that I was going to put it in my mind, that I was coming back… If it was alright with him. My mind was made up. I was going on the word, from the man upstairs baby. I was coming back…" he says with furor. "I didn't care what nobody, said!" The bartender had given Robert strength. He breathes inward, exhaling. The music stops and the people listen, attentively.

"'Let me tell you what they did to me, man. It was like that book, "The Spook That Sat By The Door." They put me in the back line, to make it look good. I looked in the front and I saw Hezikiah and Isiah up in the front line, man." Pointing to his head, he continued, "Man, ain't never been no dummy… I figured it out. I'm the chosen one to make it look good, to hide the disparity of treatment towards the brothers, man. I told the sergeant that I didn't want to be in the back, and I learned a few new words from Uncle Sam… one was an opportunist. I told him that, I wanted an opportunity to go down with the best… fighting in the front line with my brothers," says Robert.

The people cheered him in the bar. Men came over shaking his hands, telling him he's a heck of a man. Robert and Isiah look at each other teary-eyed, giving each other a strong hug. "I love ya' man, says Isiah."

"I love you too man, dig it," says Robert.

Everybody looks at Isiah to hear his story. "I kept Mama, Claf, Matri and Claudia on ma' mind. Mama taught me that the devil is a liar; and I kept on tellin' 'em he iz,' and that I waz' comin' home, with the Lawd's help."

"Man, one time I knew I was surrounded by some Vietnamese. You know the uniforms we had to wear, disguised us in the woods. The colors made us blend in with the woods. One night the cat who was supposed to be on post with me; went somewhere without tellin' me. Man it was rainin' bad that night. All of a sudden, I heard somethin' movin.' My ears waz sharp, I couldn't see for the rain. It seem like I could hear voices and footsteps… it was real dark, man. I knew I waz 'bout ta' die, if I didn't think fast. I hear shots comin' at me, man…"

Everybody in the bar was listening, by then. "Seemed like for a quick second…" He pauses, as if he hears…."I hear Mama's voice…" he turns to the right, "Turned ta' the right—it waz' like Mama made me look that way. I saw a glimpse of somethin'… didn't kno' what it waz'—but seem like somethin' told me ta' run ta' it, as fast as I could. It waz' an old truck. I don't kno' where the hell this truck come from. Man, I dive down on the ground hittin' against the truck. Mud was all over me, man. I was scared, man." He starts to rock back and forth in his seat. "Tears was rollin' down ma' face like rain… I keep feelin'… like I ain't gon' die, now. All---of a sudden, I membered what Mama would alwaz tell me, when I seemed worried. She would say… '*The Lawd say, 'Be still and know that I—am God'.*' It seem like for that minute… I become like a blind man. I didn't worry 'bout what I couldn't see, man—ma' hea-rin' become real sharp! It seem like I could hear everythang move in the woods… even a snake. I feel like it was bad enough, that I didn't start this war in 'Nam. I didn't, why I waz' puttin' ma' life on the line, and couldn't give any opinion of it. I say ta' ma'self, like Mama say, '*The devil is a liar,*' His eyes look fierce, "And nooo… I wasn't ready, ta die!"

He takes a sip of his wine. Someone puts money in the juke box, playing "*What's Happening My Brother,* " by Marvin Gaye. Isiah turns around looking back at the person who played Marvin Gaye. "Hey baby, my man Marvin Gaye."

Rufus stares at Isiah. "Leave 'em alone, let em' go through his groove. He loves that cat," says Robert.

Isiah starts singing again. "Are things really getting better like the newspaper said. Can't find no work, can't find no job, my friend. Money is tighter than it's ever been. Say man, I just don't understand, what's going on across this land. What's Happening Brother?"

Isiah stops singing and looks at the bartender. "Ya' kno' man. All that fightin' we did," he pains, "Ya' would think that, we would be treated better than this, man. Marvin Gaye... man, I love that cat. Marvin speaks for the time." Shaking his head, singing, "Can't find no work, can't find no job."

The bartender shakes his head. "That's rotten man." The other men in the bar agrees.

Robert takes a sip of his drink. Shaking his head, bitterly. "Man, I went to college to become a mathematician, and know quite a bit about electricity. Top of the class too, baby. My professor told me I was a black genius." He freezes... "But, I can't get a job. The white cats got the jobs." The look he had was venomous. "Man sometimes, I feel like I just want to do something... payback. I feel like I been had... bamboozled. I been took baby, by Uncle Sam."

Rufus and everybody in the bar was upset with what they heard, shaking their heads along with Isiah and Robert. "Send that boy home to die. Sam don't care, if we just die. It hurts man," says Isiah.

Someone played another Marvin Gaye song. The door slams, getting everyone's attention. A tall big, husky built woman comes in, wearing a beautiful dress, red lipstick, red dress and high heel shoes. She appears to be wearing a black long wig. She comes in singing, dancing to the beat of Marvin Gaye's 'Inner City Blues'. She goes over, pulling a gentleman from the booth.

Isiah gets up, asking a woman to dance. He notices that the woman dancing looks familiar, but…he says to himself, *Is that?* He looks the woman up and down. The woman looks dead in his face, boldly smiling and singing. She pulls away from the man after the song is over, going towards the bar to sit down. Isiah walks behind her, puzzled. When the woman sits at the bar, she snatches off her wig. The man he was dancing with was shocked. The bartender freezes with fear, gazing at the man. Isiah and Robert are speechless.

"Give me a scotch on the rocks, baby." Robert and Isiah continue to watch in amazement. The bartender is afraid to give the drink. Robert and Isiah start laughing. Hezikiah laughs at himself. Rufus figures it's safe to laugh.

"Man, what happened to you?" asks Robert.

"Ya' crossed over, man?" asked Isiah.

Hezikiah starts to open up. With his wig off, makeup and red lipstick still on; he really looks hilarious. The man he danced with, comes over to him, telling him he didn't like his joke. "He didn't mean no harm, man," says Isiah.

"Is ya' married, man?" Hezikiah asks.

He snaps. "Nooo, I'm not," says the man.

"Well, I didn't mean no harm," says Hezikiah.

The bartender gives the man a mean look. "Okay, he says he didn't mean no harm, let's continue to keep the peace." The man goes back to his seat.

"Man", Robert laughed, "You sure look funny, as hell."

"Frankly speaking, I really don't give a damn. I went ta' see ma' lawyer, doctor, and ma' psychiatrist, today. Man, I'm all messed up." He points to his lower part. "Uncle Sam don' messed me up. The doctor said that, I can't have children; can't or maybe never will have any more sexual pleasure, or any woman again. And on top of that, I can't find no work... can't find no job." He looks, crazed. "But, I got a plan," he nods.

Hezikiah continues, "I went ta' see ma' lawyer. Thanks ta' Uncle Sam for messin' me up. In combat, I waz' in the hole and a hand grenade waz' thrown inta' the hole, I waz' in. Got out, but somethin' hit ma' genitals. I told ma' doctor that I might as well be castrated. Told him I have nightmares of becomin' a woman, 'cause I sure can't be no man, now. He kno's that I bought a new wardrobe of women's clothes... good clothes too. I told 'em I didn't like cheap clothes." Everybody watches Hezikiah.

"The lawyer sent me ta' a psychiatrist. That's exactly what I wanted him ta' do. Today was ma' first appointment with the psychiatrist." He pauses, looking at Isiah and Robert. "I went ta' him, as a woman. And when I go back ta' the lawyer, and the doctor, I'm goin' back as a woman. Old Sam gon' pay me." He sips his glass of scotch. "I want five million dollars, cash."

The bartender, Isiah and Robert were tongue-tied watching Hezikiah. "I told ma' lawyer and ma' psychiatrist, I go out with men now, and I feel like I ain't got no use for' no woman, no how." He turns towards Isiah and Robert. "And b'sides man, ma' sister's husband hurt her bad... beat on her. He cause her ta' have a nervous breakdown. He's a woma-nizer. Come ta' find out, he had two other women pregnant, right along with her. That tore her up, and she had nothin' but respect for him b'fore. She never had a man since. Now I'm gon' fix some of these cheatin' jokers while I'm at it. It hurt me ta' see ma' sister hurt like that. I'm gon' pay back each and everybody that need ta' be paid."

CHAPTER 6

AIN'T...I A WOMAN?

Hezikiah is walking down Broad Street, dressed like a woman. She's wearing a very sophisticated brown hat with an orange, beige and brown four-inch feather sticking up. A richly colored brown suit with an orange dickey underneath; orange lipstick; brown leather gloves; gold accessories; brown leather boots and a matching pocketbook, with light brown shades.

He thinks, while smiling brightly at everybody, *Wait a minute, how do Matri walk. The only thang is, I ain't used ta' walkin' in no woman's high-heeled boots. I 'clare... oh what did I just say? I 'clare... just like Matri.* He chuckles, trying to walk like Matri. People are looking at him, as he walks down the street. *Oh, I gotta tell Mr. Shrink: I'm smokin', drinkin', screamin' and hollerin' at night.* He takes out a cigarette. *This new life is makin' me nervous. I gotta tell old Doc, I need somethin' for' ma' nerves, right away.*

"Oh here's the buildin'." He gets on the elevator. There's a fair-skinned man with a flat long nose, on the elevator. He's dressed in a dark blue business suit with a close haircut. He looks at Hezikiah, smiling. Hezikiah looks back, smiling and blushing. Giving the impression that he can't see that well, he pulls out his business card, giving it to Hezikiah. Hezikiah blushes giving him his number.

The man says, "Baby, I can't read this. I wear my glasses only in the office, bifocals."

"Well git cho' glasses baby." Hezikiah laughs and blushes.

"By the way, I'd like to take a pretty lady out. What are you doing Saturday night?" he asks Hezikiah.

Hezikiah primps, and softens his voice. "Wh... what chu' mean, am I free?" He notices he's covering his wedding band. "Well, since you put it that way, yes of course I'm free." The elevator opens. "See ya!" Hezikiah smiles.

Hezikiah walks into the doctor's office, with fake elegance. The doctor is talking to the secretary. They both look up at Hezikiah.

Speaking very proper and feminine. "Hi there, Dr. Speller, it's Hezikiah," he blushes.

Dr. Speller is caucasian; tall slim man; keen features; has an Alfalfa-like hair cut, like

"The Little Rascals," and meekly. The doctor seems a bit perturbed, but acts calm. "Oh hi, you're right on time."

"Well you know, a man works from sun up to sun down, but a woman's work is never done. I 'clare, got other things to do," he coughs, smiling.

Dr. Speller goes into his office. He slumps down, trying to give his knees room for sitting, while taking out his pad. Very softly he asks, "Okay, how do you feel today?"

Hezikiah says boldly, "Let's start with how do I look... that's what I wanna' know?"

The doctor begins tapping in, "I could say, that you look ravishing. Is that what you want to hear? How do you feel?"

"I don't kno' what that means, but it sounds good. I kno' you ain't lying ta' me. I ain't payin' ya' fa' that." The doctor appears to be very stern, as he writes.

" I need somthin' fa' ma' nerves. I'm smokin', drinkin', hollerin' and screamin' at night, and I have a strong urge to become promiscuous. This life is hectic, being a woman." He crosses his legs, batting his eyes at the doctor.

Dr. Speller looks up at him and continues to write. He says," I see."

Hezikiah winks his eyes at the doctor. "That's ma' sentiments exactly, I hope ya' do."

Dr. Speller asks as he continues to write, "Do you ever feel like you want to kill yourself?"

"Oh now look a here. Kill ma' self, do I look that bad?" " Hezikiah pants, batting his eyes, over-emphasizing his femininity. 'I'm appalled by that question."

Quietly, looking at him, "Seriously." The doctor says, "Answer the question, please."

"Well ya' don' need ta' be so formal with me. Relax and kick ya' shoes off doc, be like me." says Hezikiah.

Dr. Speller quietly chuckles, "I need you to answer the question."

Hezikiah takes out a handkerchief, fanning. "The answer is no." He gazes real hard at the doctor, bending over in his face with firmness. "If I was gon' kill ma' self, it shouldda been in 'Nam! What 'chu think somebody was tryin' ta' stop me? Do you think that's why I come back here, ta' kill ma' self?"

"Not exactly," says Dr. Speller.

"I wanna kill the person that's responsible for' turnin' me inta' a woman." He points his finger out like Uncle Sam. But then Old Sam said, "Be all you could be, even a woman, if need be... when I, git finished withca ya."

The doctor nods his head. "I see."

Hezikiah's eyes protrude. "I hope so, I don't need no blind man tryin' ta' help me. The blind can't lead the blind." He looks at the doctor shaking his head.

Firmly, the doctor says, "I can assure you, I'll do my best. Here's your prescription, Hezikiah."

"No, call me Harriet please." Hezikiah gets up to leave. "Make sure ya' do that ya' hear. I'm don' fa' t'day." He turns around modeling, walking like he's on the runway, swaying from side to side, turns around and poses. He winks his eye at Dr. Speller and keeps it moving.

Dr. Speller looks at him with no facial expression. "My secretary will give you your next appointment... Hezi...Harriet." Dr. Speller shook his head, staring at the door.

⤜ ⤛

Claudia's son brings a box into the kitchen, showing Matri. "Look auntie Matri."

Matri acts excited. "Oh honey, what is this?"

"People in a box," Paul says pointing to the box.

"Oh...I see, tell me who the people are, honey?"

"You auntie, Mama, Isiah, Mommy, Robert, Hezikiah, Sadie and Dawn" He thinks, "Roy too."

"Ummm, I must say that's quite interesting Paul. You're very smart". Matri kisses him on the cheek.

"When I'm done washin' these here dishes, I'm gon' watch Mahalia Jackson t'night. She gon' be singin' "Amazin' Grace" and "Silent Night"." Ruth shakes her head, smiling. "That woman just touch ma' soul, seem like God put er' here ta' carry out his spirit through 'er singin'."

Claudia comes and hugs Ruth. "Mama would cha' watch Roy and Paul?"

"Umm... yeah... what time ya' gon' be back?" Ruth decides to baby-sit.

"Oh thank ya' Mama," Claudia jumps up excitedly.

"Mama you're going to baby-sit for Claudia tonight?" Matri's surprised.

"Now I'm gon' baby-sit, but Claudia ya' better give 'em they bath, 'cause when Mahalia Jackson come on, I want all chirrin' ta' be in the bed dreamin'."

"Oh yeah, Mama. I did a paper on her. She started singing in a Baptist Church with the Johnson Brothers, one of the earliest professional gospel groups. She became a huge success in 1948, singing "Move On Up A Little Higher," rocketing to fame in the US, and in Europe. "I Can Put My Trust in Jesus", won a prize from the French Academy and "Silent Night," was one of the best-selling singles in the history of Norway," says Matri.

"Well Matri ya' kno' more bout 'er than me," says Ruth.

Matri is holding something behind her back smiling. "Mama close your eyes, I have something for you."

"Okay child, hurry up, now."

Pulling out Mahalia Jackson's album. "Okay Mama, you can look now."

Mama opens her eyes. Excitedly she says, "Oh ma Lawd' Matri, where in the world did cha' git' this from?"

Happily Matri says, hugging Ruth, "Mama, you can buy this at any record store."

"Matri, this sho' is a fine wo' man in the Lawd."

"She reminds me of you, Mama," Says Matri

"Oh, you stop. I'm gon' take ma' bath and listen ta' 'er t'night.

⤛ ⤜

"Mama," says Claudia. " Matri and me ready to go. I'm goin' to a party in New York with Lorraine."

Matri looks at Claudia. "You know Claudia, you're going to get enough of that Lorraine one day."

"Well until that day come Matri, let me handle Lorraine, okay?"

Isiah comes in, kisses Ruth on the cheek. Observing Matri and Claudia's attire, sniffing in the air. "Well, where you two goin' t'night, lookin' pretty and smellin' good?"

The bell rings. " I'll get it," says Isiah "Oh that's Lorraine," says Claudia.

"That ain't just Lorraine," Isiah smiles. Osmon is outside talkin' to Lorraine and she's pointin' her fingers at Osmon.

"Oh—no, I 'clare. Why is everybody tryin' ta' run ma' life, now?" asks Claudia.

Ruth looks at Claudia, warning her, "I told 'chu this b'fore, and I'm gon' tell ya' this again, don' come back in ma' house after 12:00 o'clock. Ya' in ma' house and ain't no daughter of mine gon' be comin' in here after that. Too much goin' on out in them streets. Matri, I ain't get over what happened ta' ya' yet, with that boy gettin' killed in that diner."

"Matri…" whispers Claudia. "Don' forgit ta' leave the back door unlocked. We can stay out long as we want, just leave the room door closed. Oh, leave Isiah's window open too, just in case Mama happen ta' lock the back door."

Matri laughs. "Ah-ha."

Ruth says, "Wanna chirrin,' ya' better git' out the way, they run ya' over gettin' outta' here t'night. Don' kno' what them streets do ta' them, I 'clare. Seem like the devil don' put a spell over 'em in them streets." Claudia runs down the stairs.

Claudia sees Lorraine pointing her fingers in Osmon's face. "Lorraine! Don't do that. Let me handle Osmon."

Angrily she says, "Claudia, I'm tired of him trying to come between us."

"Lorraine, Osmon is ma' friend and so iz you, now ain't nothin' gon' change that, and the sooner ya' realize that, the better you'll be."

Chewing gum, Osmon looks at Lorraine, working his jaw. "Now Lorraine, you see that woman right there. I am not going to give up on her. I made a promise to Allah and the 'cause'. I am not going to give up on her. She came from a good tree. This might sound strange to you, but we're not giving up on you either." Osmon looks at Anthony. "Is that right Anthony?"

"That's right sir, we here to rescue the black women, from the wilderness of North America."

Looking at Lorraine, "We know it's not going to be easy," says Osmon. Ain't gon' be easy, they don' got mule-headed," Osmon stares at Lorraine, shaking his head.

"That's right. James Brown said, "They've gotton' too far gone"," says Anthony.

"Okay Claudia, you go on. I'm gon' continue to pray for both of you," says Osmon.

"Bye," says Claudia, kissing Osmon on the forehead.

Matri is waiting upstairs for Ramone. The bell rings again. Isiah comes into the kitchen. "Matri who's that cat in that big black Brougham? That don't look like Thaddeus."

"It's not," Matri answers.

Isiah stares at her, amusingly. "Oh, okay." Ramone knocks on the door. Isiah rushes to get the door. Ramone is shocked to see Isiah. They both look eye to eye.

"Hey, come right on in man," says Isiah.

Matri comes into the living room. "Oh, Isiah let me introduce you to a dear friend of mine, Ramone. Ramone this is my brother." She kisses Isiah on the forehead. "Isiah, from 'Nam."

Very smooth and suave, Ramone reaches his hand out to shake Isiah's and says, "Pleased to meet you, Isiah."

Isiah says with militancy, "Yeah man."

He sniffs, "Oh Matri," Ramone says, "I made reservations for dinner. We don't want to be late."

Isiah stands, observing Ramone. Abruptly Isiah says, "Oh, don't let me hold ya' man."

"Matri yells, "Mama, I'm leaving out now."

Isiah looks out of his window, watching Luther acting as the chauffeur, standing outside of the car. He opens the door for Matri to get in, and then opening the door for Ramone. Isiah talks to himself. "Look at this cat... a chauffeur?" He pauses. " Man, ya' better be upright, don't want nothin' happenin' ta' ma' Matri now."

Ramone sniffs, looking up at the window. Isiah waves his hand at Ramone. Ramone thinks to himself, *Yeah baby, she's going to be alright with me.* Turning his head towards Matri, he thinks. *I wouldn't let anybody harm my baby... she's mine. She's going to be my number one.* Matri looks into his eyes, as he thinks.

"Matri," says Ramone.

Responding with humbleness, "Yes Ramone."

"Matri, I want to speak to you about beauty."

"Beauty?" Matri's inquisitive. She glances up, noticing Luther watching her in the mirror, with a peculiar look.

He sniffs, "Baby, come here. Kick your shoes off. Don't worry, we're going to New York." She kicks her shoes off. He grabs her legs, gently massaging her feet. Sounding quite debonair, and using his charisma, "Matri take a look at your feet. Your feet, your toes; they are perfect.."

"*Ah-ha,*" she thinks, wondering, W*here is he going with this?*

Compassionately he says, "Now, your ankles are not too small, but they are perfectly suitable for your big legs. You know Matri, an artist would marvel at such a perfect creature; craving to capture you with nothing hidden."

Imitating Claudia in her mind, she pants, "Huh... great day in the monin'... nothing hidden."

"The portrait would become legendary." Sniffing, hesitating to look into her eyes. "Beloved, your eyes sometimes frighten me. They have a mesmerizing, piercing affect. As if, looking through my soul. It makes me tempted to ask you, what do you see?" He looks slightly into her eyes, turning her face towards him, gently stroking her hair with his fingers. His eyes roam the contour of her body, from her feet to her head. "Matri, I find strength in your hair... kinky and strong. It accentuates the very essence of who you are—a real Cleopatra."

Hypnotized by her beauty, he's driven with madness; with a burning desire, by the voluptuousness of her body. Like a strike of lightening; he fantasizes, fixated on her lips. He gently grabs her hair, thinking, *Yes, I'm smitten by your physical beauty, purity and your innocence. It allures me to you.* He moves closer to her, staring; he bends to kiss her, staring into her eyes. Suddenly, like Dracula, he feels fearful and withdraws from her; looking away from her with contempt. He exhales, "Oh Matri," he sniffs, "My Matri."

Matri sits up, taking a deep breath, staring into Ramone's eyes. He looks away from her.

"I 'clare, I'm not the only one, that has a way with words."

Luther pulls up to the restaurant. "We're here."

"Ramone, you must really like the Savoy," says Matri

"It represents you Matri, classy." He looks around thinking, flashing back to the car. "Uh, here comes the waiter."

The waiter's servile, bending and smiling, "What will we have here?"

"Okay, give me number three, with white wine on the rocks," says Ramone

"I'll have number five, with Kijafa wine on the rocks," says Matri.

"I thought you didn't drink, Matri," Ramone says.

"Actually, I don't but, after the picture you drew of me in the car, I need a drink."

Ramone smiles, "Umm… I see." He kisses her hand. "Matri, I would like to take you to my home tonight. I would like to entertain you there, for awhile."

Matri thinks, He sniffs a lot, "Of course Ramone, I'd like that very much."

Another waiter comes to the table, bringing flowers. "Compliments from the gentleman," nods to Ramone. "To the lady at the table."

"Ramone, red roses are my favorite. The smell... hmmm, they're beautiful, baby."

"My beloved, you have the charisma of a rose."

He pulls out a present. "Wh…." says Matri.

He interrupts…"Please, come here baby."

Nervously she takes it, opening the gift. "Ha-uhh…" Her cheekbones rise like the sun. "Ramone… a pearl necklace, earrings to match—and perfume?" Her eyes sparkles with delight… trying to catch her breath… soffocating with excitement. Ramone takes the perfume and sprays it on Matri's wrist, kissing her hand.

Matri closes her eyes to the smell. "Ummm… this smells good." Ramone is taken by her expressions of excitement.

"Ummm, Ramone this dessert is exquisite," says Matri.

Sniffs, "Ummm, yes it is baby." He takes her fork, feeding her the cobbler.

Suddenly Matri looks to the left of the window. There's a bag lady standing there, watching them. Her face is blackened like she jumped out of a chimney. She's wearing a lot of dirty rags on her head; a big hat is sitting on the top of her head, and a great big old torn coat is camouflaging her size. She is carrying two bags. Matri thinks to herself, *The way she's looking over here, you would think she knows us. There seems to be such sadness to her. If I didn't know any better, I would swear she's pregnant.* Ramone notices Matri. She looks back at him, to point the mysterious woman out to him; but looking back towards the window again, the woman has disappeared. Matri looks back at Ramone, exhaling. "Ramone you've been great from the very beginning, up until this very moment. I must thank you," says Matri.

He holds her hands. "Matri believe me, it's my pleasure knowing I've pleased you." Matri stares at Ramone, with hypnotized eyes.

"Well baby, I think I'd better pay the waiter. We have to move on now, can't keep Cinderella out too long."

Matri just happens to look out of the window again, thinking to herself. *There's the woman again, staring. If I didn't know any better, I'd think she wanted something from me, or Ramone.*

"Let's go baby," says Ramone. "Come on, baby let's get into the car."

Not able to stop thinking about the bag lady, Matri turns around, looking back, thinking. *Was that lady pregnant? She was looking directly at us,"* she exhales, *Oh, don't be silly Matri, this is New York. Anything goes over here.*

Hour later:

Tthey arrive at Ramone's home. "Okay baby, let me take your coat. Make yourself comfortable." Ramone goes over, to mix drinks. "Here you go, Kijafa on the rocks."

Matri's looking around, admiring his home. "Oh, thank you."

He sniffs, "Matri, do you like Lena Horne?" he asks.

"I've grown to really like her. .. Ramone, do you have a cold?" Matri asks.

" Allergy. Well...you're in for the treat of your life. I'm playing ''Stormy Weather."

"Matri, let me get comfortable, I'll be right back." He goes upstairs.

Matri leans back, kicking her shoes off, listening to Lena Horne... reminiscing. *Thaddeus beloved, I just cannot forget you. Both of you have honored me.*

"Here we are Matri. Excuse me for taking a little longer. I forgot I needed to make a few phone calls... business calls." He exhales. "Say, how do you like Stormy Weather?"

"You know… I like it… and your home very much. Who decorated it for you?"

Jokingly he says, "Well Matri, that's a million dollar question."

Matri grins, "Oh?"

Charmingly he says, "Actually, I decorated myself."

Matri looks around to the architecture of the room, feeling a little intoxicated. Her eyes protrudes... her mouth drops "You 'clare? "

He mimics her. "I 'clare." The phone rings. "Excuse me, be-loved." He goes upstairs. Matri continues to look around at the designs, on the curtains in the living room.

Ramone comes downstairs. "Matri, my sister lost her keys and she can't get into the house. I have an extra set. We give each other keys in case of an emergency. So I'll be right back. Just make your-self comfortable."

Feeling a little tipsy, she says, "That's certainly, easy to do here."

Matri looks at her watch, thinking, Hour has passed...*I wonder what's taking him so long?* She looks at the stairs. *I guess I'll take a tour of the house. I'll start with upstairs.* She goes into the bedroom. *Good Lord, this is beautiful. Is he absolutely rich or what?* She pauses. Something is baffling to her. *What is that on his bed?* Walks closer to the bed. *What is this in this little glass container?* She picks it up. *Pretty glass case, but what is this white powder inside of it?* Looks around at the bed, and sees a doctor's instrument, is laying on the bed. *What is he doing with a doctor's instrument?*

She's a little dizzy from drinking. "Oh well, maybe it's just..." Then she sees a huge opened closet. Walking towards it, she couldn't help from being nosy. "All of these clothes... these suits... shoes, and what's this?" Looking up to the left of the closet in the corner, she notices a strange black bag. "What kind of bag is this?" She reaches up and gets the bag...opening it up... "What! Gynecologist! The initials are on the bag."What, Dr. Ra...Spenster!" She drops the bag and all the instruments falls out. Frantically, she snatches them up, panting." Let me close this bag and get out of here before he comes in." She runs down the stairs."

She thinks, Let me sit down. The phone rings. Matri looks at the phone... it continues to ring. *Maybe it's Ramone calling me.* She picks up the phone, and before she could speak, she hears whin-ing on the other end. She freezes. The whining continues... the person slams the phone down. Matri jumps up, startled. Calmly she puts the phone down. She hears keys in the door. Swiftly, she turns her head towards the door. Her heart is pounding. She is standing there scared stiff, with her eyes glued to the door.

The door opens slowly. She starts sweating, getting in the position to run. Thinks, *Should I run before they open the door?* While she's looking around for a way out, Ramone comes in.

"Matri please, please forgive me baby. My sister was having a very serious problem and, I just couldn't get away. So I guess…" looking at his watch … "I'd better take you home. We'll try this again."

Matri is dumbfounded, trying not to let Ramone notice how afraid she is. She thinks to herself. *Should I tell him what just happened—and the doctor's bag?*

Ramone notices Matri's reaction. "Baby, I'm really sorry about how our evening ended up. I'll make it up to you, I promise."

Snapping out of her dilemma, she says, " Oh nooo, Ramone, I think I've had too much Kijafa. I'm sleepy, that's all," yawns, "Okay let's go."

Noticing her watch. "Oh my goodness, Ramone what time is it?"

He yawns. "It's 1:30."

Matri thinks. *Oh no, I hope Mama's dead, asleep.*

Matri jumps into the car. Ramone sniffs, holding Matri in his arms. Luther's, right eye twitches, as he looks in the mirror... with an unsettling look. Matri catches, him and quickly he looks the other way.

"Matri, I almost forgot. Would you accompany me to Fort Dix? There's a big celebration for the soldiers, return." Ramones looks at Matri, with excitement in his eyes.

"When?" she questions.

"I have to go out of town for a month. Let's say, approximately three months from now. I'll call you to remind you, when I get back," he says.

"We'll see," Matri responds.

Okay Matri, here we are," says Ramone, kissing Matri on her forehead. Luther gets out of the car to let Matri out, looking away from her.

Matri jumps out quickly. Looking on the porch, she sees Claudia. "Goodnight Ramone. It's okay, it's Claudia."

Matri's worried, about Ruth catching them. "Claudia, why are you out here?"

"I just got here too. I went around the back and Mama must've locked the back door. I waz' just gettin' ready ta' go upstairs on the porch, and climb through the window."

Matri and Claudia looks the through the window. "Oh no, Isiah's there sleeping," says Matri.

"Well, that's too bad. We gotta do what we gotta do," Claudia says boldly.

Matri gives in. "Okay." They start pulling the window up.

Claudia nudges Matri. "You go first Matri. Go on now, b'fore Mama wakes up ta' go ta' the bathroom," claudia frowns.

Matri struggles to get her leg up. "Okay, first leg first." Matri falls, grabbing the end of the bed.

Claudia giggles. "Get up now, it's ma' turn." Claudia falls back, from drinking too much. Matri leans out of the window pulling her back quickly. They both giggle. "Like Lorraine say, first leg first… now second leg." Isiah flinches. Matri and Claudia grab each other, whispering… hardly seeing one another in the dark, they fall on Isiah. Both can't see, but says, "Shhhh, shhhh," to Isiah. They both lay frozen on top of Isiah.

Matri reaches for Isiah's mouth, to quiet him. "It's me… Matri."

"It's me… Claudia." Isiah shakes his head whispering, and shouting in a low tone.

Isiah feels squashed. "Will ya' two get off of me? What the hell are ya' doin' comin' in this way? If I waz' dreamin' 'bout combat, I could've hurt both of ya'," he whispers.

"It's dark in here, but this ain't no combat now," warns Claudia.

"Shhh," says Matri…"Mama… I …" Claudia and Isiah freezes.

"Oh," Matri exhales, " I thought I heard Mama. Come on before she wakes up, for sure," says Matri.

Isiah whispers, "Matri, Thaddeus called chu'." Matri stands still.

"Come on, now Matri, you go first," says Claudia.

"Okay," whispers Matri. Matri peeks at Mama's room door. "Come on Claudia." They both go into the room. Matri says, "Claudia I hear Mama." They both jumps into the bed with their shoes and clothes on, covering up with the cover.

Ruth goes to the bathroom. On her way back, she opens the door. Mama whispers to herself. "Ummm, thought I hear somethin'." She pauses, looking at Matri and Claudia. "They dead ta' the world, ain't seen 'em that still in awhile."

Four months later.

Matri slams the car door, dropping her books. "Ohh, I'm so tired, between classes and work. I'm, beat." Matri talks to herself, dragging herself up the stairs. While putting her keys into the door, she hears the phone ring. Opening the door, she sees Ruth holding the phone. "Here she is. She just stepped in."

Matri drops her books. "Hello."

"Beloved, you sound tired."

"'Ramone, you're back," her face beams.

"Yeah, I know I've been in and out of town, for the past few months. I'll make it up to you, with a ticket to Fort Dix."

"You know what, that sounds good. I've been hitting the books and work, hard."

"That's next month, the first Friday. We'll go for the weekend… okay?"

Cheerfully she says, "Oh, I'd like that."

⟩⟨ ⟩⟨

At Sadie's place, the bell rings. "Now who could that be on a Sunday?" The bell rings again. "I said, alright. I'm gettin' outta the shower, now!" Grabbing the towel, trying to dry quickly, "Wait, a minute." She looks around for her housecoat, tooting her lips out. "Dogonit, where is ma' housecoat?" Sadie says, looking through the peephole, then looking on the couch. "Oh there it is... Lawd, it's Robert." She snatches her housecoat off of the chair.

He walks in smiling, "My, don't you look pretty," says Robert.

Sadie steps back, putting her hands on her hips; squinting her eyes up. Her face and hair are wet from the shower. "Pretty?"

"Yes." Robert looks up at her hair, putting his fingers on his cheeks. "Umm, unconfined hair. There's no make up, no lipstick... you're simply beautiful."

Sadie frowns. "Simply beautiful, haaa. I 'clare... ya' must be drunk?"

Robert breaks into a smile, "Of course, see... you're in your natural state. My black pearl, that's how I need to see you. A man don't need no surprises after he marries...."

Sadie is shocked by his comment. "After ya' what?" Sadie pauses.

He pulls out a present—no chuckling this time. Squinting his eyes, trying to look serious. "Sit down for a minute Sadie. I need to talk to you." Sadie pulls her robe tightly. " Don't worry, I believe in saving the best for last," says Robert

Sadie stares at him. Very sweetly, she asks, "Robert, want some coffee and cake? I made a chocolate cake for ya'... figured ya' might be comin' over, t'night."

Robert smiles. "Hey, you really know how to make a guy feel special, don't you?" He kisses her on the forehead.

"Here you go." She blushes, giving him the cake.

"Look at you Sadie, you have a little girlish way about yourself. No doubt, you're a woman, now. A real man, likes some innocence in a woman," his forehead frowns, nodding.

"Okay... I think, I know what 'chu mean." Sadie blushes.

Robert smiles. "Sadie, we've been dating for awhile. I feel as though I know all that I need to know about you. I'm going for a job tomorrow. I'm praying that I get it." He reaches for the present.

"Come to get this, sugar. Here, open this please. It's for you... ooops. Take this first." He gives her a white rose. "Sadie, out of all the flowers to choose from... I choose this one, for you. White stands for purity and innocence. Now, open this box."

Sadie opens a little box wrapped in gold paper. "Ohh!... ohh..." Putting her hands on her throat, teary-eyed; whispering, "Robert... is this for me?"

Robert turns around looking all over the room. "I certainly don't see anyone else in here, but us." He starts chuckling.

Sadie grabs Robert, hugging him. "It's just like Matri said it would happen... you picked me." She cries.

He holds her tightly, "Hey baby, it's gonna be just you and me against the world, dig it?" He winks his eyes at her.

⟞⊹ ⊹⟝

At Dawn's place... the bell rings. Dawn is preparing a hearty meal for Isiah. "I'm coming," she yells.

Isiah hugs her. "Hey, baby. Ummm…" Isiah stands back, staring excitedly at Dawn with her afro. "Ya' not only smell good, but … ya' look… like a African Queen, baby. I really hit the jackpot this time."

"Come on baby, sit down at the table. I fixed your favorite…collard greens, steak, potatoes and sweet potatoes."

Everything was laid out on the table. "Baby let me go and wash my hands first."

She pulls the chair back. "It's nice and hot for the King," says Dawn.

"Ummm, this steak is hittin' the King's spot." He looks at her proudly. "Ya' put love inta this food, just like Mama."

"Well Mama taught me well." Isiah can't take his eyes off of Dawn, as he eats. "Ummm, give me a couple of those biscuits, Queen."

"Whatever you want King." Dawn flirts.

Isiah stops eating, looking at her. "Ya' clare?"

Dawn looks at Isiah, kissing at him from across the table. Isiah chews his food; staring, kissing back at her.

Flirtatiously Dawns says, "Baby I 'clare. You just eat until you get full. I have some pie in the stove... made apple pie for you. I know that's your favorite, too."

Eyes flutter, "Now--how ya' kno' that, baby?"

She kisses at him. "Well, let's just say, a big birdie told me."

"Are you don' eating baby?" she patiently asks.

Isiah's stomach tightens. "I 'clare, that waz' good."

"Now, you just go and have a seat on the couch."

Rubs his stomach, he says, "Okay."

She sits next to Isiah. "Here baby, you let me feed you this pie, okay?"

Isiah's eyes flutter; he blushes. "Yeah, I'd like that."

Dawn puts a napkin around his neck. "Here, open your mouth now."

"Umm, that's delicious baby," says Isiah. Dawn blushes, kissing him as she feeds him, wiping away the crumbs around his mouth.

Abruptly, he stops her... staring into her eyes, smiling. "Girl ya' kno' the way ta' a man's heart, is through his stomach."

"Okay, you're done baby. Let me relax you." She gets up, putting on Marvin Gaye's music.

Isiah's eyes brighten up, like a car light. "Al—right now, why ya' do that, baby?" He jumps up. "Ya' kno' I love that cat." He reaches out his hands. "Come to get this, sugar." He swirls her around, dancing and singing. "*Hey baby, that's alright. I know that's alright. Every day that's alright, God knows that's alright. Some of us were born with money to spend. Some of us were born for races to win. Some of us are aware that it's good for us to care. Some of us feel the icy wind, politics blowing in the air. But those of us simply like to socialize. But those of us who tend the sick and heed the people's cry. For the soul that takes pride in his God and himself and everything else.* "Woo!...Woo!..." Isiah screams.

Dawn looks into Isiah's eyes, with a sneaky seductive look.

Dawn pulls him into her bedroom. He follows her, smiling. She gently grabs his face asking the question. "Is my wish your command?" she asks.

Isiah doesn't respond. He looks at her amazingly and continues to smile at her; looking her dead in the eyes.

She says, "Baby, the Queen commands you. Lay down on that bed, right now!"

He lays down. She flips the lights out. He just lays there, waiting patiently to see what she's going to do. She starts taking her clothes off. Isiah jumps up grabbing her hands.

He starts breathing fast. "Wait a minute baby, what 'chu doin'?" he asks.

She commands him. "What do you think I'm doing? Now you just do what I tell you to do and lay down, now!"

He can't see her, but he raises his voice, "Wait a minute now wo'man, ya' orderin' me around?" Dawn doesn't respond. "Don't forgit, I'm a army man. Dawn, don't ever command me to do nothin... I had enough of that, from Old Sam!" He grabs her gently, throwing her onto the bed. He kisses her on the forehead. "Now I 'clare. This here just ain't the right way, Dawn. Now, fa' me ta' want ta' marry ya', I have ta' see ya', as somin' special ta' me. I'm learnin' what's inside of ya'. I don' need no empty package. Men always say, "If ya' could git the milk free, what 'chu need with the cow?""

Seductively she says, "Baby, do I look like a cow to you?"

"You gotta have ma' babies fa' me. Mama say ya' have ta' be careful who ya' have children with, cause she say, 'The hand that rocks the cradle, rocks the world.'

Isiah says, compassionately, "Now ya' told me ya' waz' a Queen. I can't treat the Queen any kinda way, baby. I don't wanna see what 'chu' look like, 'til I marry ya'. B'leeve in savin' the best fa' last, and ya' gotta let me do that."

They continue to talk in the dark. Dawn is angry. "Oh yeah, well you a man and men can't hold out that long."

"Now who told chu' that? Now anythang worth havin,' should be worth waitin' fa'... if he really want it. Dawn, I'm a army man. Plenty of times, I didn't have a woman in the army. I had ta wait." Furiously he says, "So if I could wait fa' Uncle Sam, I sure as hell could wait fa' ma' Queen!" He pauses, eyes fluttering in the dark. "So I' got plenty of waitin' patience, I 'clare. B'sides, I have ta' make some money."

Dawn kisses him on the forehead and says, "Shhh...." She baffles him.

He frowns. "What?...." He asks.

She kisses him on the lips, and says. "Shhh...."

"Naw, it ain't no shhh. Now what did I just git' through tellin' ya' woman?"

Dawn is disobedient. "Shhh," says Dawn.

Isiah flips the light back on. "Now ya', a mule-headed woman, ha? Ya' gon' let me be the man, woman?"

Dawn flips the light back off.

"Ya' kno' what Dawn? Ya' been by ya'self too long, that's what's wrong with ya.' Now take ya' little fiery self in that bathroom, and take ya' self a real cold shower. Ya' got any milk? I'm gon make ya' a glass of warm milk, ta' relax ya'. I'll leave the milk on the table."

Dawn flips the light off. "Shhh...."says Dawn.

"Da... Da... Dawn!...." Isiah is fidgety.

"Shhh...." He reaches into his pocket. "Dawn give me your hand. She reaches her hand out in the dark. He slips an engagement ring on her finger.

She screams. "Isiah!" She grabs his face, kissing him.

Isiah tries to hold her hands down. "Dawn! . ….. Now… now. ….. I 'clare… Dawn!..... The door slams. Dawn screams. "Isiah!"

Back in the office... in New York.

Matri is having an unusual day. Looking out of her window, daydreaming, she thinks, *This is one of these Fridays, I'd like to leave early, to get ready to go to Fort Dix with Ramone. I don't know what coat to take.* Turning around, she exhales, reading over a report. *Ummm, this case is certainly very challenging. I'll call it the 'Corporate Case'. The battle of the century; the stock market, with it's high stress factor; prodigious intellectual humbug; propaganda... same thing. Not to mention the educated thieves, as Thaddeus has mentioned in the past.* She pauses, spinning her chair around, viewing the Empire State Building. *Yes, there is something psychologically challenging about this; analytically speaking; who are the real thieves, here?*

Matri is caught up into her thinking; she doesn't hear the knocks at the door. Matri snaps out of her thoughts. "Come in!" she yells.

"Matri," Charlotte says.

Matri is lost in thought again. Abruptly she says, "Oh I apologize, Charlotte. This case I'm reading is really a brain-stormer."

"Anyway, dear heart, Mrs. Watenburg said, 'Please call her, when you get a chance today.'

Appearing to be lost in thought, "Okay Charlotte." The phone rings. "Hello."

"Matri, did I catch you at the wrong time?" asks Thaddeus.

Compassionately, she says, "For you Thaddeus, I'll always, make the time right."

"That's good news." Charlotte whispers.

Matri's distracted by Charlottes whisper. "Excuse me Thaddeus, as you were saying?"

"Well Matri, I've been calling you, and haven't been able to catch up with you."

"I know, between work and school lately…"

"And Ramone?"....

Matri pauses...."Oh yes, Thaddeus. I've been going out with Ramone too, he's just a friend."

"Matri, you may not want to hear this but…" They both pause.

"Thaddeus?" Matri's curious.

"Matri, be careful with that Ramone cat. I went to college with him. When I was a freshmen, he was on his way out. He was brilliant… a ladies' man. He was some charmer… a pretty boy. Women loved his curly red hair. The women practically fell at his feet. He was the talk on campus, but he also, as some women said, had a very cold streak too. So please Matri, I can't tell you who to go out with, but please be careful with this cat. I've been hearing some things about him, and I don't know if they're true or not. They could very well be speculations. I'll find out, and if it's true, I'm gonna…."

Abruptly Matri says, "Hold on Thaddeus, I have another call from the other desk."

"Matri… Ramone." Matri is startled.

"Matri … are you there?"

"Oh—oh, yes Ramone."

"Matri, I just want to know, if you are still going to Fort Dix with me Friday?"

"Yes."

"Okay, I have some things I have to tie up before we go. By the way, I'm setting up an office downtown, Newark."

"Oh really?"

"I'll tell you about it, when I see you."

"Okay, I'm on another line."

"Okay beloved."

She clears her throat, "Thaddeus, I'm sorry."

"It's okay."

"Thaddeus you're the best thing that ever happened to me. No one could replace that." The phone rings. She jumps up again, grabbing the other phone. "Ho… hold on… hello…"

She pauses, then excitedly says, "Oh yes, Mrs. Watenburg, I missed you too...."

"Matri, when are you coming back to visit?"

"Well... what's today? Wednesday, what about tomorrow... after school?"

"Sure, I have some special things to share with you this time," says Mrs. Watenburg.

"Okay, bye."

Matri exhales. "Thaddeus?"

"I'm here Matri."

"This is a day, that has really tested my patience," says Matri.

"Matri, I have to go out of town again, for a conference. I'm the representative for the stockmarket. You know as soon as you think this stock market thing is picking up its wings; it starts flapping downward again. I'm inclined to think, there is more than meets the eye. For quite awhile I've been seeing some pretty challenging things... that could be the apex, to this whole stock market crisis."

"Yeah, I know." Matri pauses with a suspicious look on her face.

"Well Matri, my clothes are packed, and my co-worker is accompanying me this time. He's going to be taking notes for me. I really can't say how long this is going to take. I'll call you."

Charlotte comes to the door. "Client," she says.

"Okay, Thaddeus I have to take this client."

"Bye," says Thaddeus.

Thaddeus calls Ramone. "Hello... who is this?"

"It's Thaddeus. You gave me the number, your business card, at the Savoy."

"Oh, Thaddeus, this is a surprise."

Thaddeus' voice isn't pleasant, "Yeah, I'm sure it is."

Ramone pauses. " Is that right?" asks Thaddeus.

Sliding his fingers through his hair. He speaks with charisma. "Well, what can I do for you, my man?"

"It's about Matri."

Ramone stills himself.… "Ah-ha, what about her?"

Thaddeus's nose broadens. "Matri is a beautiful person."

Ramone says quietly, "That, she is."

"And, she's very special to me.… I have future hopes for her and me."

Sarcastically, he says, "Oh you do?" asks Ramone.

Thaddeus responds quickly, " I do."

Adamantly, Ramone says, "Well my man, I could only say... may the best man win."

Proudly Thaddeus responds, "Man you don't know her, like I know her."

"The only thing I could say to that is this, all's fair in love and war."

"I will tell you this man, I've been hearing some things about you, and you better not hurt Matri," warns Thaddeus.

Abruptly Ramone says, "Is that a threat, my man?"

Thaddeus assures Ramone. "Threats don't become me... I do promises."

Cunningly, Ramone says, "Hmmm."

"By the way, what type of business, is this on this card?" asks Thaddeus.

"I'm a private detective. It's… my own business."

Thaddeus tells him, "Well, I'm going to do a little private eye, work on you. So be careful." Thaddeus hangs up. Ramone holds the phone to his ear... never moving.

<hr>

Friday evening, Claudia, Matri and Ruth are sitting at the table. Isiah comes in with bags. "What bank did cha' rob?" asks Claudia. Ruth and Matri stares, at the bags, Isiah has.

Isiah smiles, eyes glittery. He responds, "Now, I ain't rob no bank, now. Can't a man have a change of luck?" asks Isiah.

"What's in them bags, baby?" Claudia is being nosy.

Isiah pulls out a beautiful fur coat. Their eyes are fixated on the fur coat. "This is fa' ma' Queen. How ya'all like it?" Isiah asks anxiously.

Matri is taken by it. "Oh... my goodness, Isiah."

Claudia's eyes, beams in on the coat. "Yeah, I like that fa' ma' self. I could wear it t'night," says Claudia.

"I b'leeve Osmon will give ya' anythang ya' heart desires," says Isiah.

Ruth and Matri stare at Claudia. "Well why yawl justa' lookin' at me like that fa'?" Claudia is irritated, rolling her eyes.

Isiah proudly lays the money in Mama's hands. "Mama here's the money fa' the rent, the electric bill, food and the phone."

Claudia's shocked, "What we gon' pay?"

"Ya ain't gon' pay nothin' for awhile, cause ya' all been payin' when I couldn't, so now let me pay... I'm the man." He moves around proudly.

Quietly Ruth asks, "Isiah, I need ta' kno,' where ya' git' this money from?"

Excitedly, he says, "Mama, I ran inta this man in New York. A rich man, that got me a longshoreman job. That's why I been comin' in late, and sometime I stay all night doin' over time."

"Looka here baby, give me some money. That old job just ain't cuttin' it fa' me," says Claudia.

Isiah goes back to the front door bringing in another box. "Here Mama, open this... go head."

Ruth opens the box. "Lawd, Isiah...this a fur coat?"

A brown maxi fur coat, It's called. "Ruth gets up and puts it on.

Matri says with exhilaration, "Mahalia Jackson, that's who she is."

Ruth's eyes sparkle, as she blushes. Ruth prances around. " I am goin' ta wear this ta' chuch Sunday."

Ruth looks at the clock on the wall. "Well it's time ta' watch ma' news." She carries the coat in the room. Ruth turns on the tv, in the dining room; sitting down, with the coat in her hands.

"Here's Tom McKomy on the 6:00 news, giving the news on a woman, found in the alley; pregnant with no identity. After having the baby; five days later, she leaves the hospital early in the morning; disappearing with the baby, without being discharged.

But strangely enough, someone saw a bag woman, put a baby into the garbage dumpster. Now, how did that happen? What happened to the mother of the baby?"

"Phenomenal," says Matri. Matri starts thinking about the bag lady in New York. *No, of course not. What am I thinking?* she in disarray.

"It is a strange thang," says Isiah.

The news reporter concluded. "If anybody has a clue to this mysterious situation, please contact the County Hospital, or District Police station on, South 15th Street. You can also call, the 6:00 news station.

CHAPTER 7

IN THE BOX

Matri thinks about Claudia's son, putting the people in a box. "You know... you can certainly learn something from a child. Paul did a project for school. He took a box and put people inside of the box. Now, he can't explain why he did that, or the significance. As I'm seeing, virtually... is this, one great big box that we're in? Is this the prison we're in, that brother Malcolm X spoke about?" She pauses and thinks, "*But the question is... who will get out of the box?*

The phone rings. "I'll get it!" Matri yells."

"Hey, hey"

Matri laughs. "Now, who is hey?"

Robert laughs. "Okay, this is me," says Robert.

"Okay me... what's going on?"

He's been drinking. Squints his eyes, talking from the side of his mouth, drooling. "Hmmm... you know what Matri?" He chuckles, losing his balance; he tries to still himself. "Oh, what the hell... I feel hurt Matri," he says bitterly.

Matri shakes her head, caringly asking, "Why?"

"I was working for this white cat, in construction. ... Never mind, why I'm doing physical labor in the first place. I'm a bonafied mathematician, and I work with electricity... understand it better than the average cat; my professor said, I was a genius."

Matri's astonished, "That's terrific Robert, I didn't know."

"Yeah, now I got laid off. Because the white cat, got a chance to get in the Union; but Uncle Sam's man got no recognition... no special opportunities," he frowns, with malice.

Matri feels troubled. "Isiah, said the same thing."

He utters with a shrill sound, "I'm here to tell you... it hurts, real bad. I got to get rid of this pain... it could destroy me." Robert's voice switches to chuckling, to keep from exploding.

He sips his drink. "Yeah, I've been drinking, too. I told Sadie, I was going to find some work, to marry her. Uncle Sam won't help my life. I would appreciate it more if he had told me I had a 'KMA' letter, waiting for me when I got back!" Robert says angrily.

"What's a KMA letter?" Matri asks.

He chuckles, "It means, kiss my ass."

"Oh dear heart, Robert. Mama says your good works will never be forgotten by God. He will carry you through. Robert, we're all in a box, and we all have to find our way out of the box. I was listening to the news, and Dr. King is in a box too. But, believe me; he's going to find a way out. Hajj Malik Shabazz and Angela Davis are all trying to get out of the box."

Robert cries out, shivering. "You know what Matri, I'll be damned if I don't get paid. Payback is a bitch." He yells, " It's all about mathematics, and I need some money to live! I'm going to live... and I'm going to live... like I expect to live!"

Matri is teary-eyed, holding her hands up in the air; with the black power symbol, "Right on, my brother... we will have our heaven here, too!"

Robert says, "Dig it, baby."

⊨⊰ ⊱⊨

Two hours later... the bell rings. "I'll git' it," says Isiah. When he opens the door, Ramone is standing in front of the door.

"Hey my man, the door downstairs was opened," says Ramone

"It's okay, just come on in and have a seat. I'll tell Matri it's you." Before Isiah could get out of the living room, someone knocks on the door. He opens the door; there stands Thaddeus. Isiah comes to a quick halt. Thaddeus stares at, him for acting so peculiar. Thaddeus glances to the side, seeing Ramone.

Isiah tries to keep his composure, swaying his hands. "Hey, man come right on in!" he says, while looking at Ramone. "I'll get Matri."

Real cool and charismatic, Thaddeus says, "Sure, my man."

"Hey man, that's your Brougham outside?" asks Thaddeus.

Quickly Ramone answers, "Umm—yeah."

"Is that your chauffeur?" Thaddeus asks.

"Yeah." Again he responds quickly.

Isiah goes into the dining room. "Matri," he says, "Ya' have a little somethin', ta' deal with?"

Ruth and Claudia stares at Matri. "What do you mean?" asks Matri.

Isiah hesitates to answer her, "Thaddeus and Ramone, are in the living room."

"Thaddeus? I thought he left for Baltimore." Matri is startled.

Isiah shakes his head. "Well he ain't in Baltimore; he's in the livin' room with Ramone."

Matri panics. Ruth and Claudia continue to stare at Matri.

Matri exhales, "Well, let's go and handle this."

"Hey, gorgeous," says Ramone. "Are you ready?"

Cordially, she says, "Oh, I'm ready. Thaddeus you two met at the Savoy."

Thaddeus agrees. "Yes Matri, we did. And we also met in college, as I've mentioned to you."

"Oh yes, of course," she smiles.

"Well Matri, don't let me hold you up. After all, you didn't expect to see me. My partner had an emergency, so we decided to take a later flight, tomorrow." He gets up to leave. "Listen," looking back at Ramone, "I'll call you, beloved." Matri walks him to the door. He walks down a few steps, looking back at Matri. Their eyes meet... she smiles.

"Thaddeus call me soon, okay. I need to talk to you. It's important that I do."

"Sure, bye."

She closes the door, slowly turning around; looking at Ramone; who is very cool and collective.

He sniffs. "You ready?" he asks.

"Yeah, I'll get my things," she says.

Matri kisses Ruth. "Mama, everybody, I'll be back Sunday evening."

Isiah looks at Matri, turning away. "I have ta' make a phone call. I have ta' give Dawn her present". He swirls around, "Darn it, I forgot ta' show ya' Dawn's new engagement ring."

"A new ring?" asks Claudia.

He pulls it out. "Yeah, the other one, was just to hold her." He laughs.

Claudia's puts her hands over her mouth. "Oh, ma' goodness. Isiah, that's a pretty ring."

"I 'clare," says Matri. "That is beautiful. You must've paid a lot for it."

"Let's just say, it's fit fa' a Queen," Isiah says proudly.

"Bring it here Isiah," says Ruth. "Oh ma' Lawd, I ain't never seen nothin' like it b'fore." Looking up at Isiah, Ruth says, "Isiah, Dawn deserves anythang good ya' have ta' give 'er. She's a good girl."

"I kno' Mama, and I love 'er too." Isiah hugs Ruth.

"Well, I have to go. Ramone's waiting for me," says Matri.

"Hey, I have ta' go over Dawn's too." Isiah kisses Ruth on the forehead. "

Ruth stares at Claudia. "Well what chu' waitin on?" asks Ruth.

"Mama I'm gettin' ready ta' go downstairs, and smoke a cigarette; while I wait fa' Lorraine. I kno' ya' don' approve of me smokin,' in ya' house," says Claudia.

"What made cha' start smokin' anyway? Them streets gon' kill ya' yet. Smokin', drinkin' and carryin' on," Ruth shakes her head.

"Oh Mama, it ain't that bad." Claudia tries to convince Ruth.

"Go on child with ya' fool talk. I don' like the way ya' see thangs. B'sides, I'm gon' listen ta' ma' Mahalia Jackson t'night. I'm gon' listen ta' "Trouble of the World" and "Take My Hand, Precious Lord." Claudia kisses Ruth, while holding a cigarette in her hand.

Two hours later, pulling up to the base, Luther announces, "Army base of Fort Dix." He continues to stare at Matri with a strange expression on his face.

Matri thinks, *Why do I keep catching him staring at me, strangely. And why is Ramone bringing me here?* She observes the soldiers, as they look for a parking space. She thinks, *These men are certainly in a box. They can't escape no matter what side they turn. They're in a box, to kill or be killed. That's a heck of a box.*

"Matri," says Ramone. "I'm going to take you to your room, where you'll be staying… one of the best, of course. Matri, I have to take care of some business. It seems as though, I can't leave home without my business; it follows me everywhere I go."

"Okay, I'll freshen up," says Matri.

He starts to walk away; snapping his fingers. "Oh Matri, let's have a late night meal in your room. Something light, with wine or something. The phone will be turned on in about twenty minutes, and you can call your Mama." Ramone says caringly.

"Okay," says Matri.

Hours later... Matri hears a knock, and opens the door with her robe on. Ramone holds a bottle of Kijafa wine in his hands; with ice and a platter of decorated sandwiches. He sniffs, "Oh Matri, can I please apologize for the delay?"

Matri blushes, looking at the bottle of Kijafa. "I 'clare Ramone, you never cease to surprise me." Looking at herself, dressed in a robe. Matri shrugs, "But please do come in. Even though I ate at home, I could use a little something."

"I promise, I won't stay long. We have a long day ahead of us to-morrow. I'm going to introduce you to the Sergeant, and give you a tour, around old Dix."

The next day... Matri, while looking at her watch, walks towards the mirror. She prances around, having flashbacks. Imagining herself, standing in her room in the south; looking into her tall mirror, thinking about Claudia and herself, before they went out that night. She backs up, getting her pocketbook, putting it on top of her head; imagining it to be the books, that she used on her head to walk correctly. "This is the way I'm going to walk while I'm here... like a lady." Someone knocks on the door. Startled by the knock, she throws her pocketbook on the bed. "Here I come, Ramone." But to her surprise, it wasn't Ramone. Opening the door, Matri froze. Luther spits, standing at the door, looking her up and down with delight; with his right eye twitching.

"Oooh," Matri's eyes are fixated on Luther's eyes, thinking. Snapping out of it, she says, "Excuse me, I'm just tired."

"Matri, Ramone told me ta' escort cha' ta' the Sergeant's office; he's havin' a meetin' with em'." He spits out tobacco juice again.

Matri says to herself. *Chewing tobacco?*.... Eyes flutter, "Oh, let me get my coat and purse, please." Matri walks out of the door, as if she's a lady; accustomed to nothing but royalty.

Luther, is in awe of her beauty. Only seconds, short of desiring her for himself, as she walks ahead of him. He adamantly says to himself, *I envy Ramone, fer the way he got with 'er. Look how the men stop in their tracks, ta' get a good look at 'er. They're drawn to 'er. Walks like some goddess or somethin'. Ramone sure kno' 'how ta' get 'em.… He* chews the tobacco and spits. *There's somethin' very powerful about 'er. Just can't put ma' hands on it—yeah that's just it. I'll never be able ta' put my hands on 'er… boy what a waste.*

I better catch up with 'er. "Oh, Matri, right here." Luther knocks on the door. A soldier opens the door, smiling, staring at Matri.

"Come right on in, Ramone's in a meeting with Sergeant Steele. It'll be over in a minute or two. Have a seat."

Ramone comes out of the room with Sergeant Steele, wiping his nose with a tissue. He brushes off a white powder substance from his shirt. He sniffs. "Matri come in here for a minute," says Ramone.

Matri elegantly walks across the room. Ramone is proud of her beauty and the way she carries herself. Ramone introduces her to the Sergeant. His eyes are fixated on Matri, gloating over her. He reaches out his hands to hers. "Well, it certainly is my pleasure to meet such a fine lady as yourself, Matri. Ramone has told me so much about you." The Sergeant looks over at Ramone smiling. "I can see, he didn't lie at all. I mean, I'm mighty glad to meet you."

Ramone smiles, slightly.

Matri says, "Thank you. I've never been on an army base before. I find it quite interesting," she comments.

"That's the lawyer in her, always thinking. I guess that's why we would make such a great team. Me being a detective, her being a lawyer. Two great thinkers, empowering each other."

The Sergeant never stop looking at Matri. "Yes, yes of course… I see."

"Okay, let's have a light lunch," says Ramone.

Tilting his cap, "Let's go then," says the Sergeant.

Six hours later... Matri contemplates. *"Just a little eyeliner and lip-stick here... orange lipstick".* Knock, Knock. *"Oh, that's Ramone".* Matri opens the door. Excitedly, she says. "Oh my, I 'clare... Ramone, you look nice in that tuxedo."

"Close your eyes, gorgeous. This goes with the elegance of your dress. "

Matri giggles. " Close my eyes... okay."

Ramone puts the coat around her shoulders. "Open your eyes."

Matri opens her eyes, running her fingers across the fur coat. She's apprehensive. "No Ramone, you shouldn't have. I can't accept this."

Charmingly he says, "Matri, you didn't ask me for this. Take it as an expression."

Matri says, " Okay, it's an expression of elegance, power, and articulation. Thank you.."

Ramone sniffs, reaching out his hand, "Shall we?"

"Oh, wait, let me get my purse."

Luther drives up to the hall, dressed in a black tuxedo. He reaches out to Matri's hand, letting her out of the car. "Step this way please," directing them into the hall. The waiter escorts them to the table, pulling the chair back for Matri.

Ramone looks at Matri across the table, with great admiration.

Matri notices and blushes. Luther comes back, and sits at the table with them. "Oh, Matri, Luther's going to join us tonight. Actually he's more than a chauffeur; he's my business partner also." He bows his head to Matri. "Luther, assist us with the drinks, my man." He tips his head.

Ramone turns around, spotting four women, calling them over to the table. "I need you to meet Matri. I know the two of you met her at the Savoy."

Patty's black. "Hello Matri, I'm Patty."

Da'bour's white. "Matri, I'm Da'bour."

"My pleasure," Matri says, slightly bowing her head.

"As you could see, this is a big table. Sit down, ladies," says Ramone.

"Where's the Sergeant?" asks Patty.

"He'll be here in a minute." Soldiers walk by, glancing at the table smiling... mischievously.

The girls stare at Matri's beauty. Ramone notices them staring. He stares... *Yes, intriguing, isn't she?* he says to himself.

After eating feeling satiated, everyone's plate is empty. "Ramone, dinner was absolutely delicious," says Da'bour. The other girls agreed.

"Now I guess, we have to do what we came here for," says Ramone. Matri was baffled by his remark.

He notices. "What I mean is, we came here to have a great time."

"That's right," says Patty, slightly giving Ramone her attention.

"Would you ladies excuse me. I have to see what's holding the Sergeant up," says Ramone.

"Where is the ladies room?" asks Matri.

"I'll show you where it is. I have to use it myself," says Patty.

As they walk across the floor, the soldiers give them their full attention. Patty seductively walks across the floor. Matri walks like a lady. Ramone's standing in the corner, watching how the men are fascinated with Matri. "Ummm... men like a little class in this business."

"This bathroom is very nice," Matri comments.

"Yeah, I'm used to the best, but of course I make good money," Patty responds.

"What do you do?" asks Matri.

Patty pauses... "I'm a, call-girl... come on, he didn't tell you?"

Tilting her head, she asks, "Tell me... who didn't tell me?" Matri asks.

Primping in the mirror, she says, "Ramone, honey."

Sarcastically, Matri says, "He was supposed to?"

"I see... you're slow."

Matri acts sassy, putting her hands on her hips. "Really?"

Witlessly she says, "Let me tell you something' princess. I'm number one with Ramone and I will always be. The sooner you get that, the better off you'll be."

Matri's nose stiffens. Tilting her head boldly, she says, "Number one, that's interesting, I didn't know I was competing."

She walks towards the door, turning around looking at Matri. "Just do yourself a favor and go home to mommy, you don't belong."

Matri is baffled. "Ha, I don't have a clue what she's talking about. Hmm, it would be nice if I did."

After the party, Ramone holds Matri's hand. Luther watches him in the mirror. "Matri, you were a hit tonight," says Ramone.

Matri's silenced by Patty's remarks. "Are you... okay Matri?"

"I'm just tired, Ramone."

Ramone asks, "Matri, do you like nice things?"

"Why?"

He turns, facing her. "Well, you can have anything you want. We could have fine cars, fine fur coats; a better home than I have now... not to mention a big fat bank account."

Matri answers in the affirmative, "It sounds nice."

He holds her hands. "Well, let's get you to your room."

Luther lets Matri out of the car, giving her a glance. Ramone walks her to the door.

"Matri, we'll have breakfast. Then we'll pull out, a little sooner than planned. I have an emergency."

"Okay," she says, yawning.

Ramone walks her to the door, "Matri, dream about what I said to you."

"Sure."

During the twilight hours, Matri is tossing and turning. "Oh boy..." she yells. "I can't sleep." The phone rings. She looks at the clock; "It's 3:30, what does Ramone want? Hello..." No one says anything… "Hello…" Someone starts whining loudly, on the other end of the phone. Matri stiffens. She starts perspiring underneath her arms; her hands start shaking. The person stops abruptly, hanging up; Matri is frozen. Matri thinks, "I heard this same whining at Ramone's home. I want to get out of here, first thing in the morning." She turns the light on, for the rest of the night… staring at the door.

CHAPTER 8

TROUBLE MAN

Isiah is home, getting ready to hit the streets. He took the room upstairs. "Wait a minute... let me put ma' man on, while I get dressed." 'Trouble Man' is playing. Isiah is in the bathroom shaving. "Hey!" He sings. 'I come up hard baby. I didn't make it playin' by the rules. I come up hard but that's okay. Trouble Man, don't get in my way.' *This cat alwaze singin' bout ma' life*, says Isiah to himself. "Whew!..." he sings, 'I come up hard baby. Gonna keep movin' Isiah grabs his face. "Ouch, darnit. Marvin, ya' made me nick ma'self with this razor." Looking into the mirror, Isiah starts singing again. 'I come up hard but that's okay. I've seen some faces and some places, I got good connections...that's okay they don't bother me. Gonna keep movin to the top. I come up hard, I come up gettin' down.'

Isiah stops and looks down at his watch. "Gotta' get outta' here. Gotta' see the, maaan." He stands in front of the mirror; with black pants; cranberry and black parka sweater with cranberry gators; black short leather jacket; and elgrondai black hat. Looking in the mirror, he says, "Mirror, mirror... what chu wanna' tell me baby, "T... stands for trouble, man!" He chuckles.

The phone rings. "Hello."

"Hi baby."

"Give me a kiss."

Dawn kisses at him over the phone. "Are you coming over tonight?"

"I can't t'night."

"Why not?"

He snaps at her, "Because I said not, didn't I tell ya' 'bout askin' me so many questions?"

"I'm gettin' tired of you snapping at me!" Dawn warns him.

He yells, "You raisin' your voice, at me Dawn?"

Dawn lowers her voice. "Isiah, it's just that since you started working all of those long hours... I think it's stressing you out, Baby."

He pulls the phone close to him. "Baby, how you like all those diamonds on that ring?"

"I love it," She says."Dawn baby, just give me a minute. I'm not going to keep this job for long. I just need to make a certain amount of money, and I'm gonna find somethin' more suitable for the both of us... okay?"

"Okay... love you, King."

In Harlem, Isiah walks down 42nd street, at midnight. A tall little boy with long sweeping eye lashes; big afro, with an oval shaped face; wearing a black leather coat, starts walking beside him, imitating his walk. Isiah notices him imitating his walk. He continues to walk. The little boy continue to walk with him.

"Hey, man. I like that walk," he says.

Isiah keeps looking ahead, smiling at the little boy. "Why ya' like it?" asks Isiah.

Out of breath, he says, "It's cool man. They call it a "cool poze"

"What's a cool poze?" Isiah asks.

He starts bobbing his head, too. "Man I just told you... the way you walk, I like it man. You dig it?"

"How old is ya', and why ya' in the street this time of night?" asks Isiah.

He boldly says, "I do what I wanna do, dig it?"

Isiah keeps walking, without looking down at him." You can't be no more than 15 or 16, at the most."

Shrugging his shoulders. "It don't matter. I gotta live... mama say."

Isiah stops, looking down at the boy.… "Mama—say?" Isiah reaches in his pocket giving him some money. "Now take this money, and ya' git' home ta' ya' mama."

Sways his hands, "Look man, I got somin,' I got to do. If I don't do it. …. Hey, look man, I gotta go… the man. …."

"What man? "asks Isiah.

Gets tough, "Look, you better mind yo' business, man." He jerks away from Isiah running.

Isiah watches to see which way he's going. "Gotta go ma'self, gotta meet ma' man. I gotta pick. …." A car comes by speeding, almost hitting him as he crosses the street. "Hey! You stupid son of a... ya' couldda killed me." Isiah looks around for the boy. "Where did he go?"

He comes to the end of 42nd street. He turns the corner and he sees Lorraine, taking something from one of the drug sellers. She turns around looking right into Isiah's face. They both look down at her hands. The guy looks at Isiah and says, very streetish, "Hey man, ya got a problem?" Isiah keeps on walking.

CHAPTER 9
THE CRASH

Monday at work, Matri knocks on Mr. Krut's door. "Matri, you come right in." She enters his office, bringing her pad and her ink pen.

"Sit down Matri," says Mr. Krutz. He starts rubbing his forehead. "Matri I've learned over a period of time to trust you. And you've been very loyal to me. This business calls for that."

Matri notices, he forgot to puit his glasses on; you could see the weariness in his eyes; his skin seem to have shriveled, from worry, on his once handsomevface.

"Matri, I think you've also learned that, this could be a dirty business. Sometimes people don't always live up to their end of the bargain. Matri, I'm going to cut through the chase, because I can, trust you".

"Yes, you can," says Matri.

"Matri, I play a very important role in the stock market. Right now, I feel like I'm in a maze, with this thing. There is so much pressure on me right now. I could hardly figure out, how I'm going to get out of this thing alive." He pauses. "Figuratively speaking, of course. I barely sleep anymore."

Mr. Krutz sits back, folding his hands across his stomach. He says with melancholy, "But there's one thing I've decided to do. I'm not going to let this thing take everything from me. I've worked hard and long with my business," he stares off.

"Matri... Mrs. Watenburg and I, are closer than anybody really knows. I want you to go to Mrs. Watenburg's for dinner. She needs to talk to you, and don't ask me to tell you why, because I can't right now. She'll fill you in."

Matri remains firm. "When?"

"Do you have class tonight?" he asks."

"Tonight's Monday—no, as a matter of fact, no. Great timing, my teacher is out all this week—a bad cold or something."

He sighs. "Good... go tonight."

"Okay." Matri confirms.

"That'll be it for now." He swirls around, looking out of the window.

"Matri," Charlotte says, "Thaddeus is on the line."

Matri sits on the top of her desk, crossing her legs; seemingly perplexed.

She exhales, "Thaddeus, how can I help you?"

"I need to talk to you, but not over the phone," he says.

"How is Thursday, at the Town Café, on Halsey Street in Newark?" she asks.

"What time, Matri?"

"Let's see…ummm, let's say 6:00," she confirms.

"Gotcha, beloved," says Thaddeus.

"Bye, beloved." Matri remains on top of the desk, in deep thought.

⇒⊹⇐

Thursday at 6:15, Matri arrives. "Matri I thought you weren't coming, for a minute," says Thaddeus.

"Fat chance of that Thaddeus. First and foremost, this is my favorite little café. Secondly, I had to change my tire. Somehow a big piece of glass got stuck in my tire." Matri pants.

"I see," says Thaddeus

Matri opens the menu. "Well, I'm famished."

"Oh really?" Thaddeus gazes at Matri.

Matri closes the menu. "There, I'll have vegetables and... I must have my rice, I'm still a country girl." Matri looks around.

"What are you looking for, Matri?"

"I'd like to have some wine with my meal," Matri says.

Annoyed, he says, "Oh, Ramone's got you drinking?"

Abruptly, she says, "Thaddeus no, please don't do this to me now. Ramone is only a friend. I have no commitments with him."

He says with fervor, " Me either."

Matri looks at Thaddeus, putting her hands over Thaddeus' hand. "Do you want to listen to me, Thaddeus?"

Thaddeus is very attentive. "There will never be another Thaddeus." She starts shaking her head. "I don't know why I feel confused, and at the same time, I feel our souls have something in common," eyes flutters. " I can't let go."

Thaddeus pulls her face to his, kissing her... she kisses him. "I see, that's good enough for now," says Thaddeus.

"Please tell me what's going on," says Matri.

"Here's the thing. I told you I had to go away for a conference on the stock market?"

Matri thinks. "Uh—ha."

"Well Matri, it's about to..." He holds his thumb downward... "Crash. Man, I thought those cats were going to have to buy some boxing gloves. I mean, those rich white cats were saying all kinds of obscenities. My partner and me had to step in and become the mediators, between all that chaos. I reminded them, and I know they didn't like a black cat telling them... let's be intelligent about this." They both laugh. "Actually, I didn't feel too comfortable about it either. But I came there to represent and take a report back to my boss... who, is ill. I asked my boss to give me a three month's leave, to do my book, since I've been going away so much," says Thaddeus.

"What did he say?" asks Matri.

He responded with zest. "He said, after this I could take a leave of absence."

Cheerfully Matri says, "Hey, great!"

"Now getting back to the stock market crisis. I tried to lay something heavy on them. I said, first and foremost, this is infamous. Get back to the pen and pad. Start brainstorming, by pulling every collective resource that's available at hand. Also, in hindsight, go back and study what happened when the stock market crashed before.. it would be more propitious? My analysis is, a classic case of inertia, and thinking your infallible, with all of this humbug. Because you don't need to continue reiterating any carelessness, or bad judgment calls; that was and could be at present... stemming from deceit, lies, greed and distrust. Those are the forerunners that are bad for business. It's heinous, and it heralds a sudden fall, that's inevitable," he stares into Matri's eyes.

"I told them, they didn't need a crowd like this anymore, and they should get the ten top executive men: accountants and mathematicians."

"They need Robert for this, "says Matri.

"That would be great, but they couldn't take the challenge, that Robert would present to them. Their egos could hardly take me."

"I saw Mr. Krutz twice. The first night he came to the meeting, he was very quiet. The second night he came, it was a disaster. He was trying to give them, some very resourceful information, but they shut him down. Someone made a statement about Jews, and what did they do that for? Mr. Krutz started the War of the Minds." That's the title of my book, *"War of the Minds."* That, is what I've been thinking about, as the title. "

Mr.Krutz was so powerful and on point, with analysis of the figures of the stock market. He made it hard for anybody to challenge him on it... and nobody did. They were in awe of the logic he used; showing them that they have created a maze; because of their brainlessness, lack of studying and selfishness. He roared across the room, telling them, They should never, have forgotten what happened with the first crash, and that's why they are repeating it.'

Thaddeus pauses, looking to the right of the window. Matri stares at him, then looks away to see what got his attention so abruptly. Matri is startled.

Matri says, "Thaddeus if I could swear, that's the same bag lady I saw in New York."

"It could be, Matri. They take the subway too. Everybody loves New York, but they may like something about Newark too," Thaddeus admits.

Matri looks her up and down, putting her hands on her heart.

"What's wrong, Matri?" asks Thaddeus.

Matri gasps. "I have this deep pain in my heart."

"You want me to take you to the doctor?" asks Thaddeus.

She nods. "It doesn't seem to be that type of pain, Thaddeus."

"Then—what?" He holds her hands.

Matri looks at the bag lady as she walks away. "It's more of a hurtful pain. It's so many hurtful things, we as black people are going through Thaddeus... we're in a box."

"Matri I couldn't agree with you more. But we can't solve our problems at the level of thinking, we're on now. We need new minds and new thoughts."

Matri whispers "Perhaps."

⇥⁺ ⁺⇤

Months later... Friday night, in November. Ruth fried some catfish, collard greens and candy yams. You could smell it a mile away. Collard greens, catfish and biscuits with butter; sliding down the sides, melting in your mouth, makes folks start cussin.'

Ruth is in her element tonight; humming Mahalia Jackson's song, " *Go Tell It on The Mountain,*" as she spins the plates on the table, like a pizza man, spinning dough for pizza. Matri and Claudia laughs.

Someone bangs on the door. Everybody looks at each other. "Let me see who this bad person is, that got the heart ta' come bangin' on ma' doe," says Claudia. They continue to bang. "Who is it?" yells Claudia, opening the door. Dawn pushes her way through, heading straight to the dining room. Claudia backs up, out of her way, staring at her.

"Where is he?" Dawn asks angrily patting her foot. Ruth, Matri and Claudia looks down at her foot. Dawn walks out of the dining room saying, "Where is he?" She opens the door, going upstairs to his apartment, leaving Ruth, Matri, and Claudia baffled.

"I 'clare, what is wrong with Dawn?" asks Matri.

"Here she comes again," says Claudia. They all remain quiet when she walks back into the room. She goes over to the empty chair and flops down. Ruth gets up and prepares the food. "Ain't nothin' these catfish, collard greens and butter biscuits can't help." Matri and Claudia remain quiet.

Dawn looks at Matri and Claudia very angrily. "Matri... Claudia, what is wrong with your brother?"

"What do you mean?" asks Matri.

"First of all, he's acting strange. He yells at me all the time, acts like he doesn't have any patience with me, any more." She frowns.

"Oh, leave the man alone. He been workin' hard child. I 'clare," says Claudia.

Matri is thinking. "Yeah Dawn, you've got a point, Isiah is acting a little unusual. He's always on the go. I can't tell when he's working or not."

Ruth nods. "Matri sure is right... I been noticin' ma'self."

Claudia starts acting nervous. "Oh ain't nothin' wrong with ma' brother," says Claudia.

"Your nerves so bad from drinkin,' and runnin' the streets, ya' can't see ya' need ta' stop, ya 'self," claims Ruth.

Claudia stares at Ruth. "Oh, let me have a smoke." She leaves out to smoke.

The door slams. Matri whispers... "That's Isiah."

"Hi everybody."

Isiah freezes, noticing Dawn. "What chu' doin' here?"

Dawn is agitated, "What do you mean, what am I doing here? Y'all see what I mean?"

Isiah gets annoyed. "Alright now, Dawn don' start with me, okay?"

"Y'all sit down and let's eat this food," says Ruth.

Everybody's quiet at the table, except Isiah. "Ummm, Mama this food is good." He turns towards Dawn, pausing…. " Ya' gon' cook like this fa' me?" Dawn ignores Isiah. Nobody says anything.

Ruth gets up and turns the tv on. "Good evening, welcome to Black Talk this evening. We're going to brief you on the current affairs. As the preacher says in church, "There's re's turbulence in the land. We have Professor Norton and Jean Burton discussing Black Crisis." Everybody is watching attentively.

Here's Professor Norton explaining to us, ' *A New Call to Resist Illegitimate Authority.*'

"Yes, I need you to know what I'm about to explain, is a harbinger of what is to come. I've been given permission to brief you on some of the details. Because of its resistance, there will be a loss of lives. But first, I'd like to show pictures. Here are pictures of a Massive Protest at the Pentagon. Here are pictures of Vietnam War Veterans, protesting too. After experiencing the horrors of the war first-hand, they joined the ranks of the protesters. Opponents of the Vietnam War have worked to end it in many ways… some through conventional politics, some by supporting draft resistance, of attacking university complicity in militarism. Others have carried resistance further, destroying draft files and developing opposition within the armed forces. We believe that resistance to many forms of illegitimate authority, is necessary to bring health to this country. Making it a constructive force, instead of a terror in the politics of nations.

Also, there is a book on Genocide by Jean Paul Sarture. And what it entails is simply this: After the blood bath of conquest in

'Algeria during the last century, the French imposed the Civil Code, with its middle class conceptions of property and inheritance, on tribal society where each community held land in common. Thus, they systematically destroyed the economic infrastructure of the country, and tribes of peasants soon saw their lands fall into the hands of French speculators, eventually causing an act of genocide.

Matri is in deep thought. "We're all in this box, a maze… trapped. How will we get out… how… do we get out?"

"Now I would like to show you something, my people," says Miss. Burton. There's a picture of the Black Panthers, with rifles at arm. Some of these men were in Vietnam." Isiah is angered by this picture. "Stokely Carmichael says, "No matter how much money you make in the black community, when you go into the white world you are still a nigger, repeatedly."

Isiah slams his hands down on the kitchen table, charging out of the dining room. Everybody jumps up from the table after him. "Isiah," Matri yells. Matri and Dawn goes charging after him.

"Come back baby, come back to me," Dawn cries.

Ruth grabs Dawn, hugging her. "Baby let 'em go now. He got ta' git through this and he will. Come from a good strong tree… just let 'em go."

Matri and Claudia comes back inside. Claudia cries, "I want ma' brother ta' be alright… ain't never seen 'em like this b'fore Mama." Matri puts her hands over her heart. She goes to the sink to get a glass of water.

Ruth reaches out to Matri, Dawn and Claudia and hugs them all together. Claudia's sons come and grab them, hugging them by the waist. "Just like the branches of a tree, holding on by its roots, it—don' fall," says Ruth.

Sunday morning, the phone is ringing.

"Get the phone Matri, will ya," says Claudia.

"Where's Mama?" asks Matri

"You oughtta kno', she went ta' chuch," says Claudia.

"Hello."

"Matri, this is Hezikiah."

"Oh… hi."

"Matri, I need to see you."

"Okay, when?"

"What about today at 4:00, at the Town Café?"

"Good enough."

"I'll be sittin' in the back, in the corner."

"Ummm," says Matri

Matri goes into the café… but she doesn't see Hezikiah. The lights are dim.

"Over here Matri," he says.

Matri looks around. Turning around… she's at a standstill.

"Hezikiah," he says.

She's shocked by what she sees.

"Sit down, Matri please don't faint. I'll explain."

Feeling flustered, her mouth drops, the words won't come out.

The waiter comes over. Flopping down into the chair, Matri says, "I'll have Kijafa, please."

"White Saturn," says Hezikiah.

Matri gawks at Hezikiah. "Okay Matri… Uncle Sam messed me up. And I'm painin.' I no longer can be a man, Matri. That's my affliction."

Commiserating over Hezikiah's dilemma, Matri is hurtful, pointing her finger. "No…no…wh… huh? The army has debased your character, reducing you to this—this infuriates me!"

He explains, eyes glossy. "I was in a hole, and they threw a grenade in the hole… something must've hit ma' genitals. "He says… all I kno' is that… I had ta' be carried away on a stretcher." He stiffens. I was in so much pain, Matri.

Tears roll down his face. "The doctor said, I wouldn't have any feelins' anymore for a woman."

"Matri couldn't take her eyes off of him, dressed like a woman. Huge black afro wig, huge earrings, lots of make up and red lipstick, "But, Hezikiah. …."

"Yeah, I kno', why am…I dressed like this? Matri, I'm suing Uncle Sam. I have a lawyer, doctor and a shrink. I get psychiatric treatments, every two weeks. I told the psychiatrist, I don' kno' who I am no more. Isiah and Robert think it's all 'bout the money, but some of this is true. I don' kno'… what I'm gon' be."

"Matri stares continuously at Hezikiah. "You…you… prefer…?"

"Matri my sister's husband destroyed 'er. So, I guess in a crazy way, I'm also paying men back fa' cheatin' on their wives. Don't allow them ta' touch me, just play a trick on em.' They come ta' me and I go out with them… then I tell them, I'm a man; tell them, that's good for them, pickin' up anythang'; never kno' what their gettin'… tell 'em one day they gon' pick up the devil himself, for cheatin' on their wives."

Matri bursts out laughing. Hezikiah laughs too. "I 'clare." She grabs her heart,   "Y'all gon' kill me, yet." She and Hezikiah continue to laugh. "I 'clare, Mama says, "Go Tell It On The Mountain…" She pauses…. "Genocide, Black Panther's, Hajja Malik, Angela Davis, Dr. King, Veterans protesting… and sexual revolution. Yes…we have to, "Go Tell It On The Mountain… I 'clare."

CHAPTER 10

GO TELL IT ON THE MOUNTAIN

"Matri have you ever noticed how snow falls?" asks Dawn. Matri looks around at the snow falling all around her. Children are playing, having snowball fights. Some are pushing their sleds up and down the street... seeing no danger.

"The coldness kills germs, and the snow adds whiteness to the earth; representing the blanket of peace, and purity." Matri says.

"Maybe, that's a sign to all mankind," Dawn says.

Softly Matri says, "Maybe."

"Matri, let me take you for a ride through the mountains. I'll take you to a little diner... just to look at the mountains, capped by the snow; giving the impressions of ice cream cone. It brings out my artistic spirit."

"That's very interesting Dawn, lets go," says Matri.

"Matri... you seem a little out of it." As Dawn drives, she notices Matri's facial expression.

Matri confesses. "Well in a way, yeah. ... I feel like my heart's been, broken by the things of the world. The bad part is, things have to get worse before they can get better."

"Matri, just look at these mountains, while we're riding through them," says Dawn.

Matri looks at them on both sides, of her. "This is really awesome. Dr. King speaks about, 'To The Mountain Top'; Hjjah Malik (Malcolm), went to Mount Arafat; Mahalia Jackson sings about, "Go Tell It On The Mountain." Moses... went to the mountains. Yes, the mountains seem to have a lot of significance to them," Matri says.

Dawn drives up to the diner, with tables sitting in the front of it. "Here we go—Matri. Are you cold?" asks Dawn.

"As a matter of fact... a little," Matri says, looking away from Dawn.

"Well, let me go inside to get something hot to drink. We could sit here and look at the mountain top," she looks up, "The snow, seems to be stopping."

A little melancholy, Matri says, "Sure."

Ten minutes later, Dawn mentions, "Here we go, Matri. Sit here on the bench. I have to get something out of my car to show you."

Matri sips her tea, with her eyes fixated; looking at the mountaintops.

"Matri... I need to say something to you... right quick," Dawn says.

Matri is tired. She exhales, "Go on Dawn."

Sadly, Dawn says, "Matri, I've been up here a little longer than you. And I know, when to suspect someone, of being on drugs."

Eyes widens."You do?" Matri says surprisingly.

Dawn looks into Matri's eyes, holding her hands. "Matri... I think Isiah is on drugs."

Matri angrily jumps up; breaking away, twirling around. "But, why would he do that?"

Teary-eyed, Dawn says, "That's how I felt at first, but after thinking about it. Matri... 'Nam's had a very bad effect on Isiah, Robert and Hezikiah."

Matri reflects back to what Hezikiah and Robert told her. "You know Dawn, now that you brought it to my attention, It adds up. I have to talk to him. Isiah and I are very close. He'll share his problems with me."

"Here we go Matri, what I'm going to do is draw a picture. I'm glad it stopped snowing, so I could do this." Dawn begin to draw.

"Dawn, thank you for bringing me here." Matri starts thinking about her sacred spot in the south. "You know, this reminds me of my sacred place in the south. The stillness… no need to talk…." She looks around…

"Just let creation speak to you," Says Dawn

Matri stares at Dawn…"My sentiments exactly."

"That's what drawing does for me, Matri." Dawn reaches for her tea.

"Dawn, do you have some paper and a pen?"

"Yeah, let me get it out of the trunk."

"I'll sit here and write, as you draw. I'm going to, "Go, tell it on the mountain," and let them speak to me." Matri gently bites down on the pen, thinking.

"Okay," she writes. She stares hurtfully, at the mountains…. " They look very strong. They will not be moved, as Mama will say about, not giving up on G-d… no matter what. Because they are on solid ground… quietly and patiently, standing tall… at attention— Mama says, 'God is with the patient'. She says, 'God says, He never leaves the patient'. Looks up at the mountain. "You never move." She wonders, "*Is that, why Moses went there? Perhaps they're waiting for man to notice them; wanting to be understood; knowing that everything has a purpose.*" Matri stands up, and raises her right hand up in the air, standing at attention. … "No… not just to black power… but to all power. The power, isn't limited to black or white."

"Matri I'm done, look." Dawn shows Matri the picture. "It's a picture of people standing around the mountain, with different facial expressions. Some people are standing around the mountains with the expression: looking, as if they don't know what happened... while gazing at this, one woman's expression... standing before them. Her face glows; in her eyes there's peace, love and hope; emanating within, drawing them to her like a magnet. Dawn looks into Matri's eyes, holding her hands. Softly she says, "Her eyes, are the windows to the soul... that's you Matri." They hug each other.

Joyfully, Matri says, "Oh Dawn that is so beautiful, I have to show Thaddeus this. He'll love it. Maybe he could use this for a book cover, for one of his books."

Dawn's excited. "You really mean that?"

Jentle voice, "Of course, I wouldn't lie to you."

Dawn rubs her face, looking up. "The snow is starting to come down fast now."

Matri looks up, smiling. "Well, it allowed us to do what we needed to do."

"Okay, let's pack up and go," says Dawn.

CHAPTER 11
DEBAUCHERY

Time is flying and it's the end of April. It finally stops raining. Downtown, Broad Street at 1:00 AM, all the shoppers are gone. The streets are left to the night people. The bag women and men; drug addicts; dope sellers; and prostitutes.

"Man," The guy looks at his watch, pacing back and forth.

"Stop lookin' at that watch... just be cool man, they gon' have the money."

"They better not just have the white horse - they better, have that money."

"You right, about that man."

A car pulls over. "Look, I told chu, they would come." He points to the car approaching them.

The guy looks at his watch. "Hey man what took you so damn long." Two guys get out of the car with long coats and black hats. "I guess you didn't hear me man!" The two guys pull guns from underneath their coats, opening fire on both of them, and pulls off.

Later that evening... Matri walks into the house. "Mama, Claudia... is anybody here?" She walks into the dining room. "Umm, wonder where is everybody?" Turning around thinking, remembering what Dawn said. *I'm gonna check out Isiah's room.*

Matri goes upstairs to Isiah's room, slowly opening the door. *Hmmm, it's hard trying to find something in here. He is so, clean and neat... umm, the bed, underneath the bed.* She pulls a suitcase from underneath the bed opening it. Her eyes protrude. "Oh, my, God. She falls down on the bed. "No—beloved—why? My dear heart, you tricked all of us...we all love you...me, Claudia, Dawn and Mama." Feeling torn by love and deception, angrily she says, "We're going, to see you through this!"

Matri busies herself in the kitchen, talking aloud, ' *I'll bake a chicken, and put some vegetables on before they get home. Let me get some rice— love my rice. Where's the salt? I have to clean it with salt."* Matri is lost in thought, becoming oblivious to her surroundings. The water in the pot is running over onto the floor. She doesn't notice Ruth and Claudia standing in the living room door, watching her talk to herself.

"Matri!" yells Claudia. Matri turns around gazing at Claudia and Ruth.

"What's got cha' mind Matri? Git' the mop Claudia!" says Ruth. Matri comes and hugs Ruth.

"Come on in the dinin' room, Matri. Let's talk," says Ruth. Claudia follows behind.

"You boys go ta' your room and play. I'll be in there in a minute," says Claudia.

Matri holds Ruth's hands and says, "Mama..."

"Go on honey, we'll deal with it," assures Ruth.

Matri hesitates, looking at her with sadness in her eyes, "Mama... Isiah is on drugs."

"Oh Lawd," Ruth bites down on her lip, raises her head high up in the air. "Noo, oh, Lawd."

Claudia's frantic. "I kinda thought somethin' was wrong with Isiah, he alwaze rubbin' his nose and sniffin'. Lorraine told me he probably waz', too."

"Hold it chirrin'. Lets hold hands ta' gether," says Ruth. Matri and Claudia hold hands with Ruth. She speaks very humble, "Ohhh, ma' precious Lawd. Ya' say ask not, want not. And ya' say ya' listen ta' all ya' people… and if we 'member ya', ya' 'member us, Lawd. I'm hooked on ya' love." Adamantly, Ruth says, "But—ya' say, let them listen ta' ya' too'… Now Lawd…" She strongly emphasizes… "Ma' precious Lawd.'" She humbly says, "I been listenin' ta' ya'… even when I didn't understand ya'…" jently she says, "So… please listen ta' me."

"All ma' chirrin, belong ta' ya' Lawd, first…ya' only used me ta' bring 'em here fa' yo' purpose." She shakes her head. "But Lawd,' ya' maker of ma' chirrin. Isiah is a good child, but he's in a troubled world. So Lawd, 'member me and, "Take Ma' Hand, Precious Lawd" and let me guide ma' chirrin." She pauses and looks at Claudia. 'For We Shall Overcome,' King say." Ruth goes and flops down on the chair.

Matri silently yells out, dropping at Ruth's feet, placing her head on Ruth's lap. "Mama, Mama," says Matri.

Claudia cries, hugging Ruth. "Mama we gon' be alright."

Two hours later.

"Matri, the dinner was good," says Ruth. Matri kisses Ruth on the forehead.

"Claudia…"

"Yes Mama."

"Bout time ya' wash some dishes fa' a change," Ruth tells Claudia.

"Okay Mama," Claudia says with obedience.

"I'll clean them out for you, Claudia," Says Matri.

Ruth thinks to herself, "I'm gon' go and finish countin' ma' money. I been savin' that money ever since Jessie die, and leave me that money underneath that board... he almost fall through, on the day he pra-posed ta' me."

Feeling wearisome, she goes to her bedroom. Suddenly Ruth yells. "Why?... Isiah! What chu' doin' with ma' suitcase!"

Isiah throws Ruth's suitcase down and runs. "Matri! Claudia! Isiah just take ma' money out of ma' suitcase." Isiah runs pass Claudia and Matri, out of the door.

"What!" says Claudia

Angrily, Matri yells, "Come on Claudia, let's catch him!"

When they make it downstairs, Isiah is running down the street. "Here, take my car keys, I'll chase him. He's not going to outrun me, he should know better," says Matri. Taking off running, Matri talks to herself. "Now, am I zoning? Brother you look tired to me; too much partying and drugging... oh, women too?" Isiah looks back at Matri. He tries to run faster. "Ooops brother, there's a car in front of you. I'm going to catch up with you in a minute! "Isiah," Matri yells "Isiah!"

He falls over some garbage cans. An old man tries to help Isiah get up, but Isiah jerks away from him. "Oops, God is good, I'll be with you soon." Matri is right up on him now. He turns around, trying to run faster. He starts running in the streets. "Wherever you go, I'm going." They both start running between cars.

Isiah jumps over a man's car. Oh no, there's a dog coming!" Matri yells.

"The owner yells, "Come back Rover, come back Rover!"

Matri notices a stick. "Let me get this stick." Matri jumps over the car and the dog jumps over car. Matri pants. Then she starts beating the dog off of her, with the stick. The owner of the dog, catches the dog.

"Come here Rover," he says, "You are always chasing women. You are out of your league." The man looks up to say he's sorry, but Matri is long gone.

Never pausing for a breath, Matri's chasing Isiah through an alley... he falls down. Claudia jumps out of the car, crying a river of tears. "I want ma' brother back." Isiah falls. Claudia grabs Isiah on the ground, tussling and shaking him.

"Claudia," yells Matri. She grabs Claudia's face. "Claudia, get yourself together, now!" Claudia looks into Matri's eyes, like a child.

Claudia cries, "I just want ma' brother back, Matri."

Isiah starts crying. "Matri, I need help—help me please."

Matri looks away. She wants to cry, but she had to be strong for the both of them; holding Isiah and Claudia in her arms, rocking back and forth. "We got plenty of love in this family, to survive anything..." adamantly she says, "And... we will."

They all get into the car. "Isiah," says Matri. "I want to take you around the city here. The last place will be Prince Street." Firmly, she says, "I need to show you, what drugs is doing to our people. And when you see it, tell me if you still have the heart, to put a hand in destroying our people. We have to get out of this box, Isiah."

⊫ ⊨

Hours later... Isiah looks like, he has lost his soul. Tears, dribbles down his face. "We've seen prostitutes, people living in abandoned houses; crowded, decadent impoverished projects; men standing on the corners, drinking—not working; and lastly, this is Prince Street... look over there Isiah," says Matri. There are two boys, making a drug transaction. "See that guy and girl, nodding." The girl has a little baby in her arms; a little boy holding on to her skirt tail, while she's nodding. The guy nods, handing her something in her hands. "Look at the area."

An old man comes knocking on the window. Matri winds the window down. "Dig here baby, you need some dope?"

"How old are you grandpa? You need to be ashamed of your-self, out here like this," says Matri.

The old man scratches himself, opening his mouth; with all of his front teeth rotted out of his mouth. He smiles, with hungry eyes, staring.

"Oh Lawd,' great day in the monin.' Please... don't do that," says Claudia.

"Oh baby, why you wanna hurt me like that?" He continues to scratch and nod. Matri and Isiah watches as he nods.

"I 'clare, go on now. Didn't ya' hear what she say... ya' stink!" says Claudia. He looks at Claudia and kisses at her. Claudia eye-balls him. "I 'clare, grandpa go on and get some teeth, now." Matri and Isiah laughs.

The cops is coming up the street with the siren on. Everybody starts running. The cops jump out of the car, grabbing two boys. The boys keeps telling the cops to get off of them, resisting ar-rest. They're tussling with the cops, acting very tough, fearless and aloof. The cops starts beating them with their sticks.

"Why don't they stop resisting arrest, Isiah?" Matri asks.

"It's a part of the, 'Cool Poze,' he answers.

"What's that?" Matri frowns.

Isiah stares at them as he speaks. "It's a defense mechanism. It makes ya' unafraid, unflinchin,' stubborn, and destructive. It could also make ya' die early, and quick. Just look over there. Those cops is gonna,' brutally murder them, in self defense; for resisting arrest and fighting a police officer."

Matri gasps. "Let's go home, I've had enough."

⊰⊹⊱

Wednesday night... Matri comes into the kitchen with Civil. "Hmmm, where's Isiah... his car is parked outside " Noticing the garbage. "Let me take this garbage out. Claudia thinks, all she has to do, is go to work and party. Civil let me sit you here for a minute." She places Civil on the table. Opening the door, she notices Isiah standing in the yard, looking up in the air. "Oh no, he's doing it again. I have to talk to him now."

Matri goes outside. She thinks, *This is scary. I don't know where his mind is. I have to be careful... God help me."* She puts the garbage down gently; walking towards him very slowly, and stands beside him. Matri thinks, *The night has done its job, blanketing the earth for rest.* Very quietly, she looks up into the sky with him. Thinks, *The moon is at it's fullest.* They both, are just standing, watching the sky and the moon. Finally he turns his head around, teary-eyed. Matri could feel his pain. Their eyes meet. She breathes... Huh... thinking, O*h... I could feel his pain.*

He continues to gaze at her and gasps... whispering, "Where is God?"

Matri puts her arms around his waist, hugging him from the side; in a very nurturing way. His eyes are glossy. She need to say something to him, but she's almost speechless. She's in pain, too. Trembling inside, she struggles to respond, "Oh... He's everywhere... and all around you." He turns his face away, looking afar into the sky, while holding her hand tightly. She also, looks up into the sky.

CHAPTER 12
BAMBOOZLED

A weeklater:
Isiah's riding the subway, looking out of the window at the people; across the other side of the train tracks. All of a sudden, a guy comes up to a woman and snatches her bag. She tries to hold on to it, so he shoots her repeatedly. Isiah sits straight up. "Oh-no!" The lady across from him screams; getting everyone's attention on the subway car. Isiah falls back into his seat, sweating.

He thinks. *Man, is this another 'Nam? We couldda' used him in Nam, or was he from 'Nam? Some cats come back crazy... just like that. You would think that they would give us, some help when we come home... but nooo. I guess that would be asking old Uncle Sam, fa' too much.*

The conductor says, "42nd Street." Isiah talks to himself. "Here we go. I kno' these cats not gon' try ta' kill me like that, behind the fact that I'm quittin' on them." He walks toward an old furniture warehouse. "I'm walking in with a cool pose." Everyone's sitting around two big office tables; bobbing their heads to the sounds of the OJays' "Old Mighty Dollar." Isiah thinks, *Who's this woman sittin' at the very end, with her elbows leanin' on the table?* She appears to be short. There's D' Boss, a plump man, sitting at the very end. He's the head man... he calls himself, D'Boss. He's bobbing to the music laughing. Afro, wearing black and red; a big red apple cap, and a black suit with a red shirt. He flaunts a big ring, that opens at the top. Isiah thinks, *D'Boss is a flashy and gaudy cat, lookin' like he shops at a circus. The other men are wearing platform shoes, and big afros, with wide brim hats. I guess I'm the only conservative cat in here.*

D'Boss opens up his ring and tastes the cocaine. "Yeah, baby, this is the right thing." He sings, "Money, money, money, that's what it takes."

One of the guys smiles at the table, thanking him, saying, "I told you D' Boss."

D' Boss, stares at Isiah, asking, "Isiah baby, tell me what 'chu got... money, money?"

Isiah looks dumbfounded. "What I got?"

Angrily, D'Boss says, "You don't know what I mean, after all this time? He sits up, looking mean. "You playin' wit me?"

Everybody looks at Isiah, and Isiah looks back... calmly.

D'Boss looks vicious and yells, "Where is the stuff and the money man?"

Isiah frowns. "I ain't got no money, man."

D'Boss looks at Isiah, glancing around the room. "Y'all hear that? Now he over there soundin' like an old girl. 'I ain't got it.' He gets up, throwing the chair at Isiah.... Isiah ducks. The other guys jumps up, with their guns pointing at Isiah.

"No, no, put your guns away. This little girl, gon' get my money and my stuff ... immediately!"

Isiah tries to explain. "Man, ma Mama . …."

He yells. "Now you dig this. Don't care nothin'! 'bout 'cha' mama. You asked fa' it… and you or yo' mama, gon pay fa' it!" He points his fat fingers at Isiah, as if he has a gun; squinting his eyes up. "Pow!"

"Man... I want out," says Isiah.

D'Boss' eyes widen. "Oh you want out? I'll tell ya' what 'chu' owe me. Bring ma' calculator here," snapping his finger. A guy runs fast bringing him the calculator. He asks him, what took you so long? He freezes, because the calculator was just at the end of the table. "Let me see now, you owe me exactly $30,000." Isiah jumps up.

D'Boss says, "Judy baby, write it down in the books for big daddy."

Nostrils spreading, "Now ya' dig this. Man I don' owe ya' no damn $30,000!" yells Isiah. "Man, I got a Queen."

"Get it, or kiss yourself goodbye, or continue to work fa' me.… or ya' might take somebody in ya' family wit 'cha'… ya' mama, dig it!" He stares at Isiah, nodding his head."

Isiah jumps up in a rage. "You'll git' cha' money, ya' fat! Mother…!"

The door opens. A little boy comes with a cool pose, walk. Everybody watches him as he walks. Isiah is shocked. He thinks, *It's the little boy I met in the street.*

He goes over to D'Boss telling him, "Hey man. I made this… dig it." He throws the money on the table.

D'Boss looks at Isiah, tooting up hislips, and says, "This is what I'm talkin' bout'… I'm teachin' and he learnin' real fast."

The boy blushes. The woman says, "That's a good boy, I'm proud of ya."

He goes outside walking away furious. *Man, what kinda sick person is he, teachin' a child ta' sell drugs? I'm outta this. He threatened ma' family. He really don' kno' me. I ain't scared fa' me. It's ma' family. He could have me.*

Thursday night, Matri and Robert meet at the Town Café. "Matri, what is this about?" asks Robert.

Matri shrugs, "To tell you the truth, I don't know why Isiah wants us to meet him here."

"*I just have a feeling, it may not be good,*" Robert says.

Matri exhales, " We'll see, Robert."

"You know what Matri, I'm glad you introduced Sadie to me. We're getting married very soon."

Matri's eyes twinkle. "That's good news, Robert."

Isiah walks up. "Hey, what you know good, baby?" asks Robert

Matri and Robert stare at Isiah, who seems very troubled and angry. "Hey waiter," says Isiah. "Give me Scotch on the rocks." He turns around impatiently, with his eyes following the waiter to the bar. Matri and Robert watches him.

The waiter is coming, so Isiah finally turns around. He takes the drink from her, gobbling it down. "Thank ya' baby, I'll try another one," he says.

"Say, are you okay, my man?" asks Robert. Matri waits patiently for the response.

"Well…" He pauses… "I have a serious problem, man."

"Go 'head man, we with you… no matter what it is," says Robert.

He hesitates, "Man, I was selling drugs," pauses. "I worked fa' D'Boss."

Robert frowns. "Who?"

"D'Boss. I told 'em I wanted out, and he tells me I owe him $30,000."

Matri and Robert says, "What!"

"He said if I didn't give him the money, he would do some harm." He pauses, looking at Matri. "Harm ta' somebody in ma' family."

"What!" Robert jumps up in his seat. Squinting his eyes, he says very angrily, "Where are these mothers, man?"

"What!" says Matri.

Robert says, "Dig it," smiling angrily. "Let's say, I'm in the family. Boy I'm telling you, I could have a ball, with that cat man."

Matri demands, "Hold it. We have to have a plan, that's a lot of money."

"That's a lotta of money I don' have, Matri," says Isiah.

A television hangs up over the bar, with a newsbreak. "Turn it up, someone says." The news gets their attention. "We have a report on a bank robber. They call him the Black Panther Cat. This is not to be associated with The Black Panther Party. No one could catch him. He moves smoothly and swiftly like a cat, walking the beat. Whoever this person is, he knows a lot about electricity. The only clue we have is, that he loves flowers. He leaves pink petals behind, and he doesn't leave a trace of fingerprints," he gets another report.

"Wait a minute, we have another news break. In Harlem, there's a shootout, killing a pregnant woman and a young boy. Apparently, the eight-month pregnant woman was making a drug transaction with her son, who also was a part of the drug transaction. Seemingly, words were passed, causing an argument. The young boy and his mother both had guns. His mother never got a chance to shoot. She was shot three times- once in the head, and twice in the chest."

Matri places the palm of her hand on her heart, as she watches. "Oh God, this is hurtful."

The news reporter says, "The young boy, in defense of his mother, was able to kill two of the drug dealers; before being shot to death. The boy was shot eight times, execution style. One good thing about it, if I should say this," he pauses… "The baby is expected to live."

Matri's devastated, "She was pregnant?"

Isiah's eyes are glued to the television. After the news went off he heard, "Now stay tuned for the weather report."

Isiah's eyes flutter, viciously. He says, "Ya' may not believe this, but I found out when I went back ta' leave the drug business, those two waz' there. I met the boy one night in Harlem. He told me he had somethin' ta' do fa' the man." Isiah pauses, shaking his head. "I had no idea that's what he waz' talkin' 'bout."

Robert had the look of war in his eyes. "Man those low down dirty sons… I want to see them, as soon as possible," he gives a vicious, half moon smile.

Isiah gazes at Robert, holding his head down.

Matri, is enraged. "Get, your head up."

Robert says with malice, "I'm going back to 'Nam on those cats, dig it."

"Hey wait. I could get the money." Matri assures them.

Robert and Isiah stares at Matri. "I have a very dear friend. She'll loan it to me."

"I'll give up $20,000 myself," assures Robert.

"Man ya' don' have that kinda money," Isiah says.

Robert smirks, "Man, my mama told me, you never let your left hand know what your right hand is doing... dig it?" He chuckles.

"Excuse me, I have to go to the ladies' room." Matri walks away.

Isiah waits until she walks into the ladies' room. "Dig this Robert, the plan is this. We not gonna give those bastards the money. We gonna go back ta' 'Nam on 'em. I'll tell them where ta' meet us. I'll take Matri... now, I won't be able ta' stop 'er from goin'. She'll wait in the car for us. When she comes out of the bathroom, we'll talk ta' 'er 'bout it."

"Wait a minute man, I didn't want to tell anybody; but Sadie and me, we're going to elope this coming Friday."

Excitedly Isiah says, "No kidin' man," he pauses, "Ohhh man, I'm sorry about this."

Robert puts hand up, shaking his head, "We'll do it after that. We are going to Mexico for the weekend."

Matri comes out of the bathroom, like a soldier on command. "Okay, what's the plan, you two?"

Robert and Isiah look at each other. "Okay Matri, here's what we got," says Isiah.

"What about Hezikiah?" asks Matri.

"I'll tell Hezikiah what to do," says Robert.

"Okay, let me do this," says Isiah. They go into conference.

The Black Night:

"Ummm... yeah, it's dark and the Black Knight must make his move. Lookin' around out here in the stillness of the night, I kno' that I have ta' git them b'fore they git me. The Black Knight knows, his jump is powerful! I lived this long... survivin' death and game. They ain't smart enough ta' figure me out. It's the perfect time and settin' for all evil. It ain't got no boundaries or consciousness... worshipin' the father of darkness. It's time fa' a game of chess! Okay Black Knight, who will checkmate evil?"

"Here's the drug ship," he says while quietly getting out of the car. "Ummm, it's really dark out here. No one could pos-sibly see me. But I could see the ship. Who' that standin' over there? Shhh... I have ta' git' them b'fore they git' me. This gonna' be quick and easy. Well, they could call me 'The Knight'. This is how ya' wanna play, then we'll play the game, cause that's all it is. Who could play who? Only one thing they don' kno'; I'm good at chess. And chess is not just on the board. This is real and I got the skill fa' it. Pawn and the King."

Putting one foot out of the car "Okay, here we go 'Bishop'. Ooops, I'll leave ma' car on. I have ta' run back here, like a bat out-ta' hell. I could do it. Yeah, I could do it. The ship iz' sittin' pretty in the water. Here we go... what will a Knight do?...Gotta jump over this fence... time for execution. ....Throw with a strong hand now. Here... goes. ...." Boom! Boom! Boom! "Huh, huh, huh! Gotta' run fast! It's all in zonin.' Ain't nobody gon' catch me." Huffin and puffin, he says, "I could make it! That's all I know! I'm almost ta'the car. Okay baby, ya' got it." With fierceness, he rides away. "You did it baby. Check mate!"

At home, it's midnight. Ruth's having a bad dream. Tossing and turning, Ruth sits straight up in the bed, sweating profusely. "Oh Lawd." Ruth gets down on her knees praying. "Oh, precious Lawd. There is no one like ya'. I could feel trouble in the land ta' come. And it's gon' git' worse b'fore it git' betta. Don' kno' what's goin' on with ma' chirrin; they too quiet right bout' now. Ya' give me the power ta' kno' when somethin' is wrong. So please, take my hand precious Lawd, and guide me."

The phone rings in Claudia's room. "Who is this?"

Speaks loud, "Claudia, Osmon."

"Oh Lawd, Osmon I hear ya' now.

"Claudia, your mama is very worried about you."

"What fa'?"

"You know that girl... you just as crazy. What do you mean what for, Claudia?"

Claudia pants, "Don't cha' talk ta' me like that."

"I came by the house one day and your mama told me to talk to you; she's worried about you, Claudia."

Claudia is silenced by what Osmon tells her. "Claudia, it's time for change baby."

"Yeah," she looks dumbfounded.

"I'm gon' let you go back to sleep, I just wanted to drop that on ya'. I'll be seeing you soon."

Claudia sits straight up in the bed grabbing her head, yelling, "Osmon, Osmon."

"What is it Claudia?"

"I want you to come over Sunday, me and Matri's makin dinner for Mama."

Osmon pauses, "Okay Claudia, I'd like that very much... no pork now."

"Okay, we'll cook yours in a separate pot. I bought you a set of pots to cook in."

Sunday evening, Matri rinses the glasses out. "Claudia, I think this was a good idea to invite everybody over for dinner. I figured it would distract Mama's attention from us," says Matri.

"Yeah," says Claudia, " It's a good idea inviting Osmon, since she's so crazy 'bout 'me." Claudia starts thinking. "Matri ya' know where the gun is, right?"

"Shhh…" Matri looks around to make sure no one hears her. "Now I told you, I'm not going to need it. I'm just taking it, just in case."

Someone knocks on the door. "Thaddeus!" Claudia says excitedly.

Sounding carefree, "Hey babe, Matri here?" asks Thaddeus.

Joyfully, Matri runs and hugs and kisses Thaddeus.

He hugs her back, kissing her. "Oh, this is a surprise," says Thaddeus.

Isiah comes into the kitchen. "Hey man, I'm glad 'chu' could make it."

"Yeah, I decided to stop typing and come to be with my favorite people for a change," says Thaddeus.

"Everybody goes into the dining room. "Dinner iz', almost ready ta' be served," says Claudia.

At the dinner table, Osmon says, "Ruth, I didn't know Matri and Claudia could cook like this."

"It's a lotta good things ya' don' kno' bout me," says Claudia.

He assures Claudia, "I know an apple doesn't fall too far from the tree," eyes widens.

Robert winks at Sadie. "My baby, could cook too."

"Oh, you go head now," says Sadie, blushing.

Isiah looks at Dawn smiling, "Hey, ma' Queen don' do too bad at all, either." Dawn's cheeks redden, her eyes are flirty.

"Hey, where's Hezikiah?" asks Isiah.

"I don't know man," says Robert. "Can't keep up with that woman… I mean that cat." Isiah and Robert laugh.

Ruth says cheerfully, "Matri, Claudia… I'm very happy 'bout this. The Lawd give me another day, ta' be with all ma' chirrin,' and I thank Him." Looking around the table smiling, she says, "Osmon, ya' remind me of Jessie, in so many waze. Just feel like, ya' gotta' be fa' Claudia… she needs ya'."

Osmon smiles; bowing his head to Ruth.

" Well, let's hold our head down fa' the blessin' of the table. I thank ya', ma' Father, for filling all of these here seats here t'day. It's all in ya' plan. Thank ya fa' con-tinuing ta' plenish ma' table with food. Amen."

"Mama, I almost forgot. I'm going down South to clean up the house. I want to keep the house up, because I think you might want to go back home," she pauses, looking at Ruth.

"Well, I been thinkin' 'bout it. 'Cause Hattie write me a letter, askin' me if I waz' comin' back home." She bites down on her lips. "Been thinkin' 'bout it, strong."

"I figured, since I'm on vacation, I'll go down next week; taking Isiah, and Robert to help me cut the grass and do some painting. Just to see what repairs need to be made," Matri stares at Ruth, nodding her head smiling.

"Ya' say ya' goin' next week?" Ruth asks.

"Yeah, I wrote Hattie, two weeks ago, and told her that I'm coming down."

Cheerfully Ruth says, "I think that's a real good idea, Matri."

In the meantime:

Hezikiah's back at the bar. He's sitting in a corner, waiting on a date. The lights are very dim. There's a thickness of smoke and beer in the air. He's listening to music play, while men walk by, gazing at him. He looks at them, swinging his hair, and swaying his shoulders; flirting, trying to be feminine. He is dressed in a red dress, wearing red lipstick and black high heel shoes; with his hair hanging down to his shoulders.

Hezikiah thinks, *I figured I'd let ma' hair hang down t'night... they like hair. I might as well give 'em what they like, even if it ain't mine,"* He chuckles. They don't care. *I'll take another sip, maybe he'll be here soon. Oh ma' God, I forgot Matri and Claudia invited me to the dinner, for Mama t'night. I'll have ta' make it up ta' them... that's what I'll do.* He looks up and sees his date. Trying to sound feminine, "Oh sit down baby. What took you so long?" He forgets his name. "Ah... ah... Jason," he smiles flirtatioulsy.

He has a deep, slow-sounding goofy type of voice. "Shucks, I forgot my glasses again."

Hezikiah thinks. *You a liar, didn't want me ta' see those bifocals... a little cockeyed too.*

"Well Aretha, I had to take my nephew home to his mother," says Jason.

Hezikiah says to himself, "*Why, ya' blind lyin' dog; ya', just wait til' ya' really see... mee. Ya' ain't had ta' take yo' damn nephew nowhere. Ya' had a' lie ta' yo' wife, ta' git outta the house.*"

He sits down smiling, acting quiet; eyes flickering, "I'll take Bacardi and coke," says Jason.

Hezikiah teases, acting shy; but flirting with his eyes. "Kinda strong, ha' baby?"

"That's the type of man, I really am," winking his eyes. "I'm strong, baby."

Hezikiah laughs softly, acting shy. "Ha, ha, ha."

"You shy, Aretha?" he asks. "I like 'em shy."

Hezikiah says laughing, prancing his hands around. "I've al- waze been sheltered, growin' up. Ma' daddy told me that, he had ta' keep me away from the big bad wolves."

"Well, tell dad that I ain't no wolf." Sitting straight up, laughing through his nose, he says, "As a matter of fact, I'm a very gentle man... but I gotta' strong hold." Jason winks his eyes. "If you know what I mean?"

Hezikiah blushes, pushing his hair off of his shoulders. "I kno' what chu' mean."

⊸⊹ ⊹⊸

Time is passing... Jason blinks his eyes. "You ready to go baby?"

"Hezikiah blushes and says, "Yes," and flips his hair back; walking out of the bar 'twisting, way too much. Everybody stares at him.

Jason walks out, like he went trick or treating, with a bag full of goodies. "You just follow me."

Jason pulls up to the motel chuckling; pointing over at Hezikiah, telling him, "Park your car." He gets out of a used car, that Robert bought him. Walking towards Hezikiah, he says, "Now you just get your pretty little ole' self out of that car, baby. Hezikiah pulls his dress up enticing him and steps out of the car like a model.

Jason's andHezikiah are in the hotel room. Jason whistles, trying hard to see. "I'll tell ya... just look at this place. Ain't this the cutest little motel?"

Hezekiah blushes. "Yessa boss."

Jason laughs, stretching his eyes. "It ain't nothin like a woman with a good sense of humor."

Hezikiah thinks out aloud, accidentally. "I just hope ya' feel like that later on, when ya' see the real me."

Trying to widen his eyes to see. Jason says, "See what?"

Abruptly Hezikiah, laughs, "Oh, no... oh say can, you see. You know, like the Star Spangled Banner."

Jason laughs, continuing to emphasize how the room looks. "Well looka here, looka here. Will you just look at that bed, it looks mighty strong." Winking his eyes at Hezikiah, Jason says, twirling around, "Now, those curtains are so pretty... and look at the spread." He pulls the cover back and says, "Just look at, these pretty sheets, baby."

Hezikiah blushes, batting his eyes; running his fingers through his wig. "Yeah, they sure is, baby."

Jason laughs, kicking off his shoes, acting nervous and anxious.

Hezikiah kicks his shoes off, modeling; then dancing, twirling his body all down to the floor like a snake; standing straight up, legs spread wide. Jason feels thrilled by him.

"I have ta' go ta' the bathroom, baby," says Hezikiah.

Jason laughs, winking at Hezikiah. "Aretha, you hurry up now, you hear. This is the best part of the date, now. Come outta there just like a newborn baby"

Hezikiah leans back, smiling, "You 'clare?"

Hezikiah comes out of the bathroom. Jason waits in the dark. Jason pats the bed, laughing in the dark. "Now come on baby, you got your birthday suit on... ha?" asks Jason.

Hezikiah tells Jason to catch. "Now baby what chu throwing me, ha?" Reaching his hands up in the air, Hezikiah throws his bra onto the bed into Jason's face. Jason grabs the bra and laughs. Then Hezikiah throws his stockings with perfume spilled on them.

"Oooh, baby now," says Jason.

Then Hezikiah throws his wig. Jason jumps up and turns the lights on, looking at the wig in his hands. "What!... the... hell?"

Hezikiah stands there, smoking a cigarette, looking like dressed to kill; army hair cut, with a lighted cigarette and men's boxer underwear. Jason, in the nude, swings at Hezikiah.

Hezikiah swings back. "Ya' had no business cheatin' on yo' wife. Men never kno' what they really gittin'. Ya' gon' git the devil the next time." Hezikiah puts him in a headlock, with cigarette hanging from his mouth. "Why can't chu' be happy with what chu' got. Ma' sister's husband caused her ta' almost lose 'er mind, waz' a good girl too. She trusted that fool." He buckles down on his neck.

Jason yells, "You son of a. ..." They 're destroying the room.

Someone bangs on the door. "What's going on in there, I'm comin' in." The manager comes in with his wife.

"What's goin' on in here? Go back honey. You have to leave, we don't have this kinda thing in here. Now both of you, I'm gon' stand here till you get some clothes on."

Jason, is in a rage. "I'm gonna get you for this!"

"Ya' got what cha' deserve. Go home ta' your wife." Hezikiah laughs. The manager laughed underneath his breath.

Jason points his finger at Hezikiah... "Outside."

Hezikiah rolls his eyes, huffing and puffing looking at him, acting like a woman.

"Hurry up, you too," says the manager.

Jason and Hezikiah gets back to the city. Jason bumps Hezikiah's car. Hezikiah curses him and laughs at him. Jason pulls out his gun and starts shooting. Hezikiah starts driving fast, trying to lose Jason. Jason shoots at him again.

Two cops, one black and one white are sitting on the side street. The white cop says, "What's that?"

"It sounds like a shot," says the black cop. They put their sirens on, chasing Jason and Hezekiah.

"Put down your weapon."

Hezikiah drives back towards the highway. Jason continues to follow him, shooting at him. The cops call for backup. Four cars and the news reporters follow.

"Put your weapon down... now."

Hezikiah stops on the bridge. Jason hits the back of his car. He jumps out with his gun and discovers he's out of bullets. The cops jumps out of the car, with their guns aimed towards Jason; and handcuff both, Hezikiah and Jason.

A husky caucasian man, with a deep voice says, "What happened here?"

Hezikiah responds to the detective; batting his eyes and swinging his hair from side to side... then, snatching it off. "He asked me out for a date and I accepted," says Hezikiah.

Jason is huffin' and puffin'. His eyes remain focused on Hezikiah with venom. The cops and the news reporter examine the way Hezikiah is dressed. It's apparent that he is not a woman. The cops try to be professional and not laugh.

Hezikiah said, "He's mad cause he didn't kno' I waz' a man. He waz' too busy flirtin.' He gave me his card on the elevator, on ma' way ta' the doctor. He said, he didn't have his glasses on 'em, though. If he wanna cheat on his wife, he should never leave home without his glasses." Hezikiah looks at Jason asking him, "How ya' think ya' wife feels 'bout ya' cheatin' on 'er." He starts waiving to her on the news. "Hi, hi."

Jason jumps at him. The cops grab him, taking them both to jail.

Back at Mama's house, Matri says, "Mama it's time for your news."

"The weather is going to be sunny tomorrow, high's in the 70's, with maybe a late night shower. Monday, Tuesday, Wednesday and Thursday will be in the high 60's; Friday through Saturday will be high 70's, with a chance of rain," says the weather reporter.

"Good evening, here's the latest." The news shows a picture of the incident with Hezikiah and Jason on the highway. Everybody's eyes are glued to the tv. "What….?" says Matri.

"The two men went out on a date. Aretha says Jason asked him or her out on a date, when they met on an elevator, on his way to the doctor. He told Aretha… the one dressed like a woman, he wasn't wearing his glasses. He gave him a card with his phone number on it. Aretha in return gave him his number. Aretha said, he called him telling him what bar to meet him at."

"They both were taken to jail. Aretha got out. Jason was held for bail for carrying a gun and attempted murder. His wife refuses to bail him out. His brother later came to the precinct to post bail."

Everybody's laughing, harder than ever. Ruth laughs so hard, tears are coming out of her eyes. "Lawd, what's wrong with Hezikiah?"

"That's Hezikiah?" asks Sadie. She laugh herself to tears.

Claudia's little boys laugh, holding their little stomach. Everybody looks at the boys laughing, and laughs even louder.

"They just laughin', 'cause they see everybody else laughin'," says Claudia.

"I 'clare, ain't had a laugh like this in a long time. The Lawd know'd I needed a good laugh," says Ruth.

"We have another report that just came in."

Everybody stops laughing, staring at the tv.

"We have a vigilante, striking again. It looks like a drug war. There seems to be someone blowing up drug dealers and their operations, on ships sitting at the dock. This is the third bombing. We're not sure, but the bombings appear to be done with grenades." "We're assuming it's the workings of a skilled man. He bombs at night only. It looks like a one man operation. We're calling him the "The Black Knight." He's very strategic, in checkmating the drug dealers; he leaves parts of a chess game, kings, bishops, and pawns. He captures the enemy by moving into its square, with the ability to "jump over" other pieces; meaning... it's most power-ful in "closed positions." This move is one of the longest- serving moves of chess; close to where the action is. We now have the Black Panther Cat and The Black Knight. These two are certainly very clever, giving the detectives and the police force a heck of a run."

⊱ ⊰

Isiah says, pointing his finger, "Ya' kno', chess reminds me of 'Nam, man; alwaze jumpin' over the enemy; close ta' the action, and long survin' moves."

Robert says, "Yeah, those cats almost hated you in 'Nam; couldn't beat you in a game of chess."

"My goodness," says Sadie.

Matri looks at Robert and Isiah, thinking about what's ahead of them, with D'Boss. "Yes, the Black Knight and Black Panther are certainly shrewd," says Matri.

Osmon admits, "Those are some smart cats.

Robert nods his head saying, "Yeah man."

"Those are some mean cats," says Isiah.

Dawn goes over to Isiah, hugging him. "There's, something about those cats…" she pauses.

"The detectives should try to find out the motives behind this, or try to come up with a possible motive. It could be a leading fac-tor, to finding out who they are," says Thaddeus.

"Ummm, you have a point, Thaddeus," says Matri.

Now regarding the Black Panther Party, an update indicates the following:

Police raided the Black Panther headquarters in Seattle and arrested Dixon, along with section leader, Buddy Yates; on charges of stealing a radio from a bus parked outside the party offices. Police are keeping a close eye indeed in the growth of the Panthers in Washington, watching the party's progress the way a surgeon might study a malignant tumor, waiting impatiently for a chance to practice swift, decisive surgery. The increase of 39 hard-core Panthers proved disturbing and something has to done to stop the movement.

"Man ... I thought I left 'Nam," says Isiah.

"It's disheartening to come back home, to be confronted with this man," says Robert.

"I have a lot of writing to do," says Thaddeus.

"Well, so much for that. Let's have dessert," says Claudia.

Roy says, "Yum, yum."

"Yeah, let's have cake and ice cream mommy," says Paul.

"Let me help you, Claudia." says Osmon.

Happily, she says, "Okay."

CHAPTER 13

GET UP, STAND UP

On Monday afternoon... Isiah sits on the side of his bed watching tv. He bends down, holding his stomach; his nose dripping, feeling motion sickness. "Oh ma' stomach, what's wrong with ma' stomach?" He jumps up running to the bathroom, falling down on his knees, vomiting in the toilet. "Oh ma' stomach, oh... I'm sick." He grabs his stomach, rocking back and forth. "It's painin' me," he frowns, looking perturbed. Starting to have mood swings, he gets extremely angry, hitting the wall with his fist. He chuckles, as sweat flows down his face, like a shower. "Oh no!..." He whispers in a rage.… "Gotta gi… gi… git… up!"

Finally he gets up, putting water on his face, rinsing his mouth out. He grabs on to the wall, dragging himself to the side of the bed. He begins panting, shaking his head. Looking up, he sees a movie on television. A man dressed in black, is sucking blood out of another man's neck. He draws backwards. " *What*…?" he says to himself, watching Dracula. "Dracula we have somthin' in common, baby. We both feed off of other people. No matter who we hurt, we have ta' have that fix baby; that white horse." He starts sniffing, rubbing his nose, smiling. Looks up at Dracula and says, "Yeah, Marvin Gaye said it all baby." He starts singing, rocking back and forth. He says, 'Flying high in a friendly sky, without ever leaving the ground. Rest of the folks are tired and weary, and have laid their body's down.' "Yeah Dracula... while they sleep, Marvin says, 'We go to the place where danger awaits us... and it's bound to forsake us. I go crazy! ... when I can't find it.' " Yeah baby when we find it..." He pauses, smiling... singing. "In the mornin'.... be alright ma' friend, but soon the light will bring the pain.' "Marvin Gaye said it, Dracula, "Flying high in a friendly sky." Rocking back and fourth, Isiah watches Dracula going to his coffin. Suddenly, he looks around at his room, laughing and crying, intermittingly. "Oh... oh...yeah, this is ma' coffin, Dracula!"

He gets up, stands up; walking towards the mirror, like Dracula. He backs up, freezes; not wanting to look into the mirror... and whispers. "Dracula can't look into the mirror either." He starts sweating and shivering. Seems like he heard a voice... that inner voice, saying, "Look!" He looks around and says, "What?" Holding his head down, like he's got a migraine headache. At a stand-still, he cries; still not wanting to look. Slowly, he starts looking up; seems like he hears a voice again, saying, "Look!" He says to himself, "Look!" Fearfully, he looks into the mirror, slowly. He says, "Who am I? Help me somebody." He jumps, jumping up and down like Muhammad Ali. He's getting angry, turns around boxing and swinging, knocking down things.

Ruth is downstairs in the kitchen, making bread for dinner. She hears things falling down upstairs. "What is goin' on up there with Isiah... all that noise? Is somebody fightin'? Sound like Isiah fightin' the devil up there." Mama goes to open the door.

" Oh no!" says Isiah, grabbing his car keys running down the stairs, passing Mama.

"Isiah!" yells Ruth. "Isiah, come back here son!" Teary-eyed she says, "Pray and go tell it on the mountain, baby."

Isiah jumps into his car, paining; laughing to himself, like a crazy person. "Yeah, I go ta' the place where self-destruction awaits me. I kno' I'm hooked... white horse." He pulls over to the liquor store. "Yeah, I'll git a bottle of liquor; that outta' help... yeah," he sniffs.

He jumps into the car ripping the top off the bottle. He puts in the tape by Marvin Gaye, "Flying high, in the friendly sky." Hee's heading towards the highway, drinking. "It's hot out here t'day." He starts singing with Marvin Gaye, gripping the steering wheel tightly. "Flying high in a friendly sky, without ever leavin' the ground. But I go crazy when I can't find it. I ain't seen nothin' but trouble baby. Nobody really understands, help me somebody." He puts the bottle up to his mouth, wasting it all over his clothes. He chuckles; his face is wet from sweat and liquor. "Hey, ain't nothin wrong with me!" He tries to straighten his face up, sitting up tall, as he drives. Thinking about the pregnant woman and her son, he says, with tears in his eyes, "D'Boss, why did you have to do that, man? You let a pregnant woman and her son sell drugs, and get shot down!" He grips the steering wheel; eyes fluttering, putting the bottle up to his mouth again...tears and sweat, showers his face. He starts chuckling. He switches his mind to Marvin Gaye's song, singing. "Flying high in the friendly sky, without ever leaving the ground." He starts driving faster. It starts getting cloudy, raining hard. He starts singing again. "I go to the place where danger awaits me, and it's bound to forsake me. So stupid -minded... oh so stupid. But I go to the place where good feelings await me... making slaves out of men... self destruction awaits me." Again, he starts thinking about the pregnant woman and her son, and D'Boss. Angrily, he yells loudly, "Killin' women and children...you dirty...!!!!!" He starts driving fast and fierce, talking to himself. Malcolm X says, "The truth is not always pretty.' Huffing and puffing, he says, "I ain't no better... I been killin' ma' own people too!"

With a twinkling of an eye, it becomes midnight dark; lightening, raining heavily. He starts flashing back to the battlefield in Viet Nam. Gripping the steering wheel, he drives faster and faster, shouting. Sweat and tears co-mingled on his face. "I go to the place where danger awaits me."

All of a sudden the car skids off the highway. His door flies open. Falling out of the car, he jumps up; looking around, having flashbacks of Viet Nam. "Yeah we gon' kill those mothers!" He starts roaring, reaching down, putting wet mud all over his face. "Kill 'em!" He lays on the ground, grabbing a stick, thinking it's a rifle. Starts running like he's on the battlefield, rolling all over the ground. "Come on Robert, man we could do this!" He turns around running towards a hole, yelling, "Hezikiah!... Get out of the hole!" He turns, looking all around him, hearing shootings; grenades going off; people screaming and hollering. He sees body parts flying everywhere. "They all comin' for me now!" He starts acting volatile, "I ain't gon' die!" He freezes, he begins to relive what happened to him with the truck in 'Nam. "Mama... is that you?" He turns around, as if he sees something, running towards the car. Panting, he starts shooting with the stick…falling down, rolling down on the ground towards the car. "I gotta' git' ta' the truck... Mama tryin' ta' tell me." He hits his head on the car, passing out. The tape is still playing.

The storm subsides. Night has passed, and it'is daylight again. The humidity is thick, it seems like a thick fog. The car door is open. Marvin Gaye's tape never stopped playing. "Save The Children" is playing. Isiah is laying on the ground. Mud is all over his face and body. He starts moving around; feeling his head, rubbing the mud off of his face.

He jerks his head, looking all around. He's shocked at his surroundings. "Cemetery… how did I get in here?" Looking down, he realizes he's in front of an empty hole. He jumps up, stands up tall; then looks into the empty grave. He begins to feel engulfed by the grave. He looks up into the sky. "The sky is so clear and beautiful. Ya' can't find no endin' to it. Matri say, ya' everywhere." He looks at the grave again. "There seems to be a connection with life and death. God ya' had ta' show me death ta' let me see life again. Ya' let me come back from 'Nam, ta' live. Ya' want me ta' 'Get Up And Standup'." The words of Bob Marley. He pauses, standing up strong and tall, with a brave heart. He walks towards the car, like a proud soldier. He turns around. Looking up into the sky, he says, "God." Smiling, he salutes, spins around like a soldier, and proudly gets into the car.

Isiah drives home with mud all over his face and body. People driving beside him, look and laugh. He doesn't care. He turns the tape of Marvin Gaye up louder, and starts singing. "Live life for the children. See, let's save the children. Save the babies. If you wanna love you got love."

"Matri come here... come here, hurry up," says Claudia. Matri comes running to the window. "Look." Claudia points.

Isiah gets out of the car, proudly slamming the car door. Walking with his cool poze, as people in the neighborhood stares at him, covered in mud. He walks proudly into the house singing Marvin Gaye's song. Matri and Claudia runs to the door, watching him as he walks up the stairs. Isiah walks up the stairs, smiling and singing. "Save the babies, if you wanna love, you've got love."

"Alright Isiah, stop right here and come on in," Matri demands.

Ruth comes into the living room, staring at Isiah. "You wait right here, I'll be right back," says Matri. She goes to the bathroom, bringing a washcloth. "Here, don't move. Let me wipe some of this dirt off of your face. Mama, and all of us have been worried sick about you Isiah," says Matri.

"That's right," says Claudia.

Ruth stands quietly staring at Isiah, biting on her lips. He looks at Mama. "Mama let me…" Ruth raises her hands up in the air and goes into her room. "Matri, b'fore ya' chop ma' head off, let me explain. He stares. "I 'clare, I'm gon' be fine, now."

Claudia bursts out laughing at Isiah. They both stare at Claudia. "He looks so funny," says Claudia.

"I was worried about you. Love you, you do know that?" Matri asks.

Isiah smiles, "Ma' Matri, ma' beautiful sister. It's yo' kind of love, that will save me."

Matri smiles, sadly. "I believe you. Go upstairs and clean yourself. We'll talk later."

⊶ ⊷

There is a conspiracy going on Tuesday, when Matri gets to work, there's a lot of tension. Policemen, the ambulance, and news reporters are outside of the building. Everyone is standing around shaking their heads, talking. Matri walks quickly over to Thaddeus.

"Matri," Thaddeus says, "I hate to be the bearer of bad news, but..." He pauses.

Matri starts to feel anxious and nervous. "What, Thaddeus?"

Thaddeus looks back at the building. Slowly turning towards Matri, he says, "Come over here. Let's sit down..." he stares into her eyes, "Okay?"

"Matri, Mr. Krutz committed suicide. The custodian found him hanging from a rope this morning. It appears that he was there all night."

Matri grabs her mouth, panting. "Oh, my God no! What... I don't believe he killed himself... no?" Becoming overwrought, Thaddeus holds her close to him.

Matri's outraged. "Move, let me go upstairs and find out what happened, Thaddeus!"

"No Matri, it will be best if you stayed down here. Let's just get as close as we can. They may need to question you, later." Matri cannot accept this, she's bewildered.

The EMTs comes out of the building; with a body on the stretcher, and a sheet covering the whole body. Matri can't move. She's fixated on the body. Charlotte comes over to Matri, crying, hugging her. They both look into each other's eyes; perplexed, watching Mr. Krutz's body, completely covered with a white sheet. The news reporters are asking people questions.

Matri notices the bag lady across the street looking at her. *Is she?.... Every time I see her, it seems like she's looking dead at me. I could feel it for sure this time... but... why?* " says Matri to herself.

Charlotte notices the bag lady staring at Matri. Charlotte looks at Matri, wiping her eyes, feeling perturbed about everything.

Thaddeus explains, "Matri look, they took Mr.Krutz. I have to go to my office now. You and Charlotte, let's go over to the detectives, and tell them who you two are. I'll help you both with this."

Matri and Charlotte nods, as they watch Mr. Krutz 's dead body, being driven away. "After we speak with the detectives, I have to go and contact Mrs. Watenburg, Charlotte," says Matri.

"Sure," says Charlotte.

"Hello, Mrs. Watenburg," says Matri.

"Oh Matri," says Mrs. Watenburg, sniffling. "My angel, I've been crying all morning… those bastards killed him… he didn't kill himself… he was too smart for that! He out-smarted them!" she yells, trembling in her voice.

Wearily Matri comments, "I know… that… no…" She gulps... " He didn't."

"Matri, where are you my angel?"

"I, I'm at the Town Café," she says with dejection.

"Well, you stay put. I'm sending the chauffer to pick you up… we must talk, Matri."

"Okay, I'll call home and tell Claudia to have Dawn pick up my car. She has my extra set of keys."

Matri looks out of the window, and she sees the bag lady again, staring at her. Getting hysterical, dropping the phone; she runs to the door, knocking the tray of food out of the waiter's hands. "Oh, I'm so sorry."

Trying to help the waiter pick up the food on the floor, he says, "No, it's okay... you go. It seems like you're in a rush."

Matri gets up, running outside to find the bag woman. She looking around, but she can't find her. Complertely out of breath, Matri talks aloud... panting. "What do you want from me... do you want my help? Let me help you... please... where are you?"

Matri starts walking towards her car, feeling despondent. "All of a sudden, there is so much going on. God, what is going on? We all seem to be in a 'Box.' Death, crime, drugs, debauchery, conspiracy... what is going on?""

Reflecting back to the cemetery and the old abandoned building, "Who are the caretakers? I have to find purpose... but how?" She turns her head around quickly. "There she is!" The bag lady is standing near the tree, down the street. She gestures with her hands. "Now, I don't have time to chase you, something terrible happened today."

"Matri," Someone calls her name. "Are you ready?"

Matri sees the black Limousine. "Yeah... sure." Matri and the bag lady, stare at each other.

Mrs. Watenburg impatiently opens the door. Matri gets into the limousine, looking back, noticing that the bag lady had disappeared.

Entering the driveway, Mrs. Watenburg's home is big and beautiful, sitting on the edge of the mountains.

Mrs. Watenburg holds Matri, hugging her tightly. Opening the door, there's a foyer leading to the stairs, going up to the bedrooms. To the left is the guest room, and to the right is the dining room. "Oh Matri, do come in. Theodore, get us some tea, will you."

"Yes mam," says Theodore.

"Matri, I'm going to bring you into my very special room. I didn't get a chance to show it to you, the other times you came." She opens the door to her library.

Matri's mouth drops. "Huh, what a surprise you have here. Mr. Krutz, herself, and her deceased husband. Dr. Martin Luther

King; Hajjah Malik Shabazz; Marcus Garvey; Angela Davis and Elijah Muhammad…this, is a library."

"There are others Matri, but not on the wall." She stares, teary-eyed.

"Well, speaking about it… there's more than meets the eye."

Matri is smiling at Mrs. Watenburg. "You never cease to amaze me… a mirror has no color."

Mrs. Watenburg looks around, priding herself over her library. "Yes Matri," she says very stately, "I designed it myself." She pulls out one of the books, showing a book full of freedom songs.

"Matri, sit please. You know Matri, you played a very important role in helping me and Mr. Krutz save our money, before the stock market crashed." She wipes her eyes. "Those dirty two-timers. They wanted him out of the way, because they were trying to double-cross him. They couldn't, so they had to get rid of him"." With her eyes protruding, Mrs. Watenburg stares at Matri. "But we beat them to the punch!" Trying to catch her breath, slowly Mrs. Watenburg continues, while laughing and wheezing. "When they find out the money is gone, and all they did was in vain…" She squints her eyes, speaking with venom, "It will all be in vain!"

Matri gets up, hugging Ms. Watenburg. "Mrs. Watenburg, sit down. You have to calm yourself, you look faint."

"Oh my dear Matri, I'm so indebted to you, my dear heart." The chauffeur knocks on the door.

"I'll get it," says Matri. Mrs. Watenburg starts coughing furiously, wheezing, and trying to catch her breath. The chauffeur runs over to her.

"Go and get my tank," She says to the chauffeur.

Matri runs over to Mrs. Watenburg. "Tank?" asks Matri.

The chauffer brings the oxygen tank back. Matri is shocked, as she watches Theodore hook up the tank, putting Mrs. Watenburg's mask on her face for oxygen.

Matri notices, the blue eyes that were so full of life, now seem dismal. Wearily Matri says, "Oh Mrs. Watenburg, why didn't you tell me? I 'clare."

Mrs. Watenburg sits at the end of the table with the mask on, with innocent eyes staring tediously at Matri. "Just give 'er three more minutes, she'll be okay," says Theodore. Matri stares at him, nodding her head.

Mrs. Watenburg takes her mask off, breathing with relief. Putting her hands on Matri's hands, she says, "I'm okay. I was going to tell you, but you've been so preoccupied." Compassionately, Matri asks, "Are you going to be alright?"

She ignores Matri. "Matri, come over here for a minute, I need to show you something." She takes out a folder. "Matri, I've always had a heart for the poor and Black people. I was involved in the Civil Rights movement to a great degree. Well, in the movements there were songs we sung. These songs were expressions of freedom, and hard struggles. The repertoire of these freedom songs, had influential moral powers and great definitions, such as: arouse the spirit, comfort the afflicted, instill courage and commitment; uniting disparate strangers; initiating brotherhood and sisterhood of not just coloreds, but whites as well. Yes Matri, there was a group of songs from a significant and strong, Black Choral; that was traditionally, universally recognized as one of the most profoundly; moving and expressive bodies of music in the world. It was a combination of African and American Experiences." She pauses.

"You see Matri, I cherish these things. Matri, let's sit down for a minute. Here's your tea."

"Thank you," says Matri

"Matri, I need to tell you something before it's too late."

"Late?" Matri frowns.

"Yes, dear." She intently stares off, coughing and trying to catch her breath. "Late... that's precisely right.... Matri. I'm not going to live too much longer, my dear."

Matri was disheartened, asking, "Mrs. Watenburg, why didn't you tell me?"

Holding Matri's hands, she says, "As I said Matri, you have your own life."

Very meekly, Matri says, "But no, I would never be too busy to come and see about you."

"Matri, I have only a few months left," she coughs, shivering. " But, I want to make you my inheritor. Matri I know you will use it for a good purpose."

Matri is, startled. Widening her eyes and placing her hand on her heart, she gets up; stooping down to Mrs. Watenburg. Looking into her eyes, very nurturing, she says, "You want to do what?"

"I would never leave it to my daughter. My son is very ill." She stares off again. "He may or may not live longer then me. He says he's leaving my daughter his inheritance, so she won't be broke. She'll know nothing about my death... I can't find her. She won't be able to question, or refute it... because she won't know about you, at all.

"My house will go to the state as a museum. I want you to take some of my things from my library. My chauffeur will be getting a handsome amount also... after all, I'm 'filthy rich... as they say."

Matri stands up and whispers, "I don't know what to say, Mrs. Watenburg... I'm lost for words, and that rarely ever happens to me."

"Matri, I'm giving you these papers... hold on to them with your life. Oh, Mr. Krutz told me to give you your half of his money, if anything happens to him. He has no children, and one very wealthy brother in Canada. He's giving the rest of it to charity and the hospitals across the country. Make sure you do that for him, he said."

Matri is stilled like a statue. She gulps, "Huh, Lord what is happening to me, I 'clare." She looks at Mrs. Watenburg faintly, eyes fluttering, "I 'clare... you two, trust me?"

" Dear heart we not only trust you, but we were smitten by you."
She looks at Matri imitating her, " I 'clare."

"Mrs. Watenburg, can I have some of that money I asked you
for?"

"Matri I don't know what it's for, but why not... it's your allow-
ance until I die."

Compassionately, Matri says, "Don't say that, please."

"Oh, why not child? After all, I've lived a good life. And look
who I met at the end of my road. An angel, to put my money to
good use. And perhaps I will be asked, what did I do with all that
blood money; my fore-parents got from the atrocities, your people
had to endure." She pauses, with tedious eyes, "I want to be able
to say that, I left it with an angel... with a purpose."

Matri, teary-eyed, jumps up and hugs Mrs. Watenburg.

Bringing Matri closer to her by the chin, she says, "Come,
come, come now, I—'clare... don't weep for me. Perhaps we both
are catalysts for the future. Be happy we met each other."

⋙ ⋘

"Matri... Isiah."

Matri whispers, secretively, "Yeah."

"Did you get that?... Mrs. Watenburg."

"I got it," says Matri.

"Good, be ready Saturday night at 8:00. You remember what to
do?"

"Yeah."

"The train tickets?"

"Yeah."

"Wearing two sets of clothes?"

"Yeah."

"Dig it, I'm going over to see Dawn. I need to talk to 'er."

"Sure."

Is Hezikiah coming?"

"Yeah."

"Okay, I'm going to study now."

Half hour latr, Isiah looks at his watch. Knock, knock. "Who could this be?" Knock, knock. "Wait a minute, darnit!" Looking through the peephole. "Isiah?" He comes in, hugging Dawn.

"Well".... Dawn folds her arms, pushing Isiah away, patting her foot. He steps back looking at her. "That's right, I don't know where you've been!"

"I kno' baby, just let me talk ta' ya' fa' a minute," pleads Isiah.

Dawn continues to fold her arms, patting her foot. "A minute, you think that's all it's gonna take. What about our wedding date, Isiah?"

"Dawn, please sit down." He gets down on his knees, holding her hands.

Dawn exhales, "Well, if you say so."

Isiah exhales. "Baby, I've been going through so many thangs, that I just couldn't share with ya'…" He looks at her and pauses. "Ta' tell you the truth, I've been ashamed of ma' self. But I finally realize some thangs, and now I'm gon' take care of 'em."

"Some things… but you could tell me anything, baby." She pulls his chin over to her, kissing him.

He kisses her gently. "Baby I kno', but when ya' really love some-body, ya' don't want ta' pull 'em down with you."

Dawn says sternly, "Baby, we go down together!"

Isiah confesses, "Sometimes ya' don' quite kno' what ta' think, when ya' in it. I just have some thangs, I have ta' take care of. I'm not askin' ya' ta' wait for me, until I git' ma' self t'gether."

Dawn stands up like a Queen on a throne, speaking with vigor, "Baby, you fought for this country." She takes hold of Isiah's face gently, looking into his eyes, "And I'm gon' fight for you. My intui-tive love will become like a coat of armor, guiding you from the things that you cannot see… patiently waiting," looks him into his eyes with, unfailing loyalty.

He looks at her, proudly, "That's a Queen's position, on the throne." She continues to stand like a Queen, teary-eyed, "Mama says, 'When you love a thing, you free it; and if it's meant... it will fly back to you, free like a bird; knowing no boundaries to get back to you'."

Isiah says, "If anythang's worth havin', it should be worth waitin' for." They embrace, kissing one another.

Dawn says, "Okay baby." Their eyes meet. Isiah stands firmly like a soldier, saluting her. Dawn stands firmly, like a Queen. The door closes gently.

⊷ ⊶

Matri says, "Claudia, I want you to keep Mama distracted with something... Mahalia Jackson's songs. You could tell her, you repented from your evil ways," she laughs.

Claudia laughs. "Matri, ya' gon' be alright? Ya' kno' ya' too much a lady fa' this kinda thang."

"Claudia, remember down home when we went to the barnyard dance, that night?"

Claudia thinks. "Ahhha."

"I told you, I needed to give you some of me?"

"Ahhha?"

"Well, I'm going to take some of your toughness, in you, tonight. I've given you some of the lady in me; fair exchange, no robbery."

Claudia acknowledges. "Ya' right."

Matri's eyes stretches. "You know, we've been trained down home, how to use guns and rifles, now." Matri takes the gun, putting it in her boots. She turns around looking at Claudia. "How does my fro look... like Angela Davis?"

Claudia's eyes juts out, "Ya' tryin' ta' look like Angela Davis, at a time like this, Matri?"

Matri sprays perfume all over her body. "Music isn't the only thing that soothes the savage beast; so does the smell of perfume. And besides, it'll throw Mama off."

The phone rings. "Yeah, Isiah."

"Come on, Matri," says Isiah.

With a posture of courage and resoluteness; in the time of danger, for justice, "Okay."

"Go on Matri, I'll fool Mama, real good," say Claudia

⊱ ⊰

Two hours later... Robert says, "Man, when we gon' get there?"

"Just be patient, it's right over there in an old abandoned warehouse," says Isiah.

"It sure is dark out here," says Hezikiah

"There's a river not too far from here. We're gonna let the car drive off into the river. Then we'll take off our first layer of clothes, and burn them with kerosene."

"I have the kerosene," says Matri.

"We don't want no traces left b'hind. We'll cross the tracks ta' take the train." Isiah pauses. "Now Matri, ya' stay back here in the car. If ya' hear or see anythang suspicious, drive the car like a bat out of hell." Isiah watches intently, his surroundings.

"Okay, let's go. We'll walk from here," says Isiah.

One of D'Boss's boys opens the door. Isiah walks in smiling with confidence. Robert and Hezikiah walks in behind him... cool, calm and collective. D'Boss sits at the head of the table with seven other men. He'is filing his nails, as his potbelly hangs, on the end of the table. He snaps his fingers and someone comes over, bringing him some cocaine to snort. "Ummm…this is good. As a matter of fact, it's daa …mn good." D'Boss gets the attention of his boys. Isiah continues to smile, calmly.

"I see ya' got cho' boys with you man." says D'Boss. Isiah continues to smile. D'Boss and his drug dealers stare at Isiah, Robert and Hezikiah. They stare back.

Very mean-spirited, D'Boss says, "Okay man, lets roll with it… put the money on the table b'fore I get mad, dig it?"

There's a knock on the door. One of the guys gets up with a gun, walking to the door.

Isiah flinches, "Matri."

"Matri?" The guy says, looking back at D'Boss.

Isiah turns around…"That's ma' sister man."

D'Boss frowns, "Your sister?"

Isiah acts conservative, "Yup, she here."

D'Boss gestures with his plump hands, "Let er' in."

Matri steps in with black pants; and a short black leather jacket, coming to her waist; with her cleavage displayed. She has a big afro, wearing big round earrings and black boots.

"Well looka here, looka here, that's a pretty mama right there. She look like"… He snaps his fingers… "Umm—Pam Grier," says D'Boss. All the guys stare at Matri. "Now, she could work for me. I know some rich white cats, would pay good for 'er:"

"Watch it, you rhinoceros gorilla... that's mya' sister, man."

Robert laughs persistently.

Vociferously, Isiah says…. " Matri, get outta' here, now!"

Matri retaliates, "I'm gonna stay, right here!"

Isiah, angered by her remark, quickly glances at her... then D'Boss.

D'Boss gets up. His corpulent body wobbles, walking towards Isiah. He yells. "Okay man, give me the money!" D'Boss looks around at the drug dealers, nodding his head. Snatching the bag out of Isiah's hands, his eyes are fixated on Isiah, like a mad man. "The next time, ya' be real careful who you deal with!" he yells.

Robert starts giggling, staring crazily at D'Boss. D'Boss angrily turns his head quickly, staring at Robert. Robert freezes, staring back at D'Boss, like a maniac.

D'Boss slowly takes his eyes off of Robert, focusing on Isiah. "As I was sayin'. … Now, I better have all of the $30,000… I asked for, dig it!"

"Robert starts giggling again, staring at him D'Boss; like he's the embodiment of insanity, reprsenting a cause.

D'Boss pauses again, staring at Robert. Robert looks like he wants to cry, very badly. Isiah looks at Robert…then, he starts staring at D'Boss, saying, "He waz' in Nam, man... he's shell-shocked."

D'Boss looks into Isiah's eyes. "Shellshocked? Well he come to the right place, to git' shot, actin' like that." He turns, staring at Robert again. "He gives me the creeps," says D'Boss.

Robert start putting his finger on his chin, talking to himself; pretentiously having an intellectual brawl with a ghost. He says, pointing his finger out, "To be or not to be… that is the question. Ummm…" He starts shaking his finger at D'Boss. "To be or not to be." He starts giggling furiously.. D'Boss looks at Robert, who abruptly stops giggling. Then Robert looks extremely sad at D'Boss, as if he just wants to burst out crying.

D'Boss' plumpish body sways, left to right. Staring at Robert and Isiah, he says "You know what, let me hurry up and count my money, so I could git' this cat, from round' me."

Adamantly Isiah says, "Man, ya' kno' I don' owe ya' no $ 30,000 dollars, man!"

"Man, I'm gon' count my money." Looking at Isiah treacherously, D'Boss replies, "And—if it ain't all here, all $30,000… cause, ain't nobody leavin' here alive no--how. But if you didn't bring my money, I was gon' kill yo' family... starting with yo' mama."

Isiah angrily jumps back. Robert and Hezikiah pull their guns out. "Run! Matri," says Isiah.

"Run! Matri" says Robert.

Somebody turns the lights out. One of the drug dealers goes after Matri. Robert starts having flashbacks of Nam. "Kill 'em, man! Kill these mothers!"

Isiah flashes back to 'Nam in the woods at night, falling rolling down on the floor. Whispering, "Shhh… Shhh… my fear lets me see—and I ain't gon die!"

He starts looking around…"Mama, is that you?"

D'Boss says, in the dark. "Man, what's these cats talkin' bout?"

One guy says, "Man, sound like they think they in 'Nam, man"

Hezikiah starts yelling. "I gotta get outta this hole, man. They shootin' like crazy, man."

"I got 'em!" says Isiah.

"I ain't gonna let chu die! Let's kill these mothers." says Robert.

Matri is running and panting…a gun shot goes off. "Oh my God!… someone's shooting at me." Matri starts zoning, hearing another gun shot coming her way. "What!… oh—no! …." Reaching down for the gun in her boots, she almost falls, runing into a tree. Another bullet is fired. Being panic-stricken, she stands behind the tree, panting quietly. "It's dark…out here—can't see!" She hears something moving, "What!……" Shots goes off. Firing three or four times, she freezes with the gun in her hands. Five… ten minutes later, Isiah grabs her, and she starts swinging at him.

"Matri, Matri it's me, Isiah. Let's go, we gotta git' the hell outta' here, now!"

They all ran to the car, Matri jumps behind the wheel. As they drive past the warehouse, Isiah throws two grenades into the building. "Boom! Boom!" Everybody gazes at Isiah.

Isiah looks at his watch. "Look, we gotta make it ta' the train on time." It starts pouring down rain, like a waterfall. Everybody is quiet, in their own world of thoughts. As she drives with high speed, Matri broods over what just happened. In turmoil, she thinks to herself. *We have to get away. Driving is like running. I'm zoning.* Wearily, she thinks, *I… I… did I really kill somebody? Why, of—course I did—he was going to kill me—what was I suppose to do? Mama said, things will happen sometimes, that will be out of your control.* Isiah puts his hands on her shoulder, looking ahead as Matri drives, talking to himself. "Nobody will follow this up. They only do it when whites is involved. We did them a favor."

"There's a siren! " says, Robert.

Isiah and Matri look into the mirror. Two cops are coming, driving fast. They all freeze. The rain starts pouring down, Matri could hardly see. The windshield wipers are going fast. The cops' siren is getting louder, the closer they get to the car. Matri thinks to herself, *Mama says, "Rain is a sign of a good thing... don't panic. Just keep driving steady.*

"Drive steady baby," Isiah says, glancing at Matri. The siren gets louder, coming very close to the car. Everyone's frozen like ice. The cars zooms past Matri. They all exhale.

Nobody says a word. Matri continues to drive. Isiah thinks, *Man, I hate the fact that she had ta' kill somebody. If she stayed in the car like I asked her too. Damit.. ... How do I help her deal with this?* Isiah looks over at Matri, teary-eyed. He turns around, looking at Robert and Hezikiah. They both seem to be in a world of their own. Isiah continues to think,

Oh God. Matri said, 'Ya' everywhere. Well help us all, please help us ta' get out of this box. *I caused Matri ta' kill somebody... punish me fa' it.*

Matri reads his thoughts. She starts shaking her head thinking, *No. ... Don't do it, Isiah, don't blame yourself, please.*

Isiah looks at her. Matri looks at Isiah, saying to herself, *Don't... please.*

"Hey man," Robert says, "Turn the radio on, maybe we could find out what happened."

The news comes on. "We bring you the latest report tonight. Dr. Martin Luther King has been assassinated." Nobody moves... stilled like statues.

"Man, turn it up!" says Robert.

"Dr. King was dressed for an elaborate soul food dinner at the Reverend Kyle's home. King stepped outside the Lorraine Motel balcony, in the approaching twilight. Staff members were milling around in the courtyard below, with Solomon Jones and his Cadillac limousine.

Holding on to the balcony, King asked Ben to sing, "Precious Lord," and to sing it like he had never sung it before. "Sing it real pretty," King said. Jones told King that it was getting cool and he should get his overcoat. The sun was about to set. King replied, "I don't need a coat." At that moment, about six o'clock, his staff heard a loud clap that sounded like a car backfiring or a firecracker. The leader was no longer standing. An eyewitness saw him flying backward, with his arms out to his sides. He lay on his back with his knees raised and his feet pressed against the railing. Blood gushed out of his throat and neck. The high-powered bullet had exploded, passing through his neck, and severed his spinal cord.

King's voice came loudly, echoing and penetrating their hearts; like Gabriel blowing his horn, awaking the people for the coming of a final judgment.

I have a dream that one day, even the state of Mississippi, a state sweltering with the heat of injustice and oppression will be transformed into an oasis of freedom and justice. Well, I don't know what will happen now. We've got some difficult days ahead. But it doesn't matter with me now. Because I've been to the mountaintop. And I don't mind, like anybody else, I would like to live a long time. Longevity has its place. But I'm not concerned about that now. I just want to do God's will. And He's allowed me go up to the mountain. And I've looked over. And I've seen the promise land. I may not get there with you. But I want you to know tonight, that we, as a people will get to the promise land. And I'm happy, tonight. I'm not worried about anything. I'm not fearing any man.   .

It's a moment of hysteria, for what they have done... and now... King! Pacified by silence, no one says a word. Matri looks ahead. The rain pours down like it's crying for the loss of a great King. Matri thinks, *Now Mama said, rain was a sign of a good thing... how could this be? Our beloved King was just assassinated.* "She looks over at Isiah, and looks into the mirror at Robert and Hezikiah. "Yes we have to get out of the box. We as a people will get to the promise land, as King said. I believe we have to get out of the box, to get there."

Isiah says, "Slow down Matri, we comin' ta' our stop in a minute."

Slowly, the rain ceases. "Isiah observes his surroundings. Matri this is it, stop. Everybody looks around at the river. "Take yo' top clothes off, we'll burn them up. Matri. Then let the car roll off inta' the river." Pulling out a piece of cloth, wiping the steering wheel off, Isiah says, "We gonna walk a little after we cross over the train track. We'll come ta' the train station ahead." He commands, "Let's go!"

Matri goes into the suitcase, pulling out sandwiches. "Oh yeah," says Robert. "Nothin' for me," says Hezikiah. "Throw one at me," says Isiah. Let's go!"

CHAPTER 14

THE TRAIN

They all stand anxiously, waiting for the train, in the early morning. They re not talking; watchful of their surroundings, with a little paranoia. Every now and then, they're communicating by way of mental telepathy, with their eyes meeting. Some people are crying, talking about the assassination of Dr. King; others were expressing anger and revenge. Matri thinks, "He was a great caretaker, a custodian of the world."

'Hey, I'm sorry. I didn't kno' we would end up sleepin' out here all night," says Isiah.

"Hey man, things happen," says Hezikiah.

Two old women come to Matri with tissue, wiping their eyes. Saying, "He was not a perfect man, but he was a man of God."

Matri grabbs both of them, hugging them. "Yes he was, but we'll keep him alive by remembering all the good he did," says Matri.

One of the old women says, sniffing, "Mahalia Jackson sings a song called, "Joshua Fought the Battle of Jericho," and that's what King did."

Matri says with vitality, "Yes ma' am."

"Matri, here comes the train," says Isiah.

Matri hugs the two women. "I love you both, good-bye."

The conductor is a short dark brown-skinned, round shaped face; husky-framed man, with a small gap between his teeth. Dressed in a conductor's suit, he gets off the train, yelling, "Virginia, Hemingway S.C., and Florence. There are only two seats left in this car." The conductor smiles at the women, escorting them to the last two seats. He turns around, ""Everybody else, take the last car."

Matri observes everyone very closely. "Take your seats, we're behind schedule," the conductor says.

"Let's relax and enjoy this ride," says Isiah.

"Yeah," says Hezikiah.

Matri notices six people all together, including them, were on their car. Two other men comes, and sit three seats down from them. One is a thin, dark-skinned man with a short afro; with a deep scar on the right side of his face. The other, a short stocky, light-complexioned man; with a beard and green eyes. He holds a book in his hand. They appear to be into a deep conversation.

"Here comes the conductor," says Matri. He takes a seat in their car. He takes off his hat, displaying salt and pepper hair. He pulls out a book. Matri turns away, looking out of the window.

Everybody falls asleep. Matri thinks, It seems like I know him, but he's a complete stranger.

All of a sudden, Isiah starts coughing. He's bending over grabbing his stomach, rocking back and forth. "Isiah," asks Matri, "What's wrong?" Isiah continues to rock back and forth, rubbing his nose. Isiah starts crying.

"Hey man, you okay?" asks Robert.

The dark-skinned man gets up and gives Isiah a paper bag to throw up in.

"Thank you!" says Matri.

The conductor gets up, coming over to Isiah. "Come on, let me help you. Come with me." He takes Isiah behind the curtain. The conductor tells Robert and Hezikiah, "Leave him to me."

They're all sitting, waiting for Isiah and the conductor to come back. "What's behind the curtain? Where did they go?" asks, Hezikiah.

"Let's be patient," says Matri.

"Here they come," says Robert. They're all sitting there watching both of them, as they come back to their seats. The conductor pats Isiah on his back and sits down. Matri, Robert, Hezikiah and the other two guys watch the conductor with curiosity. Isiah has a brown bag. He's sucking on something.

"What's in the bag?" asks Matri

"Ginger balls, it helps ta' keep ma' stomach settled," says Isiah.

Matri looks over to the conductor and says, "Thank you... Mr....?"

In a very mild, well-mannered tone of voice, he says "Ah, Wallace...Wallace."

Compassionately, Matri says, "Thank you so much, Mr. Wallace."

Seemingly shy, displaying his gap in his teeth, he smiles. "You're very welcome, young lady."

Matri pauses, thinking, He's mild-mannered and well spoken.

"Excuse me... you know, I keep thinking that I know you. But I know I've never met anyone that looks like you, never mind, knowing you," Matri says.

He looks up at her and smiles politely. "Well... young lady, I think what we have here is "Dejavu, or alike souls attract one another."

Impressed by him, Isiah listens to the conversation

Matri thinks, He thinks before he speaks. "What does that mean?"

He pauses to think, "Ah, ahh... It means our souls have a spiritual connection, a familiarity with one another.

" Perhaps we sense the goodness in one another." Matri thinks.

"Thank ya', for helping me," says Isiah.

He picks up his book to read again. Matri peeps, trying to find out what he's reading. He notices her and tells her, "The Light of Darkness."

"What does that mean?" He looks up at her, very polished behavior. "'Right now, we've lost a great soul. There's darkness, bringing sadness and pain. The atrocity of Dr. King's death, is being heard all over the world. But his spirit, as we know him and all the good works he's done: his love, dedication, and his never ending, fearless courage. The love he had for God, made us see many great things, that we couldn't see before in a Black man. Bringing us out of darkness with a light; a light that strangely enough, to those who don't understand it right now; illuminates the world, at his time of death."

Matri pauses, "Mama says, rain is a good sign. It's been pouring down rain, since he's been assassinated... so, there's a connection. The rain brings life, and perhaps it's saying that," Matri expressed with ardor. "Dr. King brought abundant life to the earth... leaving good harvest."

Wallace says very studiously, "Yes, yes of course, rain helps things to grow. The pouring down of the rain represents the wisdom that Dr. King was pouring down. His wisdom to all of us, the unculti-vated seed. The black woman/man and humanity, waiting to be nourished by the hands of a righteous farmer, with a rich soil..." He pauses "And when harvest time comes around—ahhhh..." He stresses, "It's a great harvest. What a wonderful crop. We're living in the harvest of Dr. King's wisdom... let us pick the fruits from it," says Wallace. Everyone is in awe of what he said.

"Dr. King's wife is a very strong and wise woman," says Matri.

"She is a wise woman. Elijah Muhammad says that a woman is the mother of civilization," says the stocky -man.

The other man says, "Elijah says also, that Paradise lies at the feet of the woman."

Wallace smiles and says, "Okay, that's a great thing."

"What does that mean, man?" Robert asks.

"Yes, an old woman by the name of Annielu said the same thing" says Matri.

Everyone's eyes are fixated on Wallace. "Well, in short... she's the mother of civilization. A woman should have a strong relationship with God, because her nature bids her to bring the family into a God consciousness. Her responsibility is great, but not impossible. Women is the Society. She's responsible for the making of the society; making it or breaking it, starting in her home with her children first, and foremost. 'Hands that rock the cradle, rocks the world.' God has charged her with the responsibility to bring about a righteous society. She must learn her God. She must learn to obey and make her obedience to God, and not to man! "Her footsteps can lead us back to the Garden... of paradise. She's been equipped by God to do it," says Wallace.

Isiah says, "Ya' kno,' just look at me. I never thought that I would become a victim of drugs. I thought when I come back from 'Nam, that ma' life would be straight. Just look at me with ma' nose runnin', man. I feel like 'Nam lynched me, man. Took me down and left me hanging."

Matri got some tissue and started rubbing Isiah's face.

Robert crosses his legs, shaking them nervously, turning towards Wallace; squinting his eyes up and staring into Isiah's eyes.

Isiah says, "Yeah we all got this pain man, it would be good if we could explain the justification fa' the pain." He holds his head down, thinking. "It's like a deep hurt..." He gulps. "What do we do with it, don' kno' how ta' git rid of this hurt. The sad part 'bout it iz', we don' even kno' why we had ta' kill—and every time we killed... we got ta' the place where we waz' proud! I waz' proud of killin' another human bein'. My adrenaline thrived off of killin', man!"

Hezikiah cries out. "I still smell the stench of blood! And I don't feel like a man, no moe. I don' kno' what I am...a freak! I can't live no normal life like no man!"

The two guys came holding their shoulders. One says, "Hey, my brother let me say something to you, about the military, please.

Whenever a soldier is injured, the protocol is to get to safety, treat the wounds and heal. ... Recover and get back to the battlefield, as a new man." Emphatically, he says, "Yes, you've been injured emotionally, psychologically, and physically. Now you desperately need to know, what is the protocol now? In a sense, how do you get back to the man that you, never got a chance to know before you left?"

The other man says, "Look brothers, you continue to destroy yourselves because you can't fix a wrong with revenge. You'll self-destruct, in a minute."

Matri gets up like a soldier in command, looking around. ... Raising her voice with great vigor, expressing with all of her heart and soul, saying, "It's going to be alright, you must believe that!"

Wallace gets up and says, " Man must look into the mirror, and learn the spirit of the man, presenting no color barriers. If he does not, then he is no better than those who have oppressed him. Man's errors are only in the pursuit of his perfection. Meaning that… he strongly emphasizes. "Man never intends to do wrong. In his wrongdoing, his intentions are only to do good. His nature bids him to do good, to listen to that good voice. But something interrupts that... let's say... Nam, in your case."

⇥ ⇤

Isiah asks, "Time sho' is passing…where do ya' change conductors, Wallace?"

"Hemingway, South Carolina," says Wallace.

"That's where you're going? says Matri. That's where we're going."

Wallace chuckles, "Oh boy, destiny sure has a way of taking over."

"Where you two going man?" asks, Robert.

"We're going to Florence."

"You know that's not far from Hemingway," says Wallace.

"Yeah, we know," says the other guy."

Matri says excitedly. "Here, take my home address in Hemingway. Robert and Hezikiah and Isiah will be there for a month. I'll only be there for a week. Hattie will come over with lots of food, helping the boys clean up."

"Hey man… Isiah… you gonna need some help with that little monkey…?" asks Wallace. They all stared at Wallace. "What I mean is that, since I'm so close by, I'll drive by and help you get that monkey off your back. You could do nothin' til' you get 'em off."

Robert says, "Man, he's right. He could help us all... I believe."

"Wallace looks up at all of them and says, "Man never knows where his absolute destiny will lead him. He could be traveling on a road, then all a sudden it's no longer the road he intended."

They all look at Wallace. Matri says, "Please help them."

⇒⊹ ⊹⇐

Eight days later:

The wind is blowing fiercely, with the rain. Matri comes home, getting out of the taxi. Mama watches out of the window. Matri looks up, noticing Mama watching her. *How am I going to act like everything is wonderful, Mama is so intuitive… guess that's her gift from God.* Mama opens the door. Claudia and the boys stand behind Mama as Matri walks up the stairs.

Matri smiles jovially, "Oh Mama!" She puts her suitcase down at the door, hugging Mama and Mama holds her tightly. *She's been worrying,* says Matri to herself.

Claudia grabs Matri, squeezing and hugging her... teary-eyed. "Matri," says Claudia. Mama looks at Matri and walks away quietly.

After dinner, Matri later goes to Mama's bed. She lays at the end of Mama's feet, massaging them. Mama doesn't respond. "Mama are you okay?" asks Matri. She doesn't respond. "Mama," says Matri.

Finally Mama speaks up softly, "When is Isiah, Robert and Hezikiah comin' back?"

"They say as long as it takes to get the house in shape... besides they wanted to get away for awhile." Mama refrains from saying another word. Matri falls asleep at her feet.

CHAPTER 15

LOVE AND WAR

Month later:
The phone rings, "Matri beloved."

"Go out? Why, I'd love to go out tonight… Lena Horne? The lady I heard singing in your home? 9:00… Ramone, I'd better start getting ready, it's 7:00… bye." Matri looks at Civil. "Let me feed you, dear heart, before I leave."

The phone rings. "Hello, who?..." Matri frowns… "Lorraine?... okay, hold on."

"Claudia!" yells Matri.

"Hi girl!" Claudia rolls her eyes at Matri.

"You ready, Claudia?"

"Yeah… ohh, the kids…"

"I'll watch them—I don' want them in the street, and comin' back home late at night," says Ruth.

Claudia turns around looking at Mama. "Mama said she'll watch them," says Claudia.

"Girl, I got a black eye… two, as a matter of fact," says Lorraine.

"Girl, what happened?"

"Umm… I'll tell you later. I put a lot of make up on them to cover it up."

The bell rings. Matri looks out of the window, yelling to Claudia. "Claudia, it's Osmon."

Osmon frustrates Claudia. "What he want now? I 'clare." Claudia frowns.

Lorraine, demands Claudia, "Get rid of 'em," puts her hands on her hips.

"What did I tell ya', 'bout orderin' me round' now, Lorraine? Ya' ain't ma' man, or mama, okay?"

Lorraine sucks her teeth," I'm ready. I'll be downstairs."

Osmon walks in the door. Claudia goes in the room, to get her pocketbook. Osmon is left standing in the living room. "Oh Osmon," says Claudia. "I'm goin' out. I told Lorraine I'll be waitin' outside."

Osmon smirks, "Who said I came to see you?" Ruth stands at the kitchen sink, biting down on her lips.

Osmon sways his hands, "No, I came to see ya' mama. Go on," says Osmon.

Claudia rolls her eyes at Osmon... takes her pocketbook, her cigarettes and walks out the door. Osmon shakes his head

"She didn't even say good night ta' her children," says Ruth.

Osmon feels defeated. "Yeah, Ruth." Osmon walks over to kiss Ruth on the forehead.

Biting her lips, Ruth says, "I sho' need ta' see ya' bout Claudia... we'll wait til Matri leave too."

The bell rings. Matri comes out of the room, noticing Osmon sitting down watching TV with Ruth. "Oh, Osmon, I didn't know you were still here. Where's Claudia?" Matri asks.

With a sullen face, Osmon says, "Hmm, that's a good question."

Someone knocks on the door. "Who, is this?" asks Matri. Thaddeus stands at the door, with flowers and a big long box for Matri's birthday. Ruth and Osmon watches Matri and Thaddeus. Matri is startled. She gulps, "Thaddeus... wha... why didn't you call me, and tell me you were coming?"

He blushes, "I wanted to surprise you, for your birthday."

Matri is flabbergasted. "Oh my God, Thaddeus I forgot about my own birthday. As a matter of fact, we all forgot, turning towards Ruth, Matri stares...

Thaddeus delightfully, takes a moment to explain, " I couldn't forget yours, because we were born almost like twins... same day. To hear Ruth tell it... a few hours apart, literally speaking. The big 27."

" Oh, I didn't forgit, I birthed ya'. Made cha' favorite chocolate cake. But, didn't git' a chance ta' tell ya, for everybody else pullin' on ya'," says Ruth.

Humbly, Matri says, "Oh Mama, I'm so sorry. Will you please forgive me, dear heart?"

The door slams downstairs, drawing everyone's attention to the door. Ramone walks up the stairs with flowers. They're all still standing in the middle of the floor, with the door opened. Matri peaks around Thaddeus' shoulder. "Huh, it's Ramone," she's nervous.

Thaddeus notices a peculiar expression on Matri's face. Glancing to the side, he notices Ramone coming with flowers. Suddenly, her body feels heated. Her hands are feeling moist. She becomes mute, twisting around towards Osmon. They all continue to stare at Matri. She exhales, "I 'clare." She turns looking at Thaddeus, then looking at Ramone.

Ramone and Thaddeus smile. Noticing each other's smile, they both stop. Looking at each other hardheartedly, is very noticeable.

Imitating Matri, Ramone says, "Here beloved, these are for you... I 'clare."

Matri gently takes the flowers, smelling them. "Umm....These are beautiful, Ramone."

Thaddeus opens up his box, pulling out a long beautiful brown, maxi fur coat. He jently puts it, around Matri's shoulders.

Ramone is devastated. Thaddeus notices Ramone's expression, and smiles proudly.

Ruth and Osmon continue to stare at Matri.

Matri stares at Thaddeus and then Ramone again. She turns around, looking at Mama and Osmon, for help.

Osmon calls Thaddeus to the kitchen. Osmon takes out a piece of gum. "This is the time for chewing. Here man, chew some gum." Thaddeus takes the gum. "Chew, man. Osmon chews, smacking his lips. Tilting his head, he says, "My brother, you gotta play your cards right."

Thaddeus chuckles at Osmon, chewing his gum to quell the situation. Balling up his fist with tenacity, Osmon says, "You gotta tell yourself... you the man!' He pauses, "Don't even sweat this. It's about time, brother. There's a season for all things. All's fair in love and war. He beat chu' out this time... 'cause he did one simple thing... he called first." Osmon chews vigorously, "So it goes to the caller, at this time," he thinks, " It's like this song, ah... ah... ah... Amaz..." snaps his fingers, "Help me out man."

Softly Thaddeus says, "Amazing Grace."

Osmon looks at Thaddeus, eye to eye. "You're amazed by this... right? Well, you gotta back out gracefully."

Thaddeus chuckles at Osmon's serious sense of humor. "Tell 'er you didn't come to stay, no how. You have to go and work on your book... you have a deadline," tiilts head.

Thaddeus stands straight up, "Hey man, you're right. It ain't over."

Matri comes into the kitchen. Thaddeus kisses her on the cheek. "Hey babe, I have to go home, to do some work on my book. Yeah, have to get it out soon. Happy Birthday," says Thaddeus.

"Thaddeus, the coat is awesome. I love it, happy birthday my twin birth brother, to you also." She kisses him.

Thaddeus says "Yeah, how about that... what a coincidence. Same time, same place." They both smile. He winks his eyes at

Matri, kissing Ruth on the forehed, nd walk out of the kitchen in a dignified manner. Glancing at Ramone, he says, "Dig it."

"You bet," says Ramone.

After everyone leaves, Osmon says, "Oh Ruth, before we talk. I need you to know that, I want to ask Robert, Isiah and Hezikiah if they want to work for me. I have my own construction business."

"They'll be back tomorrow. Matri say, it would only take then a month, ta' git the house ta-gether fa' me."

"Ummm, I see," says Osmon, looking at Ruth in a curious manner.

"They went down south ta' fix ma' house up. I think I wanna go back home," Ruth shakes her head.

Osmon is disturbed by Ruth's remark. "Ruth... what is it?" he takes hold of her hands.

Ruth says disheartedly, "Ma' heart been actin' up on me some kinda bad. I fainted a few times here by ma'self, but the Lawd been pickin' me up," says Ruth, with weary eyes.

Osmon is upset and takes out another stick of gum. "What Ruth... did you tell anybody?"

"I'm gon' be alright... I trust that. Just help me with Claudia fa' these chirrin' sake. I been so worried 'bout Claudia. That old Lorraine girl ain't no good fa' Claudia ta' be with. She keep 'er in that New York place with those Ra-sta-ssa and hippie people. And she justa' drinkin' all the time, like a fool. As much as she love them boys... she don' pay them boys too much tention' no mo'," Ruth shakes her head.

Osmon sits up, "Ruth, I know you know... I got somthin' in my heart for that girl... can't seem to get it out. Know she come from good blood. That's why I'm being patient waitin' things out with her, cause everything got a season."

Ruth smiles, while looking afar. "Ya' put me in the mind of ma' self, bout' Jessie. Tell ma' chirrin,' he put somin' in ma' heart...

that I just couldn't take out, and wasn't tryin' no how." She stares off, blushing.

"Ruth let me tell you somthin' good. I ain't gon' let that Lorraine girl hurt our Claudia. You best believe that, when I tell you'," Osmon gives her a serious look.

Ruth holds Osmon's hands. "Osmon, Claudia have somin' in her heart fa' ya' too, I kno' ma' child. It's just that, I been worried bout' all ma' chirrin. Somin' been goin' on with all of 'em, and I been puttin' them all up in prayer... in the twilight hours of the night. When everybody sleep, I been goin' ta' ma' sweet Lawd, asking Him ta' hold ma' hand.

Osmon starts shaking his head up and down, jaws moving rapidly. "I'm gon' end this thing with Claudia... tonight," he says firmly." I'm tired of playin' with Claudia. Don't you think, I don't know Claudia have a soft spot for me in her heart, Ruth?" His jaws starts jumping again. Barely able to talk, chewing his gum vigorously. "Hmmm, I know where she is tonight. And I'm declarin' war on her tonight," eyes protrudes, " I'm gon' end this nightmare!" says Osmon.

Hours later... Osmon and his Brothers arrive at the club.

"The Highest Peake is a hot spot," says Brother John.

"We need to soldier out here sometime," says Brother Anthony.

"Anthony, how I look man?" asks Osmon.

Brother John and Anthony look at each other. "How you look Brother Captain?" asks Anthony.

Osmon sits like a soldier with his uniform on. Osmon says, "Yes?"

With militancy, he says, "Brother you look like one of Elijah Muhammad's soldiers," says Brother John.

Osmon looks at Anthony smiling. "You know I had a long talk, with Claudia's mama tonight." He exhales, "I got to help Claudia.

Got to pull her away from that Lorraine girl. We gon' try to convert Lorraine, too... can't give up on a sister."

"Here we go man," says Brother Anthony, getting out of the black meticulous Brougham, looking militant. Osmon pulls out a stick of gum. Anthony opens the door for Osmon. People that are standing around talking, stops, staring at them. Osmon puts his feet out. His shoes has a gloss to them. Wearing, a dark blue uniform with red crescents on the shoulders; professionally pressed to impress. His FOI fez, fits his head perfectly. Anthony stands still, as if Osmon is an ambassador of some sort, until he's out of the car. Brother Anthony and John are wearing the same type of uniform and fez... immaculate.

"Stay in the car Brother John, and stay on guard," says Osmon.

He responds quickly, "Yes sir."

Osmon and Anthony steps inside of the Highest Peake, like soldiers. Everybody stares at both of them. People at the bar stop drinking, and stares at them. Osmon starts looking around at the people, with a very firm look. Anthony stands behind him, posing as a bodyguard. One guy calls Osmon.

"Hey man, go through that door." Osmon stills himself, looking at the guy, then proceeds towards the door. He hears a lot of music. He pauses, turning around looking at Anthony, then opens the door.

They both look at each other, noticing the psychedelic lights. Their walking around like soldiers, looking for Claudia and Lorraine; looking into the faces of the women, as they dance. Their eyes flinch as the lights are flashing off and on. Everybody's turning around, looking at Osmon and Anthony, as they walk through the crowd in slow motion. Anthony looks around, observing everyone as he walks behind Osmon. The women blush when they look at them, trying to entice them; with their dance, and their bosoms shaking like Jell-O.

Osmon freezes, when he sees Claudia. Anthony freezes. Claudia is drinking at the bar, laughing with a guy. She's wearing a short tight skirt, with big earrings, and a big afro; and her cleavage showing. She doesn't see Osmon. James Brown's song starts playing. The guy at the bar grabs her hand to dance. She starts dancing seductively to James Brown's song. Osmon starts walking towards her, arduously chewing. The lights are flicking off and on. The music continues to play, "Say It Loud, I'm Black and I'm Proud." Osmon stops right at her, while she's dancing. Brother Anthony is right behind him, staring at her. She turns around, turning into a cube of ice. The guy walks away.

Looking dead into her eyes, Osmon asks her forcefully, "Are you coming with me to marry me, or are you going to stay in the mud sister, and die a second death?" He looks around at the place and the people. His eyes dilates. Emphatically he says again, "Is this what you want!"

He becomes stone-faced, walking all around her, like a sergeant at arms. Anthony does the same thing. "Just look at you... happy to drink that stinkin' liquor, that puts you to sleep. Keeping you in a comatose, state of mind!" He yells like a sergeant, "Is this what you want! Huh Claudia?" He looks her up and down. "You can't even stand up. Look at cha!" Claudia tries to stand up. "Are you a mother? Claudia, are you a mother... is this a place for a mother! Look at the way you're dressed, you're shaming yourself, looking like a prostitute... Claudia!" The other women are trying to cover themselves.

One woman tries to cover her cleavage. One, starts trying to pull her skirt down. "Do you hear the song, Claudia?" With vigor, Osmon and Anthony start singing the song with James Brown; while walking around, looking everybody in their eyes. "Say it loud!" Everybody starts singing, "Say it loud, I'm Black and I'm Proud. I say we won't quit movin' till we get what we deserve." He freezes, staring at Claudia while continuing to sing. "We've been duped and we've been scorned, but we can't quit till we get our share. Say it Loud, I'm Black and I'm Proud." He continue to walk around, as the lightsflash. Anthony follows behind him. Osmon and Anthony sings, with great spirit "Now we demand a chance, to do things for ourselves. We're tired of beatin' our heads against the wall, and working for someone else." As the lights flash, he turns around walking in slow motion towards Claudia... she seem, to be afraid, and regretful.

"I'm sorry," says Claudia crying.

He stand erect, "No! don't ever say your sorry."

Claudia freezes, looking baffled, with her mascara smeared from crying.

"Claudia, I'm here representing the 'We' for the "Final Call." Looks around at the women, "And we came here, to pull you precious women, out of the mud to respect yourselves."

Osmon says, "Claudia repeat after me! Say... I am the cream of the crop."

Claudia repeats, like a frightened little girl, "I am the cream of the crop."

Forcefully he says, "I am the most beautiful black woman, on the planet earth!"

Claudia gulps. "I am the most beautiful black woman, on the planet earth!"

"I am a lady... and I am a mother," says Osmon.

"I am a lady... and I am a mother," Claudia repeats.

Osmon says compassionately, "And this ain't no place, for a lady like me."

Claudia sniffles. "And this ain't no place... for a lady like me."

Osmon smiles at Claudia, and says, "It doesn't, become me."

Wearily she says, "It doesn't, become me."

He turns around looking at the other women, as still as trees, staring at him. "Now this ain't no place for you, and it ain't good enough for you... lost sheep of America."

Some of the women told Osmon he was right, and they wanted to come to the Temple. Lorraine comes over to Osmon with a man, rolling her eyes at Osmon and Anthony. She's street-walking, towards the door smiling, shaking her rear end.

Osmon shakes his head at her. "Sister look what they did to you... damaged goods," says Osmon.

"My sister, I love you with understanding," says Anthony.

"Some of you, ya just can't save. Come on Claudia, your mama's worried about cha," says Osmon.

On the way home, Claudia and Osmon sit in the back seat. "Look man, at how the people are coming outside, staring at us," says Brother John.

"We have to get their attention man. And we did tonight, right Brother Anthony?" asks Osmon.

"We did, Brother Osmon," says Anthony.

Claudia continues to cry. "I'm sorry Osmon," she says.

"It's gon' be alright, Claudia."

"It will, Claudia," says Brother Anthony.

"Hey Anthony, let's give Claudia a tour of what the Muslims are doing here, in Newark."

He answers blissfully, "Yes sir."

Claudia, here's Clara Muhammad's school, named after Elijah Muhammad's wife. Elijah Muhammad said, "We should teach our own. Looking around, I see all types of buildings, needing work done on them. I'm good with my hands. That's why I have my own construction business. Elijah Muhammad freed me." He holds Claudia's hands. " Claudia, I wanna marry you, and put your sons in this school. I need you to be my secretary, if that's what you wanna be, until you make up your mind about school. "

Claudia says, "Okay Osmon."

"Here's the restaurant across the street. Lord, these sisters can cook. They been trained in the MGT classes. Elijah Muhammad said, "The man that feeds you, controls you. We have sisters that are very skilled, in sewing Muslim Girls Training (MGT) uniforms; and teaching other sisters how to sew; and wear very modest attire. The messenger said, "We need to get out of massa's wives clothing, they're not respectful enough for our women. The MGT classes, is consist of teaching the sisters how to be better mothers, wives and ladies at home and abroad."

Osmon gestures with his hands. "Take us downtown, Brother John. We have our own newspaper. Elijah Muhammad said, "We can't trust the local newspaper... they been lying to us long enough. It's a form of control. Malcolm X said, "The pen is mightier than the sword. See the bakery over there. We have the best, natural, old fashion bread. Elijah Muhammad said that the chemicals are killing us. He speaks about the 'Hereafter,' the beginning of a new world for us. We are a new people, who will not look up into the sky for survival, or waiting for the crumbs that fall off of massa's table. We will be the new people, that's independent of massa. We'll have a conglomeration of things: land, our own schools, new schools of thought, stores, factories, doctors, and friends in all walks of life... you name it. Fair trade will exist, with equal opportunity."

"That's sound like a lot of things that we need ta' do," says Claudia. Osmon stares at her.

"Brother Anthony, we better get Claudia home now. I don't want Ruth worryin' no more, about Claudia. This wild goose chase is over. Me and Claudia gon' get married. If that's alright with Claudia."

Claudia says sweetly, "It's alright, Osmon."

Osmon looks up, "Let's go home to Ruth, my Queen."

CHAPTER 16

THE CREAM OF THE CROP

Saturday afternoon, Brother Anthony opens the door, letting Claudia out of the limousine. She, is wearing an all-white MGT uniform, with a white headpiece: white shoes, white pearl earrings and necklace. Getting out of the limousine, it seems like the sun comes and stops right at her feet... bowing to her; bringing out the most illuminating smile for a lady; adding a glow to her pecan skin... which has, not one blemish. The people gather around whispering, and watching them, as they capture some of the sun's radiance. Queenly, the cream of the crop... her prince has finally come to free her. No longer, a 'Black Cinderella,' in the wilderness of North America. She is in her glory... finally, a Prince has found her slippers, in the wilderness. ...

Holding her head up in a stately manner, like a Queen. She holds onto Anthony's hand, as he leads her to her Prince. He reaches out to her gently, holding her hands, smiling at his Queen, with so much love and compassion. They both hold each other's hands, walking in slow motion with the sun, smiling brightly... just like the sun.

Twenty minutes later, you could hear a pin drop. Claudia and Osmon face each other, as the Minister spoke. Osmon's eyes are teary, thinking, "The hunter finally captured the game," says Osmon to himself. "My heart are well-pleased and my eyes are delighted with what I see. Thank you Allah."

Claudia blushes, seeing the tears in Osmon's eyes, expressing love for her. She thinks, "I kno' he loves me. I 'clare, with—ma'—fool self, what waz' wrong with me… shoudda' married this man a long time ago. He sure looks good. Come ta' think of it—he sure reminds me of daddy," she says to herself.

Matri holds Ruth's hands. She squeezes Matri's hand.

Thaddeus keeps looking across the room at Matri, daydreaming about Matri and his wedding. "Yeah Matri, maybe one day this will be you and me. That is, if I could get Ramone out of the picture."

Isiah looks across the room, noticing Dawn. She notices Isiah looking at her. She blushes. Robert looks at Sadie, winking his eyes at her. She looks back at him, with love.

Hezikiah peeks at the sisters. "These is some beautiful looking women. I ain't never seen no women like these before." He holds his head down. " But it ain't no use in me lookin." Eyes gets glossy,"' Cause I can't have not a one of 'em. I'm ruined fa' life." He says to himself.

Matri comes over to Claudia, giving her a dozen red roses, "For the lady in you."

Claudia kisses Matri, prancing around with her head up high. "Thank ya' ma,' beloved."

Fifteen minutes later, Claudia and Osmon are standing before the cake. "I want everybody to meet my family," says Osmon. Everybody gathers around to meet his family. "This here, is my mama Ethel, my step-dad, Albert, my sisters: Denise, Violet, and Carnella."

A FOI says, "Wait a minute, Captain Osmon. Let me take these pictures of you and the Queen." Osmon pulls Claudia to him. They both blush as the Brother takes the pictures.

"Wait a minute," says Claudia. "Take my sweet little boys' picture, with their mama and new step dad." Her sons are dressed in dark blue suits with blue and white bowties. Their hair is cut very closely.

Brother says, "Okay now, let the boys stand together in front of you two… perfect."

"Matri you and your mother come over here, you'll take a picture first, then his daddy. Mama and my sisters will take one next."

" Yes Mama," Osmon calls Ruth Mama. He's hugging, blushing and smiling from ear to ear.

Everybody comes over to Osmon and Claudia, congratulating them. Lieutenant Kareem comes over, hugging Osmon. "Sister, you got a fine, strong… good man."

"No doubt," says Lieutenant Larry.

Osmon says, "Where's my man, Brother Anthony? Now, you got to take a picture with me and my wife." Anthony comes over smiling. Osmon puts his hands around Anthony's shoulders. "Now you see this brother; he played a big role in helping me with this woman." He pauses… looking Anthony straight in his eyes. "Thank you man," says Osmon. They both hug.

"Hey my Brother Osmon, you made a good choice. I took some really good shots of you and Claudia outside, my camera takes excellent pictures," says Thaddeus.

Brother John says, "Brother Captain, I know we don't do this but, I got a Brother by the name of Brother Wayne. He's from another community. He sings, so I decided to give you a special present, from me. Is it alright?"

Osmon looks at the Lieutenant. He nods. "Yes, my brother."

Brother Wayne says, "Brother, this is your day. We have his equipment set up already." He smiles.

A stocky short brown-skinned brother, comes forward. With shyness, he says, "I'd like to dedicate this song to my brother and sister. I wrote this song in dedication to Allah, thanking him. It's entitled, "Thank You Allah."

Thank you Allah. For your will, you willed to me. Thank you Allah, for your will, your will to me. You gave me a will, filled with love. You gave me a will, filled with joy, yes you did. You gave me a will, filled with dignity. You gave me a will, filled with truth. You gave me a will, filled with patience. You gave me a will, with justice for you, justice for me. You gave me a will, filled with harmony. You gave me a will, faced with peace. I wanna thank you Allah for your will, you willed in me. I wanna thank you, thank you Allah, for your will, you willed in me. You gave me a will, filled with happiness. You gave me a will, with kindness. You gave me a will, filled with affection. Thank you, thank you Allah, for your will to me.

Everybody seems to be hypnotized by his song. He brings tears to everyone's eyes. Ruth nods her head back and forth. The Muslim Sisters takes out tissues, handing them out.

"Where's mine?" asks Robert.

"Where's mine too?" asks Isiah.

Osmon grabs Claudia's hands, staring into her eyes.

Thaddeus bobs his head. "Oh man, this touches the soul."

Matri places her hands on her heart, saying, "Beautiful."

Robert says, "Hey listen up, I want to say something right quick. Come on over, baby," Robert, looks at Osmon and Claudia. "Sadie and I just want everybody to know that we eloped and got married three weeks ago. We couldn' tell you, because there was too much going on."

Everybody cheers them on, congratulating them. "Come here man" says Osmon. He hugs Robert, congratulating him. "I wouldn't trade this day for nothin'!" says Osmon " And no gum today," He laughs. "What I want to say is this... Y'all see this woman?" He looks at Claudia, smiling. "Meet my wife. I want everybody to know that I married this woman, not just because there was a need for a wife. I married her because of what The Honorable Elijah Muhummad said about our women. I married her because of what's inside of her. I saw that I had somethin' to work with... she came from a good tree. She has strong southern values. And her Mama instilled God in her. And my mama told me, when you find a good woman, you find a good thing. Treat it accordingly, my step-daddy told me. Come here dad." He comes forth. "Now my dad Albert told me that, sometimes our men make good women out of martyrs." His step-father starts nudging him. Osmon looks at him.

His step-father. A slim, short dark-skinned man with keen features says, nodding his head, pointing his slender fingers. "Yes, men do make good women out of martyrs.

"Now, I'm gon tell you what that means. Well, what it means is this. 'I'm talkin' ta' ya' brothers. You with ya' old fool self. You meet a good woman and you abuse her; cheat on her; spit on her. Ooh yeah, some of you do that too. I know, with your foolish selves. Then when she leaves you or dies, you start thinking about all the good things she did for you. That's when you want to love on her again. There is no need trying to love on a dead woman, because she can't feel anything, when she is dead. She is gone on to somebody else. Every woman you meet after that, you lose her, because you can't stop talking about the one you are haunted by. You walk around in love with a ghost, and that's your punishment." Everybody laughs, telling him that he's right.

"Now everybody, come on now." A jolly big-boned sister, with a happy face, comes up to the front. "Alright everybody, time to cut this delicious cake, I been sweating over the oven with."

All of the cameras were crowded around Osmon and Claudia, like celebrities, as Claudia cuts the cake. Cameras are flashing, all over the place. When Claudia reaches to give Osmon a piece of cake... at that very moment, their eyes meet with tears of joy. Osmon says to himself, *Matri always says, 'The eyes are the windows to the soul'....* "I believe I met my soul mate," says Osmon.

Claudia says to herself. *I'clare I'm the happiest lady in the world, right now.*

CHAPTER 17

MAN TO MAN

Matri and Ramone meet at the Town Café, on Hasley Street, next door to his business. "So, tell me Matri. How did you like Lena Horne?"

"Ramone, I think she's truly awesome. It's needless to say, how beautiful she is, and I really like, "Stormy Weather.""

Ramone gazes at Matri. "Matri, needless to say, your beauty is an icon. It carries its own symphony."

"You sure know what to say to a girl." Matri blushes.

Ramone says, "Matri there's something I've been wanting to say to you, for a while."

"What is it?" she asks.

"Matri, you can have anything you want, and more, if you come with me into my world." Ramone pleads with Matri.

Matri is perplexed. "What world is that?"

Ramone tries to entice Matri. "The world of fine cars, minks, beautiful homes, and traveling all across the universe. ...Be extravagant.... if you want."

Matri is being facetious, "Hmmm… it sounds inviting."

Sounding charismatic, Ramone continues, "You can meet some very rich white influential men and women, who get anything their heart desires." He pauses, "You know Matri, a man would pay quite a bit of money, just to spend one hour with you... black or white. Of course, you wouldn't waste your time with a poor black man. He's a waste of your beauty and time."

Matri interrupts him. "Ramone, I have to go to the ladies' room."

"Sure, baby." Ramone thinks to himself, as she walks away. *My heart seems to be torn between business and pleasure.* He looks at Matri and he starts to feel for her. Filled with passion, he slowly starts withdrawing away from her. *I've never felt this way before. It's no use in me trying to have her for myself. I wish that I could, but I couldn't appreciate you baby.* He hits the table. The people turns around, looking at him. Acting schizophrenic, he switches over his personality to a cold calculating person. *I could make big money off of her. White men would kill, to have her.* He pauses. "Yeah baby."

"Ramone... Ramone... are you still with me, here?" Matri sits down.

He coldly stares at her, blinking his eyes quickly, "Oh, I'm sorry baby. I guess I drifted for a minute."

Matri seems a little disturbed. "Ramone, it's a little late. I don't want to worry Mama."

"Yes, yes of course. But Matri, you never got a chance to see my office next door. I got everything set up for business. Just take a look at it. it'll only take fifteen minutes."

He opens the door. "Okay, here we go."

Matri's eyes roam the place. "This is very impressive, Ramone."

He questions. "Do you think you could be my secretary for a minute, until I find one? I have to go away for a week on business. When I come back, we'll talk about the things we've discussed at the café. I'm leaving this Monday. I'll be back Sunday."

Matri accepts his proposal. "Okay, that's a sure shot. Besides, I'm not working now anyway, since Mr. Krutz's death."

"Matri, you couldn't prevent his death, so don't trip over it, baby," says Ramone.

Matri exhales. "I know."

"Well, let me get you home. I need to pack."

Sunday at 8:00 am... the phone rings. Thaddeus says, "Man I need to talk to you."

"Oh yeah. My pleasure baby, you wanna meet at my home?" asks Ramone.

"Okay, my man."

Ramone looks at his watch. Hour later... the bell rings. Thaddeus walks in with dignity, wearing a long black cashmere coat, hat with black gloves. He observes Ramone's place. Ramone, who is wearing an expensive bachelor's robe. He proudly watches Thaddeus, observing his home.

"This is some pad, you have here, man."

He sniffs, taking off his coat. "Thank you, have a seat. Can I get you something to drink?"

"No man, this isn't exactly... a sociable house call," warns Thaddeus.

"Okay," says Ramone, sitting across from Thaddeus on the couch.

Sounding debonair. "I'm going to get right to the point, my man. I have a book to complete. I want you to leave Matri alone. You and I both know that you're no good for her."

Ramone tilts his head, and charmingly says, "Is that right my man? I have just as much right to the lady as you. Now, we both know the problem for both of us, is a matter of who she wants."

"Ramone, I'm so glad destiny led me to her path before you did. I had a chance to instill in her mind, what real beauty does for her. Believe me, she knows it's only for a chosen few, that can capture the true essence of it. Not some worldly charismatic, charmer." Thaddeus gives a slight smile.

Flaunting himself, Ramone says, "Yeah, my man. Let me teach you something. I've always hung around older women." He sniffs, "My uncle taught me quite a bit about women. He was a womanizer. He would say, 'Just be real tender with them. Flatter them, they're very vain'. "You know what made it so great man?" He proudly stands up. "I was already in college and was no dummy. But of course, you know that I was on the Dean's list." He swirls around, snapping his finger, "Da... damn, I was smart," He says with arrogance. "And good-looking, of course," he chuckles.

Thaddeus sits with his face resting on his fist, studying Ramone. He quietly says, "Umm, condescending. Don't flatter yourself too much, now. You revel in the lowest part of the gutter...with a combination of a saint and the devil."

Ramone flinches, "Ah, ah, ah, let's be nice about this," he says cunningly, "I read books on the anatomy of the female body. After all, I was in school to become a gynecologist," he smirks. "I began to understand what the body needed for stimulus and responses. Have you ever wondered why the women called me, 'Doc, Baby'?"

Facetiously, Thaddeus says, "You're good man, very charismatic." He sniffs, rubbing his nose.

Thaddeus is curious about him sniffing." Man you have a cold?"

He ignores him, "Man, women love a smooth charismatic man. Demonstrating to them, that I loved their bodies more than they did... they loved it. In a very melodious way, I would always describe their bodies from head to toe." With disgust, he says, "They are so very vain. They should be barred, from church!"

Thaddeus analyzes Ramone. "Ummm... is that right?"

Ramone boasts, "So it's easy to convince them, that they are a commodity. And no man should have it for nothing. And no matter how hard they try to be something, they'll never amount to anything, without me."

Thaddeus holds him in contempt. "Beauty and perversion, what a book I could write: "The woman who is disdainful." One woman's poison, is another man's cure. You'll meet your match sooner or later... they're out there man... no doubt," says Thaddeus.

Ramone stands away from Thaddeus, walking gracefully back and forth. He's watching him as he talks... like a game of chess. "You know Thaddeus, I believe like the hippies. It's your thing, do what you wanna do with it." He prides himself. "I liked Cain in the Bible." He stares at Thaddeus, intensely. "You do know, there is such a thing as evil people, like us around?"

Thaddeus snaps his finger, "You're clever, my man. But then, the devil is very clever."

"Yes he is, that's why I used everything. Learning what made them laugh, cry, and even blush. When they were sad, I was their best listener, using compassion and psychology. When you get the mind, the body automatically comes." He smiles, "You know, they are funny creatures. Actually, I'm intrigued and amused by them." He looks up shaking his head. "They possess a kind of power and charm, that they are not aware of," he exhales, "Thank goodness."

Thaddeus gets up, walking around graciously; standing erect like a lawyer. "You know what Ramone. I sat there very patiently listening to you, because I found you in college to be a very interesting guy, older of course. The carnal passions, that women had for you in college, fed their vanity even more. Even though, some said that you seemed to have so much disdain for women. I always wanted to know what made you tick, and now I know."

Ramone smiles at him, cunningly. "What... what?" asks Ramone.

Thaddeus makes a gesture pointing his right finger. "Man, isn't it a shame you can't feel. You're numb to the fact, you're clueless my man. Wouldn't you just love to..." He pauses. "No... that's too strong of a word for you... wouldn't you..." Emphatically he says, "...just like to be able to experience feelings, and real emotions of love?" Thaddeus says with passion, "Man, you oughtta try it. There ain't nothin' like it, man."

Ramone's eyes flutter. " Who me?" he says.

Thaddeus says sympathetically, "Oh man, I figured you out. You just wish you could have Matri. But I realize, there is no real war here. You can't have her, even if you wanted to. You'll destroy any woman you touch. And it kills you to know that."

Ramone yells. "You don't know what the hell you're talking about!" He grabs Thaddeus viciously and Thaddeus flips him onto the floor.

Thaddeus breathes furiously. "Man, I don't fight a man in his home!" Thaddeus reaches for his hands, to let him up. Ramone refuses, pushing away from Thaddeus, getting up. Closely encircling each other... staring into each other's eyes.

"What happened to you, my man?" asks Thaddeus.

Ramone starts acting schizophrenic, sniffing, and laughing crazily. His face frowns, crying out with agony. "Yes! Man, I envy you." He starts walking slowly around, staring at Thaddeus with expressions of jealousy and envy. "You're right, man." Gritting his teeth, looking away, "Oh, I want her. I'm mesmerized, by her exotic beauty. I have strong feelings for her." Breathing heavily, he says, "Like a poet's passion." His personality changes again, viciously saying, "But my woman-hating passion, is still very much alive. And... sometimes, on the flip side of the coin, I hate her with a passion, as well."

Thaddeus, is fixated on him, shaking his head, "Mannn."

Ramone exhales. Eyes flutters, looking nauseated and tired. "I... I'm sick... hurting, man—you're right!... I feel so damn empty... shallow, man," eyes riams ariybd, " It's so painful because...." He pauses, gazing at Thaddeus with jealousy and contempt. Emphatically he says, "I'm not like you... I'm tor... torn-man...." He looks queerly, "Is this love I'm feeling?" He grabs Thaddeus's arm, shaking, looking at him with gloom and resentment.

Thaddeus says with compassion, "Man, this is deep. My man... as Black men, we all are in pain, for one reason or another. Some are conscious of it, and some aren't." He holds tightly on to Ramone's arm. "We've been hurt bad. We don't realize that we have a soul. And we've been down so long, that we don't even realize we're down, man. My father, man. I've never met my dad, man." Looking teary-eyed into Ramone's eyes, he continues, "Mama says, he died before I was born. Just wish to God, he hadn't before I got a chance to know him. Sometimes, I feel a void because of it. I just wished that I could've held his hands, and taken just one walk with him before he died. I watched mama work so hard man, for me. We need that man's strength. Slavery has done a job on the Black man... always taking, but never giving us anything."

Ramone pours himself a drink, while leaning against the fireplace, staring at his mom's portrait. "I used to see women as a divinity. Hmmm, but now, I see them as abominable, unchaste 'things.' As much as I love my dear beautiful sister, and all that she is. I'd prostitute her...given the chance."

Thaddeus stares with shocked eyes. He shakes his head, buckling in his lips.

Ramone looks up at the portrait, mouth shivering with pain. "My man, I never told anyone but, my mom made me ill, when I discovered who she really was. I had to go on a sabbatical... taking off for two years after high school. My little sister talked me into going back to school. Yes, my mother was a rolling stone. Slept with any man she rolled up on... skilled charmer. Her husband, who I thought was my dad, used to beat her. I loved my mother, she was so beautiful, mulatto. I used to want a woman that reminded me of her. I could never understand why dad would beat on her, so viciously. I thought mother was a madame, until..." He pauses...."I found out, they were just alike. I caught her in the bed twice, with my dad's brother and with the man next door ... I used to smell the stench of sex on her. I heard men talking about the things she used to do to them…" He cries, yelling, " She was a damn whore! I don't know who my real dad is, man," tormented eyes, he says, "She lied to me, man."

Both of their faces were filled with gloom. "She charmed me. I put her up on a pedestal, and she let me down man!" He yells, with tears flowing downing his cheeks. They stand, in the middle of the floor, holding each other's arms. Finally, they sit down on the couch.

"You know Ramone… I'm writing a book entitled, "Estranged Soul of The Black Man." "Man, we have to go deep."

Ramone says, "Sad part about it, I don't know if I can change man. I don't even have the desire… and that's where it starts. You talking about damaged goods… here I am in living color, baby."

"No, don't ever tell yourself that man," warns Thaddeus.

"Man, I was a gynecologist at St. Luther's Hospital. I was damn good, too. I kept having this hurt. This deep pain inside of me, man. I got tired of it. I decided to numb it with drugs, so I started stealing drugs from the medicine cabinet. I mean, who would've ever thought it was me. One day the head man of the hospital caught me with a needle in my arm. He then figured it out… how the last two patients died. He couldn't understand why I was shaking, while performing surgery on these women." He pauses, "They didn't want to ruin the reputation of the hospital, so they did it secretly. They said that I had a nervous breakdown from too much stress. I went to a convalescent home, but could never practice again. But I didn't give the drugs up completely, I'm still in pain. I snort cocaine, from time to time." He sniffs." That white horse, the Madame."

"Matri says, we're in the box. I see it more and more man… just how we're going to get out, is one thing," Thaddeus says.

"Matri's got a good point," says Ramone.

"We can't give up." Thaddeus pulls out his pen.–A Muslim Brother told me that 'the ink of a scholar is worth more than the blood of a Martyr'. I have high visions and aspirations, of helping to change the world, for the better. Sometimes man, I'd rather write about it, than live it."

"Man, you got me thinking," says Ramone.

CHAPTER 18

THE DEPARTURE

Tuesday noon, Matri gets an unexpected phone call.
"Hello Matri"

"Hi! Mrs. Watenburg, are you okay?"

Voice sounding very weak, "Matri…."

Matri's feels troubled, "What is it, Mrs. Watenburg?"

"I need…" She coughs, wheezing. "I need to see you…" coughs again. …"Right, away."

"Today?"

"Yes, please."

"I'll be right there." Civil starts making noise in the cage. Matri looks back at Civil. "I'll be right back. I know, I said I would spend the day with you and Mama." Ruth comes to the door, staring at Matri. "Mama I have an emergency at Mrs. Watenburg's. I'll be right back." Ruth starts humming, and walks away.

⫤ ⫣

At Mrs. Watenburg's home, Theodore opens the door. "Where is….?" asks Matri.

You could see, a unsettling look in his eyes,"Come upstairs Matri, she's in bed."

Walking on the white plush carpet, Matri's feet sinks down, at least three inches. Mrs. Watenburg's laying in her bed....a bed fit for a Queen. She's wearing a light olive, silk night gown. Her room is decorated with beautiful, rich green, elegant interlaced curtains; made of the finest brocade. A lavish, olive and green bed-spread; and mint silk sheets, of the finest fabric, adorns the bed; along with huge embroidered olive and green pillowcases.

Mrs. Watenburg's gown, looks like she's going to a ball. But she, wearily watches the sand in the hour glass... seeing the countless sand diminish. Her facial expression, has the facade of one who sings opera, performing with a high pitch... over and over. But she must finally bring it to an end... because of tedious exhaustion.

Straining to speak, she says, "Matri darling, come... come here and sit down beside me. I need to talk to you." She starts coughing and wheezing, getting out of breath.

"Mrs. Watenburg, please sit up a minute." Matri holds her up, putting a pillow behind her back.

Her eyes are weak and weary. "Give me some water, dear," voice trembling.

Quietly, Matri says, "Yes ma'am."

"'Lay me... back down, Matri." Matri starts brushing her hair back, out of her face. She exhales, "I'm better this way, for now."

Matri begins to worry.

"Matri...." Mrs. Watenburg pauses.

"Yes," Matri looks in her eyes with love and compassion.

Her voice shivers. "I, I... want you to take me, to that place in the south, where you took Mrs. Annielu."

Matri's heart starts beating rapidly, remembering Mrs. Annielu's same request. Matri looks straight-faced. "Why... Mrs. Watenburg. Why on earth would you want me to take you there?"

Mrs. Watenburg becomes oblivious …eyes Sparkles. "I saw mother last night... just as plain as day. And some, of my other relatives were here, too."

Matri felt a chill. Breathing slowly, she stares into Mrs. Watenburg's eyes. …."I'll take you... to my heaven. When do you want to go?"

Her eyes twinkle. "Matri, can you take me there, tomorrow. We'll… need to leave early. We'll take my private plane," she looks over at Theodore, " Theodore will take us."

Matri looks at Theodore, "He knows, how to fly a plane?"

Winking at Matri, she says, "Yes, he's highly skilled, in a lot of ways. I need to see it as soon as possible," with the look of death in her eyes, she thinks, "Death, is on me."

Happily, Matri says, "I need to take you, in the twilight hours."

"We'll stay at a hotel, that day," says Mrs. Watenburg.

With teary eyes, Matri hugs Mrs. Watenburg, kissing her on the forehead. "Okay, I need to go home and get ready."

She waives at Matri. "You go, my angel… go," says Mrs. Watenburg. As Matri walks away, Mrs. Watenburg starts coughing, terribly. Matri runs back to her side, yelling to Theodore. He runs back into the room. Matri steps back, looking at Theodore put the oxygen mask on her face... their eyes meet with despair. Mrs. Watenburg immediately calms down. She start staring from afar, as if she sees something or someone in her room. Matri and Theodore looks around the room, to see what Mrs. Watenburg is looking at. Then, slowly looking at each other with sadness.

Theodore slightly smiles. "Go Matri."

Matri runs to the car, panting. She thinks to herself, *"What was Mrs. Watenburg staring at, what did she see that we couldn't see? Hattie said, that in childbirth some women don't make it. Three women died right before her eyes, and she saw that same stare, that Mrs. Watenburg shows. It was told to her, that before death, you see your relatives that went before you. Now, I don't know if I want anybody coming, to me…. I think I'd rather see them when I get there.* Matri pauses and chuckles to herself. *I think I need to forget about this, and concentrate on getting home to pack.*

Hours later. Matri is in the room, packing. "Matri. Lawd child, where ya' goin' now?"

She hugs Ruth. "Mama I'm going south with Mrs. Watenburg. I'll be back Thursday."

Ruth just walks away, shaking her head. Ruth says to herself, *I'm just not gon' say nothin', ain't no use in me talkin' no moe..."*

The bell rings. Matri looks out of the window. She notice, Mrs. Watenburg is looking upstairs, smiling at her. She thinks, *Hmmm, strange... she look so beautiful. That's, that same smile, with those blue eyes and red hair; she had when she took me, out to lunch that first day."* Matri runs into Ruth's room, kissing her good-bye. "Mama they're here. Tell Claudia to take care of Civil until I get back, if you're not up to it."

⇌ ⇌

It's Wednesday... The sun is about to decline; approaching the night, like a ship passing through the sea; with its workers, retiring after a hard days work.

Matri, Mrs. Watenburg and Theodore quietly ride down, the black asphalt country road, in a rented Limousine.

Matri thinks, as she looks out of the limousine. *Who said, you have to be rich, to be able to see the best scenery? Hmmm... well, what they are about to see, is majestic.*

Theodore says to himself, smiling. *I can't wait to see, what Matri has to show us.*

Mrs. Watenburg glances at Matri from the side, thinking, *Yes, my angel... that's what you are to me.* Imitating Matri's phrase, she thinks. *I clare... you, my dear Matri, gave my heart something, that I've been longing for. ...Matri beloved, if all the oceans in the world were full of gold, shining with glitter... the love you gave me would out-shine them all... money can never buy it. Dr. Martin Luther King, Hajjah Malik Shabazz, Beloved Marcus Garvey, and Honorable Elijah Muhammad, had an undying love for people and humanity...yes, so full of love... just like you my angel.*

Matri Thinks, *Nostalgia isn't always so pleasant.* Matri looks around at the scenery of the south, as they ride past the spot where Nosa and Claf were killed.

"Theodore, turn the air conditioner off. The trees are blowing, and I want to smell this fresh country air, as it hits my face," Mrs. Watenburg insists.

Matri says, "Well Mrs. Watenburg, this is where I was born."

"I must admit Matri, the country scenery has so much life. The different colored vegetables, seem like they are laying in their own separate beds. So are the colorful flowers, decorating the fields. Of course, this is nothing like the city, with its people and its bright lights. It's a circus, with everyone stepping on one another's foot." Mrs. Watenburg pauses, looking at Matri, with a big smile. "I could sense a tranquility, and a naturalness. I could visualize you, in this southern scenery," she looks up at Matri.

As they approach Matri's safe haven, Matri feels, a chill run through her body. "Here we go, let's get out... here," says Matri

Theodore and Mrs. Watenburg, takes a long look, at this peculiar spot of Matri's.

"Come, come, I need this too," says Matri.

Theodore, lets Mrs. Watenburg out of the car, helping her to walk up to Matri's heavenly abode. Mrs. Watenburg looks back, as if looking into a whole new, dimension.

Matri gestures with her hands. "The time is right, come over here... right here. Don't say a word... just look. Then... I'll let you enter your own cave... in, your mind." Matri looks at both of them saying, "We should all have our own cave to enter, when we need it."

Matri, Mrs. Watenberg and Theodore are standing at the edge of the cliff, holding hands.

At that moment, the twilight has snuck in. The stars lay like dice, thrown against the black velour of the night. It is the most beautiful, captivating, picturesque scenery; that would make anyone, want to take just one glimpse of it… before leaving this world. No one moved, no one said a word. They, are just looking on, into the galaxy. Time is an illusionary part of the imagination… hypnotized, by total peace.

Mrs. Watenburg thinks, eyes twinkling, *Yes, yes my angel, I could certainly understand, just why Mrs. Annielu would come here. You could never get this kind of peace, anywhere else. I'm seeing my whole life flash before me.* She giggles inside. *I feel like a little girl again.* Mrs. Watenburg starts breathing deeply. *Ohh, I feel so youthful.*

They continue to stand still, in silence. Matri's face beams. She thinks, *Isiah… you asked, 'Where is God…?'* She exhales. Humbly she thinks … *God said, 'Be still, and know that… I Am God.' He's everywhere, beloved.*

Mrs. Watenburg's aura is radiant, just like a shining star. She thinks. "*Yes, my eyes have seen the coming of the glory of the Lord. And I may not get there with you, Matri… but I hope to see you again.*" Mrs. Watenburg looks over at Theodore… standing peacefully, with the biggest smile on his face. All of a sudden Mrs. Watenburg turns around, looking towards the cave, and says, "Mrs. Annielu?"

Matri and Theodore slowly turn around, staring at Mrs. Watenburg. Matri looks at the cave. Mrs. Watenburg stumbles backwards. Matri and Theodore catches her.

"I think we better go now, I'm very tired," says Mrs. Watenburg.

They walk Mrs. Watenburg, slowly down to the car. "Mrs. Watenburg, I'll sit up front with Theodore, you need to lie down… you're tired," says Matri.

Matri and Theodore remain very silent, as they ride down the road back to Hotel Balley. No one could see each other, because of the pitch darkness, of the southern night. They are still reminiscing, from the beauty they had seen. They are communicating to each other, through mental telepathy. Mrs. Watenburg, never said another word. She lays resting, peacefully. Matri looks back at her, seeing only a glimpse of a silhouette ….thinking, she says, *Ummm, she seems so peaceful, sleeping.*

Theodore exhales, pulling into the hotel's parking area. "We're here, Matri. I sure could use a good night's rest, after this wonderful experience you shared with us. Thank you, for wanting to share it with Mrs. Watenburg and me."

Theodore looks back at Mrs. Watenburg. He pauses, staring at her, calling her name. "Mrs. Watenburg."

Matri looks back at her, lying in the back seat with her eyes closed; seemingly, without a care in the world. "Mrs. Watenburg, she calls again."

They look at each other and jump out of the car. Theodore opens the door, yelling and shaking her. "Mrs. Watenburg!"

Matri gulps, "Oh, my God… Theodore." Matri and Theodore stares at each other, grabbing Mrs. Watenburg, holding her.

⇒+ +⇐

At the funeral, Matri and Theodore are the last two standing at Mrs. Watenburg's gravesite. Matri looks around, as if she could feel a presence…Theodore holds her arms, tightly. "Throw, Matri."

Matri threw the dirt on the coffin. Then she placed a white rose on her coffin, saying, "Mrs. Watenburg, I may not get there with you, but I hope to see you again." Theodore looks around, as if he could sense a presence. Matri holds his hand tightly. He throws the dirt on the coffin. Matri and Theodore walk towards the limousine. Theodore opens the door for her to get into the car, saying, "Madame, where can I take you?" He bows to her bowing.

Exhausted, Matri says, "Please take me home."

"Matri," Theodore says, "She wants you to keep this limousine. Told me, it's for a lady."

Matri stares off, "Theodore, we'll talk. I'm just tired, right now. After all, you're going to be at the house for awhile. I don't want anyone to know about what she left me."

He respects her wishes, taking orders from her, now. "Okay, I'll take you home."

CHAPTER 19

THE UNFOLDING

It's the month of July and Taresa gets a visit from Dawn. "Oh, Taresa it's so good to see you. You look beautiful.," says Dawn.

Taresa's dressed in all white Muslim MGT attire. Her husband smiles from ear to ear.

"Yes... this is my wife, my queen's restaurant," her husband says.

Osmon and Claudia, stares at each other, smiling and blushing. Everybody starts laughing. "What y'all, laughing at?" asks Osmon.

"Man, I gotta give it to you, this food is good. These sisters sure know the way to a man's heart," says Robert. Sadie frowns at Robert. "Ah, come on now. You know they don't have anything, on your cooking, baby."

"Ya' sure 'bout that Robert?" asks Sadie.

"I'm darn sure about that." He chuckles, winking at her, real hard.

Isiah says, "Osmon, Dawn and me wanna' thank ya' for givin' me the job. 'Cause it's sure helpin' us look towards the future, for marriage."

"Yeah man, it's helpin' me 'til ma' case comes through, too," says Hezikiah.

Osmon proudly says, "Hey man, I have an obligation to help my brothers, and b'sides we're family."

"Hey, did anybody find out what happened to Lorraine?" asks Taresa.

"No, I just don't kno' what happened ta' that girl," says Claudia.

Brother Anthony quickly walks in, with a paper. "A s-salaamu 'alaykum."

"Hey, my brother you need to sit down for a minute and get yourself some food, you been at it hard," says Osmon.

"Brother Osmon," says Brother Anthony. "I know we don't read the newspaper, but I was out fishin,' and ran across this brother. He was tellin' me about this girl that got killed. He said her name was Lorraine, and I asked to see the paper, and there she was. A picture of our Lorraine."

Everybody echoes, "What!"

Claudia grabs the paper. "Oh, ma' God. It say, she was shot in the chest four times, and the head once. She waz killed by a old rich cat, 73 years old... a white cat."

He said, "She used him, so he shot her five times, because she got five thousand dollars from him... five times."

"Let me see that paper Claudia," says Osmon.

"Well you both tried to save her," says Taresa.

Taresa's husband says, "I saved my Queen. Now she's my beautiful wife." Taresa blushes.

"We better eat up, 'cause the meeting starts in an hour," says Osmon. He gives Claudia a gentle hug.

"Sure," says Robert.

"You know, I just want to thank each and every one of you for supporting me at my restaurant tonight," says Taresa's husband.

"Yeah who kno's, we all might become Muslims," says Hezikiah.

Osmon has a big smile on his face.

Two weeks later.... Saturday night. Matri answers the phone: "Hello."

"Matri, Ramone wants you to meet him at his new office."

"What time... 9:00. Okay, I'll be ready." She watches the bird as he sleeps in the cage. "Civil you look so peaceful there, with your soft white fur. Representing innocence and purity. I gave you the right name... Civil. So peaceful, never bothering anyone." She pauses, "Oh Civil... sometimes I feel very guilty, for caging you in like this." Reaching into the cage, she kisses him on the forehead. "I have to leave you again. I promise I'm going to make it up to you, and Mama both."

Upon arriving at the office, Matri rings the bell... feeling a presence behind her. Turning around, she notices the bag lady across the street, starting to come towards her. Getting nearer to her, Matri heard her whining, like a very disturbed person. As she walks by, she keep staring at her, whining. Luther opens the door, with an over-exaggerated smile. His piercing blue eyes distracts her away from the bag lady.

With a southern drawl, he says "Why ya' just come right on in, and have a seat. Ramone will be back in a minute. He had ta' make an emergency call. You kno', with the type of business he's got, clients call him all times of the day and night. It's almost like bein' a doctor," he shakes his head.

"Well okay, I have nothing but time," says Matri.

"Matri," he says amiably, spitting out tobacco juice," Why don't cha,' let me fix ya' somin' ta' drink?"

Pleasantly Matri says, "A coke."

Cordially, he says, "A coke? Ya' sure, ya' don't want somthin,' a little stronger than that?"

Matri reflects, "I use to drink wine, but I stopped."

Obliging her, he says, "Okay, let me go in the back and see if we have a coke." Luther goes in the back room. "I'm sure we do," he says to himself; pulling out a little bottle, pouring whtie powder, into Matri's coke. "Let me give this wench somethin,' ta' put 'er just where I need 'er to be, with no problem." He comes out of the back, acting very obsequious. "Okay gal, now here we go." He spits again, spitting the tobacco out, with his right eye jumping. He's fixated on her, with the devils work on his mind.

Matri looks at him, for that quick second. When he used the word gal, and chewing tobacco. She has a quick, flashback… sort of a deja vu. She thinks quickly, Umm, that southern expression, too.

His eyes twinkle, staring at her with lust, as he drinks rum and coke. "Let's just chit -chat, until Ramone comes back."

Matri thinks, *There he goes again… another expression. He's from the, deep south. I never recognized his voice like that before… strange… not necessarily, just a coincidence, maybe.* Matri drinks the coca cola.

"Now, ya'-sure drink that coca cola, like ya' real thirsty."

Matri gulps. "As a matter of fact, I am."

"Well, don't hesitate ta' ask fer' another one, if ya' want. We might as well keep ourselves busy til' Ramone git' back. What kin-da music ya' like gal?"

Matri stares at him again. "Oh… okay, do you have any of Lena Horne's music… "Stormy Weather?""

He gazes at Matri. "I see Ramone is rubbin' off on ya'—I tell ya', seem like that's all he like." Luther gets up, walking to the corner to a small record player.

Matri listens attentively. She begin to feel, very dizzy. "Oooh, can—I have another coke please."

Mischievously, he asks, "Are ya' sure now, gal?"

"Ah-ha", she says, smiling.

He goes in the back room again. "I'll put a little more of this in 'er drink, don't want 'er ta' kno what I'm doin' to 'er."

Matri drinks half of it, while listening to Lena Horne. He watches Matri, staring at her with lust and viciousness in his eyes. She's just too stupefied, to notice it.

"Hey Matri, want chu' ta' come with me fer a minute... need ta' show ya' somethin'."

Matri gets up feeling, dizzy. "Ohhh... ah... O-kay."

He takes her to the cellar door. "Now ya' just watch ya' step gal."

He flips on the cellar light, helping her down the stairs. Getting her to the bottom of the steps, he knocks her out cold, tying her to a pole on the floor.

Breathing angrily, he says, "Ya' black wench."

An hour has passed. Matri comes to, in the dark. The drug is almost wearing off. Realizing her feet and hands are tied up with a rope, she starts twisting her hands around to untie it, but she can't. She keeps looking around, not able to see anything. Now, she realizes that she's in trouble. She starts panting, feeling afraid of the unknown. Laying quietly, eyes roaming around in the darkness. She jerks, "Huh?" Feeling something big, going across her legs, nibbling at her toes, and scratching her. She jumps, thinking to herself. "Ohhh ...a mouse, no... too big to be a mice—a rat!" Fifteen minutes later, she feels something slowly crawling up her legs, all over her body. She thinks quickly, "Oh, God, a snake?!" Being scared straight... the thoughts come to her mind like magic; "God said, 'Be still, and know, that I—Am God'. Freezes, like a block of ice; closing her eyes, not breathing; going to her favorite spot on the cliff, looking into the heavenly abode... not saying a word... no need to talk..

Finally, it stops! But, still no light. Twenty minutes later, she begin to hear something breathing hard, then sensing a warmness on her face. It feels like a hand starts rubbing on her, slowly moving to her breast; untying her legs, separating her legs as he rubs her down to her feet... then all over again. Then a voice says, "Ya' kno' massa, always did like ya' black wenches. They say he like the smell of your body." He sniffed across her hair, face and neck. The smell of tobacco and slob slithers down her face. "Always wanted ta' do that. Now, I come across one of the prettiest black wenches, I ever seen in ma' life." He whispers, "They call 'er... Matri."

Matri listens, realizing it was Luther.

With squinched eyes he tells her, "Gal, Ramone was gon' make ya' his number one call gal. That's how much he wanted chu."

Matri finally, speaks up. "What do you mean, a call girl?"

He twitters. "Now gal, ya' don' kno' what a call gal is?"

Wearily, Matri says, "No."

Eyes widening, staring at her crazily, "Member when we went ta' Fort Dix?"

Matri frowns. "Ummm."

"He took ya' there ta' break ya' in, and ta' let the soldiers and the rich men, git' a good look at cha'. And I mean when we left, Ramone's phone was jumpin' off the hook. Wooo," he whistles. "Ya' shoulda' heard the prices, them men give 'em for just a half-hour wit' cha. Four rich men wanted to buy ya' fa' themselves, as a steady call gal. I tell ya', all the other prostitutes was jealous."

Matri's heart is paining over the news. Defiantly she says, "Tell me why I should believe you, of all people!"

"Well if ya' gon' b'leeve anybody, ya' better b'leeve me outta all people. Cause the night when ya' was wit 'em, after ya' went ta' see Lena Horne, he told me how he present thangs ta ya'. Like fine homes, cars, travelin'... I mean what chu' think he was tellin' ya' them thangs fer'." He grabs her hair. "Now darlin', he got this business right here, prostituting gals all over different states and countries. He ain't no private detective no-how, now. He pass a millionaire... it don' made 'em filthy rich, already."

Matri realizes, there is some truth to it. She becomes quiet, disheartened.

He tattles. "He use ta' be a doctor, but he messed that up, messing with drugs. He killed two women on the operatin' table, cause of it. They found out and fired 'em fer' it."

Matri's mind went back to the night she was at his house, and saw a doctor's bag in his closet.

He gets up from the floor, turning on the light. Matri hollers. With squinting eyes... Luther stands before her, with a big snake around his neck, chewing tobacco. He starts playing with it. "Oh he's harmless, not all snakes bite cha'. Just look at 'em… this is what was crawlin' on ya'. Don't fret I'm puttin' 'em away. Got somthin,' gotta git from ya'. Somin' real nice… then, I'm gon' kill ya," says with venom.

He comes back, kneeling down on the floor, eyes piercing. He puts his hands on her chin. "Yeah, I'm gon take it." He spits in her face. " Ain't gon' give ya,' nothin' fer' it now. Ya' kno' Ramone have a, love hate fer' ya' too. He want cha' just fer' himself, and then he hate cha' at the same time. He got a deep hatred, fer' ya' gals too.

He comes closer to Matri, rippin' her blouse open. Matri spits at 'em, he slaps her in the face twice. "Now wench, what chu 'gon' do that fer'."

Then Matri has another flashback, to the south. Thinking, she visualizes him standing on the porch when her and Claudia was going out one night. "People say your family was suspected, of belonging to the KKK," she says with hostility, "I, know you. You used to come home every summer, from the city people."

He smirks. "Now, what take ya' so long ta' figure me out, Matri. Ma' family, is the KKK. I got it in me too." He spits. "They say, ah apple don't fall too far from the tree."

"You venomous, diseased...." She spits at him again.

He pulls out his gun, pointing it in Matri's face. He unties Matri's feet. "Get up, nappy head wench!" He yells, getting the whip off of the table. "Now I'm gon' treat cha' worse than massa, b'fore I have sex with ya—I'm gon' whip ya,' like a dog. Then I'm gon' have sex with ya.' And I ain't gon' pay ya' nothin' fer' it!" Looking psychotic, he gazes at her. "I hate cha' just as much as Ramone or more…ya' black wench…." He pauses. "Ya' see,

Ramone don' kno', I planned ta' win his trust and take everythang from 'em, in time... even you. But I'm gon' kill ya'...I—gotta... ya' kno' too much...." He spits on 'er.

"Is that--right" A charismatic voice comes across, from around the stairs. Ramone has his gun pointing on the back of Luther's head. "If you move, I'm going to blow your sick head off."

He spits, then chuckes,"Now, the pot can't call the kettle black now, can it?" asks Luther.

Treacherously, Ramone says, "You fool, don't you know I made a pact with the Devil! There is such a thing, some people gave their souls over to the Devil. I'm his product... his son. Luther, the devil don't trust anybody...in the worlds of the Devil. There is no such thing as trust, because he don't know what—he might do... the conscious is gone, my man. Why-I scare myself sometimes. That's the nature of the Devil. Luther, my man, if I can't trust myself... how in the hell could I trust you.... excuse my expression, please... will you? You've played a very risky game, of Russian roulette, dig it?"

"Well—ya' right, ma'—man. The game is on—if you don't remove your gun..." He presses his gun to Matri's head, twisting the tobacco around in his mouth, "It's Russian roulette," he chuckles, "Thats-right."

Matri sees her life, flash before her eyes. "Yes Mama... I love you all. And I may not get there with you but, I hope to see you again." Ramone and Luther listens to her.

"My beautiful, black pearl... I won't let him harm you. The very part of me, that wants to love you dearly, has the power over me right now. " says Ramone, with love in his eyes.

In the meantime.... It's midnight, Ruth's tossing and turning in her sleep. She sits straight up in the in the dark. "Matri... Matri...

Lawd, I'm feelin' ma' child, Matri." Ruth gets up out of the bed, and gets down on her knees, praying in the dark. "Lawd', she always git' at the end of ma' bed, layin' cross ma' bed, justta massagin' ma' feet." She say, "Heaven lay at the feet of the mother." That's the most beautiful thang, a child could say ta' er' mother. If that's true Lawd', she don' a lot of good fa' me. Ma' child Matri is justta troublin' ma' spirit. Wherever she is, I don' kno'… but take ma' hands precious Lawd, and let me touch 'er and guide 'er back ta' me safely." Ruth starts humming and singing to the Lawd. "Oh ma' Lawd, you a precious Lawd."

In the basement… "Luther, put the gun down man!" Ramone commands him.

Right eyes flickering, he nods his head, "If you say it again, I'm gon' kill er!"

Then all of a sudden! The snake comes out of the closet. Luther looks away at the snake. Matri grabs the gun. Ramone grabs Matri's hands. They all start tussling with the gun. The gun goes off, and Matri screams. Ramone yells, "Oh—no—Matri!" Three shots are fired. Ramone said, "What!—Oh–no! Then, five more shots are fired. Psss… psss … pssss… pssss . ….The snake hisses… moving slowly, then freezes like a block of ice.

CHAPTER 20
THE LETTER

Monday morning, while sitting at the kitchen table having a cup of coffee ... Verna tries to find a verse in the Bible, to send a card, with the words that will comfort the family. Eyes looking bewildered, her slender fingers, holds onto the Bible tightly. Slamming the Bible down, she gets up from the table, pacing back and forth. Looking at the paper again, raising her hands up in the air, she talks aloud to herself. "Okay, okay... I have to do this! If now isn't the best time, when is the best time? Come on girl, wake up and smell the coffee! I'm not going to work today. It's early, I should be able to catch them ...it's only 8:30 a.m." She walks into her bedroom, noticing she hasn't taken her rollers out of her hair yet. "Oh girl, never mind your hair. You don't have time to worry about hair right now. I'll take the parkway, hopefully it isn't backed up."

Time is passing... Verna keeps ringing the bell impatiently. Stepping off of the porch, looking around the side of the house, she thnks, "I don't see anybody's car around. Then looking up at the windows. "The curtains are closed... from the looks of it, there's just...no one home...Ummmm, I know what to do... I'll put them in the mailbox. Let me see if I have a paper clip in my pocketbook… Oh, thank God, here's one. Oh how I treasure you, you little thing, you. I'll write this…please give this to Mama… she'll know who to give them to, the names are on the letters." She clips them together, putting the letters in the mailbox.… "There." She exhales. "That's better than waiting, too late. Okay mama, I did what you told me to do. You'll turn over in your grave if I don't do this… don't want you haunting me."

⊷ ⊶

The court is in session at 9:00 a.m. A pot-bellied white policeman stands adjacent from the judge's seat, with his hands folded in front of his stomach. He stands beside the court-reporter, and remains standing until a robed justice is seated, following the traditional chant. Everyone is trying to sit patiently, until the Judge comes out for the verdict. Another policeman, standing up like a soldier on guard, is next to the court reporter.

A voice says, "Here comes the judge, now. Everyone rise please, and remain standing until the judge is seated. At the sound of the gavel, please be seated." Everybody stands up quickly, like it's judgment day, waiting to be judged. The judge comes out, wearing bifocal glasses. He has thick black hair, a very thick mustache, and part on the side of his head. His appearance, remids you of Hitler. He looks around the courtroom… his facial expression is, knavish. "Sit." Everybody sits immediately.

"Hey, this white cat looks like Hitler, man," says Robert.

"Yeah, I see man," says Hezikiah.

Suddenly, a door opens. Robert and Hezikiah freeze, looking up at the judge. The judge looks ahead, and everyone turns around to see who it was. A tall dark brown-skinned woman, drags her feet with chains tied around her ankles, and chains around her wrists. She is wearing a big black, crinkly afro.

Ruth cries, "Oh Lawd, ma' Matri."

220

"Oh Mama," says Isiah, "It's gon' be alright. This ain't the end, this is only the beginnin'." Dawn leans her head on Isiah's shoulders, crying.

"Matri!" Claudia cries out. Osmon holds onto Claudia. Robert holds onto Sadie as she wipes her eyes. Hezikiah just stares, with shock.

The judge slams his gavel down.

"Quiet in the court." The silence is, immediate. The judge stares at Matri with silent obscenity. She looks through the judge, saying to herself, *My best weapon is to remain aloof. Not a word, not even a facial expression.*

It seemed to anger the judge. Matri Cameron, you were found with a deadly weapon, such as a gun. Upon the screening unit, reviews of police reports and interviews, there were no witnesses involved. Not enough proof of self-defense, for bodily harm. Self defense is a justification for conduct that would otherwise be a crime of Involuntary Manslaughter."

"Homicide is the killing of one human being by another, either lawfully or unlawfully. However, murder and manslaughter are unlawful. Consequences for the conviction of Murder may potentially include: Up to life imprisonment, Life in prison with or without parole, or the Death penalty. He looks up at Matri. "You were caught with an illegal weapon, fingerprints prove you cold-bloodedly killed two men. One white, shot in the head and once in the face; and one black, shot three times; once in the head, once in the heart and once in the private area.." He looks up over his glasses at her, saying …" And a snake, shot twice."

"I find you guilty beyond a reasonable doubt, with no witnesses, Guilty of 1st degree murder in both cases. I sentence you to the death penalty. You will be taken to Caldwell Penitentiary until sentenced for the death penalty... the electric chair..." He slams the gavel down, leaving the courtroom with everybody hysterical. Matri cringes... hear pumping fast.

Ruth grabs onto Isiah's arms, yelling "She didn't do it. Ma' baby wouldn't do such a thang." Claudia, Dawn, and Sadie burst out crying. Robert and Hezikiah jumps up flinching, almost going back to 'Nam... ready to take arms. All the policemen put their hands on their guns, staring at Robert and Hezikiah. Isiah notices what's going on, he looks at Robert and Hezikiah, with the facial expression... telling them *no*, then looking at Ruth. Getting their attention to Ruth, they humble themselves. Isiah holds onto Ruth, trying to comfort her.

Ruth's looking up in the air... "Oh Lawd, I kno' she didn't do it. Lawd, Ya' kno' she didn't do it." Ruth looks into Isiah's eyes, pitifully. "She wouldn't do such a thang. Isiah, ya' kno' she wouldn't," Ruth stares away from Isiah, speechless...

Isiah's eyes juts out and flutters, as he tries to hold back the anger, to comfort Ruth. "Mama, I kno' Matri wouldn't kill nobody," he looks up at bench with a vengeance.

Osmon tries to comfort Claudia. She's hysterical. "Come on Claudia, don't let Mama see you like this. Try to be a little strong for Mama," says Osmon.

Thaddeus goes over to Matri, hugging her. "Matri, it ain't over yet. We'll free you."

Robert and Hezikiah walks over Matri, hugging her. "We'll get you the best lawyer to reopen the case. I know it didn't go down like this. There's more to this, I know it is," says Robert.

Matri looks into Ruth's face. She smiles, trying to comfort Ruth. The policeman grabs her by the arm. Matri looks down at his hands, looking up into his face. "It's time to go, let's go," says the policeman. When he pulls her away, Matri looks back at everyone, as she walks, almost tripping from the chains on her feet.

Time seems to have stopped for Matri... as she gets off the bus for prisoners, Matri begin to feel like she's losing it. Too hurt to cry, she thinks to herself, paining. *I... huh... Luther, you and Ramone set me up for a fall,* she shivers, " *Luther, you let a rat and a snake crawl* *all over my body... how cruel... torturous,"* eyes weary, feeling sick to the stomach,* *Ramone, you tricked me too. I thought you adored me, and all along you hated me. You wanted me to sell myself to other men. How dare you!* She trembles, *I 'clare, now don't you know I'm, a lady!* Pitifully, she says, with a straight face, "Ha... don't you know that?" Matri stumbles, putting her hands on her heart. The prison guard holds onto her.

The door opens. A masculine female correction officer, with a very penetrating voice, says, "Step this way," leading Matri into a room with water hoses. "Okay, take everything off."

Matri yells, "Wh... what!" Looking around to run, Matri 's hysterical and emotionally bruised.

The officer demands, "I said, take your clothes off." Matri becomes stubborn, she won't move. The correction officer comes up closer, yelling in her ears, "I said for the last time... get naked!"

Matri's paining. She stares at her, shivering, and speaking with defiance, "I will—not!"

The officer roared at her, eyes scanning out Matri's entire body. "You will!" says the correction officer. She calls for another correction officer.

A black, short husky woman; wearing a afrong; hard-core, corrections officer with teeth protruding; encircles Matri... who stands fearlessly, looking the officers up and down. The husky officer yells, "Get naked! By the time I count to three, you better start taking your clothes off!"

Matri snaps, feeling violated. Smoke comes out of her nose like a chimney, as she becomes the matador for the bulls. In a frenzy, she says, "Go- to-hell... now!" They grab Matri. She blacks out, fighting them viciously.

The officers drags Matri, hurling her to the floor, of a small room in the basement of the prison... bam! She closes the small door, huffing and puffing. The husky correction officer says, "That oughtta cool Ms. Prissy off."

"Yeah... let that wench stay for a week. When she gets out, she'll be good and damn ready to obey the rules. She'll be stripped, before she comes out of that hole."

The next day.... Ruth says with anxiety, "Verna, come on in here and sit down. We got some talkin' ta' do."

Verna sighs... eyes expresses deep conern, "Ruth, my mama gave Matri these letters, to give to me before she died. She said the truth had to be told, 'cause she didn't think Hattie would ever tell you." Ruth holds her head down, shaking it back and fourth. "I'm so sorry, for not telling you sooner." Verna watches Ruth intently, as she reads the letter. "But I didn't know, when would be the best time."

"Oh Lawd, ma' heart is so heavy right now," says Ruth crying, holding onto Verna.

Eyes filled with dejection, she says, "Ruth, I could only imagine, how painful this is for you... with what's happening with Matri... now."

Ruth rocks back and forth, biting on her lips. "I guess ya' did the best ya' could do. Just can't b 'leeve Hattie hurt me like this," says Ruth.

Verna looks tedious, nodding her head. "Ruth, just try to think how much Hattie loves you. She wouldn't do anything to hurt you intentionally. There has to be a good reason behind all of this." Ruth gets, very quiet.

Verna pauses, with sympathetic eyes, "Ruth… are you listening to me, now?"

Ruth reaches her hands out to Verna. "Just leave me be… just leave me be fa' now," says Ruth.

Verna looks at Ruth and sighs. "Okay Ruth, I'm going to leave you, to yourself for now, but I'm calling you tomorrow. I hope you answer the phone, 'cause if you don't... I'm coming back over here." Verna hugs Ruth and walks out of the door.

Three days pass. Matri's feeling exhausted, from no food. They did give her a little water to drink, from time to time. Matri wakes up in the middle of the night, in the dark. Feeling fatigued and hot and not eating. Her mouth is dry from the lack of water. She has feelings of delirium, no light to see by. Trying to come to terms, thinking about Luther and Ramone. *Ramone, I thought you were a friend of mine.* Still paining, placing her hands on her heart, Matri is overtaken by melancholy. She's looking around for air. There is hardly any air in the room. She jumps... "Oh—what is that?... A rat!" She crawls quickly across the floor, laying against the wall.... She jumps again... thinking she feels something crawling across her body. "What! ... A snake!" Sweat pours down her face profusely... delirium has set in. She's crawling across the small room in the dark, rapidly running from wall to wall from the snake... and the rat. Nooo!—noooo!—noooo!... Mama!... no—no. Her head and eyes are turning quickly from side to side. She's panting, feeling all over body, shivering and jumping. Suddenly, telling herself, "Be still! She yells.

⚡ ⚡

In the meantime. It's midnight... Ruth is on her knees again, praying. "Matri ya' gonna wear ma' knees off. Lawd, I could barely go on...this is a hard pain fa' me Lawd. They gon' kill ma' Matri... Lawd, this is so heavy on ma' heart... but... I hurt silently. Matri ma' baby, 'member what I teach chu' child. Ya' gotta pray while ya' in there, with them crazy people." She pauses, "Yay, I walk through the valley of the shadow of death," she says with conviction. "And I will fear, no—evil."

Ruth falls back on the bed, thinking about what Verna told her, holding on to her heart. "Lawd' what this woman tell me, bout'

Hattie lyin ta' me… I could hardly take it. How could Hattie hurt me like this?" Ruth frowns, shaking her head." And Matri don' kno'... how could I tell her at a time like this? Ohhh Lawd, I'm tired now. Now Lawd, ya' tell me if I be patient, ya' would never leave me. Oh Lawd, they gon' give ma' baby the chair. It' hard fa me to hold on this time…I feel like I'm fallen Lawd… and ya' say ya' put no mo on me than I can bear…but Lawd? Ma' precious Lawd." She looks up, "Please forgive me, but seem like ya' don' put too much on me this time, Lawd…" She cries… "Please Lawd, remove this burden off me… I'm in alotta pain, this time." Ruth pauses, holding onto her heart again. "Ma' heart is beatin' fast! Oh Lawd."…"I'm so hurt…" She passes out.

At the prison… It's 12:15 a.m. Matri pauses… "Oh yes, Mama… I walk through the valley of the shadow of death… and I will fear no evil!" She yells, fainting.

Later, Ruth comes to… yelling out, "Claudia! Claudia… help me, help me."

Claudia comes to the room, screaming. "Mama, Mama! What's wrong, Mama?

Ruth pants, "Turn on the light child!"

Claudia tosses and turns nervously, forgetting where the light is. She finds the light.

"Oh ma' Lawd, Claudia!"

Claudia goes to her bed. "What is it Mama?" she cries.

Ruth lays stretched out on her back. She says calmly, "Claudia, didn't I tell ya' ta' turn the light on?"

Claudia gulps… looking back at the light. Her two sons are standing at the door, watching them. Frantically she says, "Mama now, I 'clare... ya' kno' the light is on."

Ruth whispers, "Baby, I can't see. I'm hurt so bad inside." Ruth starts shivering.

Claudia's sons come over to Ruth. Roy and Paul ask, "What's wrong?"

"Grandma, what's wrong?" says Roy.

Paul says, "You always say, trust in the Lawd, grandma."

Somebody's knocking on the front door. "Go get the door Roy," says Claudia.

"Isiah…" Claudia cries… "Mama… Mama… can't see."

"Mama! yells Isiah…"Mama!."

Back, at the prison:

Matri wakes up, hallucinating. "Oh Civil, I miss you dearly." Matri talks to herself, aloud. "Civil, I see you looking at me." Wearily she says, "Why are looking at me like that... what have I done? Oh, you're in your cage, so I' need to go into my cave... okay…. virtually... I know. Let's talk Civil… will you talk to me? Civil I'm lonely, what about you? Yeah I know, think about how lonely you must be. I'm so very sorry Civil." She puts her hands under her chin, thinking. *There you were Civil, just flying around in the air, with more freedom then man could ever imagine. I never thought about your family and how they love you too. Birds have families too. There I was, just like massa, waiting for the right time to capture you.* She speaks aloud, "Stop it---stop looking at me like that Civil. Yeah, how could I not think about your freedom, when I know the pain and agony of freedom, being taken away from our race—and here I go, inflicting pain on you… like you don't have feelings. Don't look at me like that Civil, please.

"I now realize the importance of your freedom, but I never thought about it until now… until mine is taken away. You know I'm sentenced to death, but I'm not afraid Civil… I have to admit Civil," she laughs wearily… "I never thought I would die like this."

She says compassionately, "Civil, I have an affinity for birds. I bought a book on birds and found out that they have feelings and they're intelligent. The Owl…" She pauses. "Hmmm, I sure wished that nosy owl who polices the air, would've seen what happened with Ramone and Luther, maybe he could've been my witness."

"But Civil I need to know one thing, that the books didn't tell me. I always wondered about this…how do you hold yourself up in the air without falling?" She pauses, staring as if she sees Civil, waiting for the answer…"Huh, oh my God!" She shouts out…God,' that's who holds them up. "Why did God allow me to capture you Civil?" She stills herself… "Well that's an interesting question… why did he allow our race to be captured by massa? Is it because everything has a purpose? And this was your purpose Civil, to be captured by me, to free me for a purpose. I was a part of your destiny and you were a part of my destiny, because even a bird has a destiny, and a purpose to fulfill."

Matri stills herself…"But, your purpose was to let me know this before I die. Am I going to tell it to someone?" Thinking….."Tell it to Thaddeus, to write about, before my death. Guess I better get out of here first… I'll tell him to write, "The Purpose of a bird."

"Thank you, Civil. I'll tell Isiah to take you back home and free you. You've completed your destiny. You must go back and fly like a free bird… soaring high across the sky. And Civil, just like we both have a purpose, we both have a destiny to die and leave this world." She stares as if she sees Civil. "Yes Civil, I could see you as plain as day." She smiles… Very compassionately, she says, "And you may not get there with me, but I hope to see you again". She hears someone opening the little door to the hole. "I'll apologize to them, and get cleaned up... yeah, that's what I'll do."

━━┽ ┾━━

It's Saturday, afternoon. Matri waits for her visitors. She's well-groomed, looking quite different from the last time they saw her. There is a lost of weight in her face and body. Her afro is big and full, accenting her high cheek bones.

Claudia comes in first. Matri is very calm. Claudia sits on the chair. "Hi, ma' beloved sister." Claudia starts crying.

Matri whispers, smiling. "Hey, Claudia don't weep for me. I need your strength, Claudia… Claudia look at me… look into my eyes, right now."

Claudia looks into Matri's eyes. "Answer my question… do I look sad?"

Claudia shakes her head, from left to right. "Ah-ah," says Claudia.

Matri cautions Claudia, "We have to make this brief."

"But Matri, I have to tell you somethin'." Matri sees a worried expression on Claudia's face.

"What happened, Claudia?"

Claudia's eyes tear. "Matri, Mama's in the hospital, we took her last night."

Matri asks anxiously, "What—happened!"

"She gon' be just fine. The doctors is taken' real good care of 'er…" Claudia pauses…. "Matri, I have ta' give you this letter, from Mrs. Annielu's daughter. She tell us, to give one to Thaddeus too. I didn't open it. She said, ya' need ta' read it right away."

Matri sighs, looking at the letter. "Okay…"

Claudia looks teary-eyed, saying viciously. "I heard these prison woman could be cruel. If I could come back there with ya', I'd fight every last one 'em!"

"Claudia, calm down. Please don't worry about me, I'll be fine. Remember I said, sometimes you would have to give me some of you, and you would have to take some of me…Claudia, when I saw you walk out of that limousine, I clare, you we're walking like me…a lady, and you never had to practice it, either. So you took some of me." She points to Claudia and herself. "I'm going to watch, pray, and fight… if I have to."

"I love ya', Matri. Bye", says Claudia

Matri smiles. Thaddeus comes in. Matri puts both hands on the glass, holding the glass dearly to her. Thaddeus sits down, putting his hands on the glass, matching his with hers. Neither one of them says a word. Looking into each other's eyes, feeling love. After minutes of looking into one another's eyes, Matri puts her lips on the glass. Thaddeus puts his lips, connecting his with hers. A correction officer comes out, telling them to hurry if there's someone else coming in. They slowly withdraw...Thaddeus gets up, showing her the letter that Claudia gave him. He gets up, walking away… he stops, turns around… looks at her again… and walks out.

Isiah comes in. Matri abruptly says, smiling, "I'm fine."

"Matri mama's in the hospital. We gon' see if we can get chu' out ta' see her, cause we appealin' the case. I waz' told we might be able ta' accomplish that."

Very calmly Matri says, "Isiah, destiny will take the higher hand. Just like Dr. King and Hajja Malik- MalcolmX, they knew they couldn't fight destiny… so they embraced it."

"Thaddeus found us a good lawyer. He say he b'leeve he could spin some wheels fa' ya', ta' see Mama."

With glossy eyes, Matri whispers, "I- see."

"We gon' get chu' outta here ta' see Mama. Matri ya' didn't kill nobody!" He exclaims.

The correction officer comes over. "Time is up."

Eyes dazzling, she says, "Isiah, I'm inside of my cave… it's beautiful—no-one could get inside but me." Matri gets up, giving Isiah the biggest, peaceful smile. She turns away, looking back at Isiah smiling, walking away gracefully. Isiah stands, dazed by her strength, as she walks away.

At the hospital… Thaddeus sits in the waiting room. He pulls the letter out of his shirt pocket, staring at it... reading it again. He jumps up, staring out of the window. He closes his eyes, listening to the rain as it falls... beating down on the window. He says to himself, "Who is that person I'm seeing, standing out there in all that rain?.... Seems like he's troubled…crying… or is it just, the rain falling heavily down on him?" Someone takes hold of his arms, he never turns around or opens his eyes, to see who it is. He continues to see the man in the rain. He just holds tightly to the person that holds his arm. …. She doesn't disturb him… she closes her eyes, leaning against his shoulder, listening to the rain as it falls against the window.

Five minutes later, lightening strikes! "Bam!" Thaddeus and Matri looks into the window, at one another.

"Ms. Cameron," says Dr. Batcher. Matri and Thaddeus turn around looking into each other's eyes. Dr. Batcher reaches out to shake their hands. "Ms. Cameron, the nurse is getting your mom ready to see you. …Give it about twenty minutes."

"Doctor?…" Matri pauses…. "Is she?" asks, Matri.

He says, "Her heart is very weak," The doctor pauses. … "She lost her sight. So, you can't see her for long."

Matri is overtaken by melancholy. She painfully smiles, and nods. "Thank you Dr…"

Thaddeus looks out near the door, seeing a police standing outside of the door. He didn't notice before, that Matri is hand cuffed. "Matri," says Thaddeus… "Sit."

Matri sits. "Thaddeus, this is all my fault. I kept leaving Mama at home by herself. All I could think about was going out in the streets, like she said. I should've seen this coming. Since… I'm such a thinker!" Her mouth trembles, " I put the streets before my mama." Matri feels tormented.

Paining, he says, "Matri, I'm not going to let you exacerbate the situation, with what you're trying to do to yourself!" says Thaddeus.

Her eyes are very penetrating. "Why didn't I see this coming, then?"

Thaddeus grabs Matri, gently looking into her eyes. "Matri, things happen in life to all of us. None of us are perfect. Sometimes, it could be the way destiny wanted it to happen. … It could be a means to an end to something… a means to show you, what your purpose in life is really about… and you have to go through this, to see it. That's all!"

Then she notices a beautiful picture, reminding her of Yotha and Claf, when they were in the hospital. Hypnotically she walks toward the picture. It's a picture of a person in a boat, paddling down the river. It's dark and cloudy… the waters seem troubled… but as you look on, this bright sun seems to be waiting further ahead, for this person… *Ummm… ummm.* She thinks, turning around looking in Thaddeus's eyes. Smiling, she says, "I'm torn between truth and love. Why does he have to be my brother? This hurts so deeply. Thaddeus stares back, painfully looking at her in chains and handcuffs, thinking…Why does she have to be my sister? This isn't fair, oh- God," he turns away, trying to hide his pain.

Matri turns away quickly, staring at the picture, looking for strength. Continuing to think, as she observes the picture. I just want to love him…it was you Thaddeus, that I always wanted. I need to love him right-now." Calling on her deceased brother, Claf. Oh Claf, I need you. Annielu, why?" She grabs her heart, stumbling back.

Trying to be strong for Matri, Thaddeus comes over to comfort her paining, putting his hands on her chin… looking into her eyes with compassion. "Oh my beloved… Matri." He exhales, "I know, Matri… it's hard for us… but we're going to survive this. We're going to start out… by redefining a lot of things. We're going to change the pages of history… including, redefining love," he says with ardor, " Matri, I will write your story."

Matri stares at Thaddeus smiling, eyes glaring. She whispers with pain, "Yes."

Sounding melodious, Thaddeus says, "Oh Matri, they say that Humpty Dumpty sat on the wall; Humpty Dumpty had a great fall; all the Kings men, and all the Kings horses, could not put Humpty Dumpty back together again." With so much hope, fighting the tears in his eyes, he says, " We're going to change that story Matri… we are a people that had a great—fall; but my beloved"… He smiles, staring deeply into her eyes, saying with passion and vitality, "We—will be put back together again!" Thaddeus hugs her tightly.

The nurse comes. "You may come in now. Ruth's falls in and out of sleep."

Matri looks, at the handcuffs.

"Matri… she's blind, she can't see you," Thaddeus reminds her.

The nurse closes the door. The policeman stands outside the door.

Ruth's eyes are closed. Matri goes to the end of her bed, laying down at her feet. She begins massaging and kissing her feet gently. Ruth's feet, starts moving around. Matri tickles her feet.

Ruth opens her eyes… not being able to see. "Matri is that you?" asks Ruth.

Matri says, very nurturing, "Yes Mama, who else?"

Ruth reaches out for Matri, with tender arms, "Matri," says Ruth.

Matri gets up, kissing her on her forehead.

Slowly Ruth speaks, smiles, "Matri … is ya' alright?"

Matri backs up, not wanting Ruth to know she's handcuffed. Very loving, she says, "Mama, I'm here and I'll never leave you. Mama I was supposed to carry you. You're too sick to carry us," says Matri.

Thaddeus comes to her bedside kissing her on the cheek, holding her hands.

"Thaddeus…" says Ruth, feeling his hands jently.

He calls her mama, "Yes Mama," says Thaddeus, looking at Matri.

"Thaddeus… I had a dream… I see Jessie again, in ma' dream. I had this same vision, while givin' birth ta' Matri. In that dream… Jessie had a baby boy in his arms. I'll never forgit that dream, for some reason. When I had the dream this time, I see ya' standin' next ta' Jessie. He had his arms 'round ya' shoulder, smilin'. Ya' both waz' standin' there, justta' callin' me." Thaddeus and Matri stares, at each other.

"Mama, what do you think that dream was telling you?" asks Matri.

Ruth didn't respond. Matri asked again, "Mama... Mama!" She yelles "Mama!"

"Mama!" Thaddeus yells. The nurse comes running into the room, with the doctor.

CHAPTER 21

THE WITNESS

At the Town Café... Hezikiah says, "Snap out of it Isiah."
"Man, I'm just thinkin' 'bout, when I used ta' come home from the service. Mama would be so happy ta' see me. She would fix me the best meal in the world, and I kno' it waz' just fa' me," says Isiah

"Yeah man, she alwaze made me feel like that, since ma' mama died. She would be the best second mama, she could be for me, man," says Hezikiah.

Abruptly Isiah asks, "By the way man, did ya' find out anythang yet?"

"No man, not one lead, to the murders."

Isiah feels dismayed. "We gotta' do it fa' Mama. I been walkin' the streets ever since, Matri went ta' jail. Man, it saddens me not ta' find out any clues... but I got a gut feelin' that, there's somethin' out there ta' be found."

"Ya' kno', Osmon got his boys lookin' around too. Somebody gon' come up with somethin'," says Hezikiah

Thaddeus says with contempt, "Man, I'm so hurt by this ..." He pauses. "I knew Ramone was nothing but trouble for Matri, but I never in ma' wildest dreams, thought it would end up like this."

"Here comes Robert," says Hezikiah

"Man what chu' smilin' like a Cheshire cat fa'?" asks Isiah.

Robert sits down calling the waitress. "Give me a slow gin, mam." Isiah and Hezikiah stares at Robert. Excitedly Robert says, "T stands for trouble baby. Here's the deal man. I was coming out of here, just yesterday, and this cat stopped me. He asked me about Matri. I froze… because I wondered what did he know. So the cat told me, he was a witness and he had another witness." Everybody comes closer to Robert. "And he wants us to get on the case and talk to a lawyer, because he knows, him and the other person can free Matri." Isiah, Thaddeus and Hezikiah jumps up excitedly, making army sounds.

Hezikiah says with exhilaration, "Is, that- right- man?"

Smiling from the side of his mouth, proudly. "As a matter of fact, I told the cat to meet me here tonight!" Robert looks at his watch. "He should be here, in about twenty minutes."

"Isiah looks up, towards the door. A tall man, almost 7feet; fair skinned, oval shaped face. He appears to have been in a fire, wearing a patch on his left eye. Demeanor… very cool, leaning to the right with a dip in his walk.

"Is this the cat, Robert?" asked Isiah.

Robert turns around, reaching out his hands to Gil. "Hey man, you made it."

He swings his arm around, like he's dancing. "Made it my brother, If I had to crawl. I was gon' make it, baby."

Robert chuckles. "This is Gil." says Robert. Isiah, Hezikiah and Thaddeus shakes his hand anxiously.

Isiah pulls out a seat for Gil. They all impatiently watch Gil, to see what he was going to say. Robert calls the waiter. "What do you have baby?" asks Robert.

"Oh man, just a ginger ale on the rocks… don't drink no more." Says Gil.

They all look at his skin, and the patch on his eye. "Well let me get to the meat of it. I don't know if you noticed, but there's

a coffee shop right across the street, called 'Litle's Coffee Shop'."
He points, acting cool, with his hands. "It's adjacent to this place. I
go over there a lot, especially when I'm not working. Me and some
cats go there and talk about different things, dig?"

Everyone listens attentively, and anxiously.

"This night, Saturday... I was the only person in the coffee
shop. Sittin' there,   thinkin', I happened to look, and I saw this
beautiful woman ... reminded me of Pam Grier, man. I couldn't
take my eyes off of 'er. She went to ringing the bell... and... I saw
this white cat come to the door, smiling. Now I saw the black cat
and the white cat go into the place a lot. As a matter of fact, I assumed the business was owned by the black cat. Because he was
always dressed in a suit, being chaffered by the white cat. But five
days ago, I noticed the black cat putting suitcases in the car, like he
was going away. That's why I couldn't understand, why this woman
was going there... and that time of night."

All eyes were fixated on Gil. "I decided to go upstairs to my
apartment... there's four apartments upstairs from the coffee
shop. So, I went upstairs and took a bath. I decided to watch movies that night. Say, round' bout' 11:30. I just happened to look
out of the window, and noticed the woman's car was still there.
For some reason, I found it a little peculiar. I still didn't see the
black cat come back yet. I kept watching the office. Every now and
then, I dozed off for a minute. I woke up again, and looked out of
the window... then I noticed the black cat getting out of a taxi. I'll
say about fifteen minutes after he went inside, I saw the darndest
thing..." He pauses...They all look at him, with anticipation. ....
"I saw this girl go inside. He must've left the door unlocked accidentally." Gil Pauses again.... "Now at first, I couldn't tell, if it was
a girl. I stopped looking so hard at women, like I used to." He
pauses again.... "I was a womanizer, pretty boy... you know? Man,
one woman got tired of my lies, she...." He felt his face, looking
at them real hard with his one eye. .... "Threw lye at me, burning

my face a little, good thing I was able to duck. Some of it got in my eye... I lost it. Good thing, somebody was around and threw some cold water on me to try and get some of that lye off of me."

"Wheeew," says Robert. Isiah shook his head.

"But anyway, after this girl went inside... I say about another 15 minutes, I heard nothing but gun shots go off. I saw the girl running out of the office as fast as she could, leaving the door opened. I was devastated by then. About forty-five minutes after that, I saw the cops coming. Somebody heard the shots besides me. Just as the cops and detective were going towards the door, the pretty babe came to the door holding a gun in her hands, lookin' like she been to hell and back. They handcuffed 'er and put 'er into the car. The detective, and a cop went inside. When they came back, they were shaking their heads, staring at the woman in the cop's car.

"Man, when the ambulance came, taking the bodies out... I knew they had to be dead, cause' the sheets covered them up from head to toe. Man, the sheets were bloody on both of them. Then... they brought out this big snake, the people standing around jumped, including the cops and the detective. I heard the cops say, "The snake was shot too."

"So man, what happened ta' the girl. Can ya' help us find her?" asked Isiah

"Man this is the good part," Gil pauses. "I found 'er. How do they say it, a criminal always comes back to the scene of the crime. It was six days later. Saturday night, at about midnight, the girl came back. She went across the street, and grabbed on to the doorknob whining, and crying a river of tears. I immediately ran downstairs to help her. After I saw that woman accused of murder in the papers man, I just had to try and help her."

I went to the girl grabbing her, holding her with love. I still got the touch, man. I was able to get her up to my apartment. Man it's sad, it's sad. When she told me she did it, and why she did it, man it almost broke me down to tears. Man, what that black cat did to er' man, he deserved to die… So I convinced 'er, that we would make a move with the truth, but it had to be done right. I'm letting her stay with me for awhile. She don't have, no where to go."

"Well—anyway, the next day I went down stairs to get 'er somethin' to eat, that's when I met my man." Gil turns around towards Robert. They all cheered Gil on, shaking his hand and hugging him.

Thaddeus says, "Here's the thing. The attorney I have for Matri, asked if we could work on finding a witness for him. Now we're good to go. He says that, he got an appeal for her, appealing to the appellate court for an oral argument. Generally, the appellate court focuses on the lower courts' facts and findings. Depending on the application of legalities of the lower courts, examining all records, making sure there's no legal defect in the decision." Everybody listens attentively to Thaddeus.

"Now, if by chance there's a defect, challenging defects— it can be what they call…ah…as de novo, meaning completely challenging all the facts and its defects. In which case, the lower court resolves the case, granting pre-trial motion, or dismissing the case for summary judgment.. Umm… I believe without any trial testimony."

"Man, Matri didn't stand a chance, because she didn't have any witness. So, this sounds like a piece of cake?" questions Robert.

"Yeah, she wazn't given a chance, by Judge Hitler," says Hezikiah.

"We'll meet with Attorney Dean Shaw, a white cat... Monday. We have to get her out of that disgusting place. A beauty like that cannot be locked up," says Thaddeus.

"Hey, man." Isiah hugs Gil compassionately. "Man, thank ya' for havin' a heart ta' help ma' sister."

"Man, for what that cat did to that girl, if I thought lying would help your sister, I would." He pauses, staring at them. "Man …" He smiles boastfully. "I was what they called a good liar… some say, a compulsive liar." He chuckles.… "Baby, lying was my game plan, for the women. …. So now my man, I don't do those things no mo.' But I will lie for the good. All them lies we been told by massa, you gotta lie ta' survive massa's world. I'll take the stand, and I'll be the most skillful liar, you've ever seen… dig it?"

Robert pats him on the back. "You sound like you should've been a lier… lawyer, my man." Robert and Gil chuckles.

"Well, let's bring this night ta' an end." says Isiah.

They all say, "Dig it."

⋙⋘

It's Monday, at 3:00 a.m. Matri is dreaming, that she's sitting at the edge of the cliff. The wind is gusting… there's a sudden darkness appearing, and clouds begin to waltz slowly across the sky. Matri is taken by this unusual happening on the cliff. All of a sudden, she feels something or someone exhale. It's blowing wind on her face, making her close her eyes… bringing peace and calmness to her. Finally, she opens her eyes. There stands the most beautiful huge, white bird with big black piercing, crystal clear eyes… looking into her eyes. She says, "Yes, the eyes are the window to the soul. Oh Civil, you've forgiven me." The bird starts flying away, looking back at her. Then all of a sudden, Matri sees someone with white wings, flying with Civil… dressed in white. "Who… is that flying with Civil?....It's me! …Yes Civil, no one will take my freedom away from me. I'm free," says Matri. Matri starts tossing and turning, throwing the cover off the bed.

At 9:00 a.m. she wakes up. Closing her eyes… Matri hums, turning from left to right, massaging her body with the soap, as the water trickles down her back. "Ummm, this water feels so good. It's about the best thing around here. But this is a prison, what do you expect. Ummm, nice and warm." She continues to hum…

The door slams. "Matri," someone yells. "Matri."

"Yes ma'am. I'm over here, the last shower."

The correction officer comes over to her. "Matri the warden needs to talk to you, right away."

Matri stands still, water running down her hair and face. Feeling perturbed, she questions, "What did I do, or didn't I do?"

An hour has passed:

Matri is sitting before the Warden, Miss Callahan. A harsh-looking, short woman; with manly features, wearing bifocals. She has jet black hair, combed back in a bun, with a masculine voice.

She says, " Matri, I have good news for you. Two witnesses came forth. You're going to appear in court tomorrow at noon. Chances are, from the sound of it, this will be your last day with us."

Matri was astounded by the news. In her quiescent state, her emotions took her from one extreme to the other. She starts to feel like she hadn't left the showe. Beads of sweat, begin pouring down her body. Her hands begin to feel cold. She starting to quiver, rubbing them together. Matri stares at the warden... who's looking at her, waiting for a response. Finally noticing the warden, she tries to clear her throat "Miss Callahan, sure… sure." She places her hands across her heart.

"Are you okay?" asks Miss Callahan.

She gulps, "It's… it's just… this is breathtaking. I'm elated over the news… it's just so unexpected…" Her forehead crinkles, "Who?… I. …."

"Matri, I have someone waiting to see me about this, so you can go now. I believe your attorney will be coming to see you at about 4:00 p.m."

Matri whispers, "Yes ma'am."

Wednesday: A sharp, slim; very friendly secretary, known for her discerning. Steps out of Attorney Shaw's office. "Good morning, how can I help you this morning?"

"We're here to see Mr. Shaw," says Thaddeus

"Sure… would you like some coffee?" she smiles, with the walk of a model.

They all say, "No thank you." She goes into his office and comes back out. "You fellows, can come right in," she says, with big bright eyes, flickering.

An astute Caucasian man with a keen nose, twirling his mustache with his fingers, reaches out his hand. He shakes everybody's hands. "Yeah man, this is the main cat we want you to meet," says Thaddeus.

"Gilbert Jones, man," says Gil.

"Pleased ta' meet you, Mr. Shaw," says Hezikiah, Robert, and Isiah.

He pulls up to his desk. "Is someone missing?"

"Yeah, the girl who committed the murder. You can rest assured that she'll be in court. She's kinda strange… she stepped out to the store, and I couldn't wait for 'er."

"Okay let's think positive, she'll be there. Here's what we're working with. Whenever a trial judge makes an error, including or excluding evidence, you take it to the appellate court; a court that hears cases, in which a lower court, either a trial court or a lower level appellate court has already made some decision; which at least one party to the action wants to challenge, based upon some legal grounds that are allowed to be appealed, either by right or by leave of the appellate court."

"In Matri's case, I know that there's probable cause. for more evidence. It wasn't given enough time for evidence. I'll use the time factor, to reopen the case for lack of evidence. The appellate judge asks questions, based on their review of the records.

"I want you guys to know that, in this business, if you're in it long enough… sometimes your heart gets wrapped up in your case… if you still have one. " He pauses, "Irregardless…" He looks at all of them. …. " Meaning, I didn't have the evidence at hand, when I went before the appellate judge. I had to take a chance and go on "blind faith" instead of "blind justice". He shakes his head, "Furthermore, I'm tired of justice – *just us,* as a white race. One day I looked in the mirror fellows, and I didn't like what I saw…my conscience can't take it any longer. Maybe the man upstairs, will forgive me for lying so much, to make a living." They 're stunned by his speech.

At the prison:

The correction officer comes to her cell. "Matri, someone's here to see you." Matri freezes.

A tall skinny, toothless white woman; looks like Hagatha the witch; with sunken eyes, in the cell with Matri, asks her, "What are you freezing up for? You should be jumping with joy, girl. Sounds like you gon' get your freedom back. I'm never leaving out. Nobody tries to understand why I killed my husband. He hagged me down, that's why I look like this," she yeslls, "Look at me! I'll never love again, that's for sure. That no good, lying cheatin,' no good for nothin.' I told 'em he'd never amount to nothin'…" She pauses.… "Come to think about it, how can he amount to somethin'?…I killed the bastard." She rolls over, back onto the bed, laughing hysterically. As Matri walk out of the cell, the woman yells out. "And I ain't sorry, neither!"

⋙┿┾⋘

Friday in court.… The family is occupying the first row. "Hey you girls," whispers Thaddeus. "This is, attorney Dean Shaw."

Claudia, Dawn and Sadie nods. "I know we got this all sewed up," says Thaddeus, emphatically.

Mr. Shaw winks. "This is a piece of cake. I'm leaving no room for doubt." Everybody watches the lawyer attentively, as he speaks.

Osmon whispers to Anthony, "Man it kills me to see a sister in chains, like an animal."

"Yeah man, no doubt," says Anthony.

Angrily Isiah says, "Seein' ma' sister in chains, rips ma' heart out, Dawn."

Dawn holds Isiah's arms tightly. "She's free, now baby," says Dawn

A piercing voice says, "Court is in session." The marshal continues, "Those present, at the sound of the gavel, rise and remain standing until the robed justice is seated, following the traditional chant.

Judge Timbers presides. He's a tall Caucasian, very long nose; very meek-looking man, wearing a close haircut. His eyes stroll around the courtroom, getting a feel of everyone.

Everybody thinks to themselves. Claudia thinks, *Well, what chu lookin' at?*

"Ya' look, but cha' better kno' what chu' doin' man, I'll die this day," Isiah thinks.

"Man, don' make us go back ta' 'Nam t'day," Hezikiah thinks.

Robert thinks, "You better free her. We're ready and fully equipped," says Robert, giving the eye to Hezikiah and Isiah. They all nod to each other, Robert has a bag on the floor.

The judge tells Attorney Sawyer to approach the bench. "Yes your honor," says Mr. Shaw. "I have two witnesses for the case of Matri Cameron. She was sentenced to death for the murder of two men. During her first trial, there were no witnesses. Within the last two weeks, there are two witnesses coming forth, to testify on Miss Cameron's behalf. Gilbert Jones, and the one who committed the two murders, came to testify to the fact. Miss… Antanette Smith." He turns around, looking at Thaddeus for the other witness. Thaddeus and Gilbert turns around, not seeing her. He turns around telling Gilbert to come to the front and take a seat beside him. "Your honor we're going to give Miss Smith a little more time to get here… perhaps she got caught up in traffic." Looks at Gilbert…. "I understand she's taking a bus here." The judge nods his head, patiently.

A door opens, everybody turns around. A cop brings Matri out, uncuffed this time. She's wearing clothes, brought to her from home. A pretty blue dress and pearl earrings. Her Afro, is combed out very neatly. Matri walks with dignity to her seat. The judge is taken by her beauty… but prudently, he watches as she comes forward. She looks at everyone, sitting down, quietly in the front seat.

"We will get started until Miss Smith comes, we're wasting time. I want Mr. Jones to take the stand." A policeman comes to Gilbert. with a bible in his hands. "Do you swear to tell the truth, and nothing but the truth?" asks the officer.

He puts his hands on the Bible. "I do."

Mr. Shaw asks, "Mr. Jones will you please tell us how you are a witness to these murders?"

He sits up proudly. "Well, I sure can, now." He's very neatly dressed, in a brown suit and a tie. "It started when I was sittin' in Litle's Diner. I live on top of the diner. At 9:00 I noticed a beautiful woman…" Pausing, he's looking at Matri, with astonishment.

"Please continue, Mr. Jones."

Gil snaps back. "I noticed this woman, going into the private detective's office. A white cat opens the door for 'er."

The judge looks at him, because of his expression. Mr. Shaw says, "Be more specific, please."

"This white man opens the door for 'er. I went upstairs to watch tv, and just happened to look out of my window. I noticed the woman's car, was still parked outside, and it was gettin' late. I thought to myself…11:30. I saw another girl go in the office, bout' 12:00 midnight. For some reason, it looked suspicious. I went back to watching tv… and I fell asleep. All of a sudden, I heard shots… then I woke up. You know, it took about forty-five minutes b'fore the cops came. That's when I saw them take the two bodies, the snake and Ms. Cameron away."

About the next five days… late at night, I saw that same girl, leaning against the office door. Just crying, a river of tears. So I went downstairs to help her. I figured I might find some connection with the murder." He looks at the Judge.… "I did. She told me she committed both murders, and killed the snake, 'cause he was sneaky just like them."

All of a sudden the door opens. Everybody turns around. The judge looks towards the door over his glasses. A medium height, bag-lady comes into the room... whining loudly, continuously. The policeman confronts her, telling her she can't come in. "Please you have to leave the court," he says.

She refuses, pushing him away. Looking straight ahead at Gilbert, pointing her hands and says, "Gilbert wanted me to come… I told him, I would come to free Matri."

Everybody's bewildered, making a sound of, "Ummm" in unison. Gilbert's aghast, by her presence, thinking…."*That's not the person I have staying with me….*"

Matri grabs ahold of her heart, feeling faint. Thaddeus goes over to Matri. The policeman looks at the judge for a decision. He tells her to come to the front, taking a seat next to Matri. Everyone's eyes follow the bag lady to her seat. She sits next to Matri, whining.

Matri thinks, "Oh my God, this is the bag lady that kept watching me… and this is the sound, I heard at Ramone's house—and she called me in my room at Fort Dix!" Matri feels faint, she exhales slowly. The bag lady has a horrible stench all over her body.

"Quiet in the court," the judge says. "Please continue, Mr. Jones."

'Well, your honor I heard a guy was asking around for witnesses. So I told him I'd meet him at Town Café, to tell him I found the person, who had committed the crime." He looks across the room to the bag lady.

"That will be all." Mr. Shaw turns towards the bag lady…He pauses… "Ms. Smith will you please take the stand."

She gets up whining, as she takes the stand. The Marshal takes the Bible to her. Everyone looks at her appearance. Her face is dirty, and she's wearing big stuffed pants with clothes, hanging out from the side. Three rags covers her head. She has on big army boots and carries a big bag, with all sorts of things in it. She holds onto her bag, as she takes the stand. The judge requests that she leave it at her seat. She tries to fight the policeman. The Judge says, "Very well, let her take it."

Mr. Shaw asks her, " Miss Smith, will you please tell us in your own words, exactly what happened." She stops whining abruptly, staring at Matri. Matri is weary and hurtful.

Speaking like a bruised little girl, she says, "I went to Ramone's office to kill him and Luther." She starts rocking back and forth, looking distraught. "He made me prostitute. I ran away from home with him. He told me I was pretty… and that… I had a very beau… ti…ful… body. He said he would marry me. But first I had to help him make some money. He said I should be like the hippies… it's my thing… I could do whatever … I… want to." She changes abruptly… "But…" Acting frantic she says, "He lied to me! He got somebody else to make money for him. He said I wasn't makin' enuff money, no more. He started beatin' on me. Giving me black eyes… kicking me in my stomach when…" She pauses, and starts whining again. The Judge and lawyer are very patient with her. Suddenly she stops whining…."Kicking me in my stomach, 'cause I told 'em, I was pregnant."

The people in the court room said, "Whoooo!"

"Order in the court," says the judge.

Pitifully she says, "I loved 'em so much." She pauses, saying treacherously. "I beat up the other girl with a bat. He found out and spit in my face and broke my jaw. I was in the hospital for a week. He beat me so bad one time, I had a nervous breakdown in the street. A woman came and took me to the hospital. She let me stay with her for three months." She started acting frantic again, rocking back and forth. She blushes, "I love 'em, still… he's my daddy." She looks at Matri with jealousy and resentment. Her voice tremors, she yells, "But he wanted you!" pointing her finger at Matri.

Matri starts shaking her head. Sorrowfully Matri says, "Oh—no."

She massages her bag, as she holds on to it dearly. "So… I went to his office that Saturday night, and I killed 'em. I tiptoed down the stairs, and I saw Luther holding a gun to her head." She points at Matri. "Ramone was holding a gun to Luther's head. They all start fightin,' so I shot Luther in the head and she fell, musta hit 'er head on the floor or somthin'. Ramone thought she got shot. So I shot Luther again in the face. Then Ramone turns around to see who it was shootin'… and it was me," viciously she says, squinting her eyes nodding her head. "Boy, was he shocked. I shot 'em in his head. He fell to the floor, so I took his gun and shot 'em in the head again, then in the heart and his private part, one time. I shot the snake and laid it across both of them. I left my gun near Matri, and took the other two guns, to throw the cops off when they come." She starts whining, rocking back and forth, and staring at everyone in the courtroom. Patiently, the Judge waits for her to stop.

She starts trembling. Angrily she speaks, looking at Gil. "Gil told me, a woman's like the finest of crystal, and that she could be broken very easily." Dispirited, she looks around at everybody in the courtroom, yelling and crying. "And—I–can't be fixed, 'cause he broke me into too many pieces!" She sounds like, a lost little girl, "And I don't know how to fix myself." She yells, grabbing her head, "I shot 'em in the head cause… he took my mind…" She pauses, speaking with no remorse, "I shot 'em in the heart, cause he kept on hurtin' my heart… killin' my babies." She says crazily, "I shot him down below… cause I was a virgin, and he took that from me too, and made me sell myself for him," she pauses, "I killed the snake because, he was evil just like Luther and Ramone… so why should he live."

Everyone was shaking their heads. She brought tears to the peoples' eyes in the courtroom. Dawn pulled out a tissue, passing it down to Sadie and Claudia. Osmon pulls out a piece of gum.

Anthony put his head down, shaking it back and forth. It is a tear-jerker for Robert, Isiah and Hezikiah. They looked at each other teary-eyed, because they understand pain. Thaddeus is just sitting there, silenced by it. The judge and the lawyer shakes their heads.

Appearing insane, she cries out, "He took everything from me! My mother and my father... brother... I have no one to love me! And now---I'm too dirty for God." She looks at Matri and says, "Will you please tell God I'm sorry... maybe he'll listen to you, cause," She softly says, "Matri, he'll listen to you, cause you the finest of crystal, and you ain't been broken like me." She stands up proudly, holding her bag, gently massaging it. " All he left me with... is a bag."

The guard starts to approach her. The Judge tells him to go back. "Let her talk," says the judge.

"I want everybody to know, that I am the bag lady that put the baby in the garbage disposal... that baby was Ramone's. He said he would kill me, if I ever got pregnant again. When I got pregnant, I had to disappear, because I didn't want to kill my baby this time. I became a bag lady, so that he would not know who I was. I figured that if I put her in the garbage, somebody would find her, and take care of her." She looks over towards Matri. "Will you find 'er and take care of 'er for me. I have nothin' to offer 'er... not even myself."

Stares at Matri. "Ohh, and Matri, when you went to my brother's funeral, you looked right at me. Yes, that was me with the big hat and shades on. I often watched him, too.

Vehemently she says, "So for every woman in here, I want you to know that I killed him, not only for me... but I killed him for all women... I wanted him to die!" She starts whining as she steps off of the stand, walking towards the policeman to handcuff her.

Everybody stands up in the court, watching her as she walks away, handcuffed. She looks everyone in the face, smiling with the brightest smile and bright eyed... she walks proudly. If you didn't know any better, you would think this was her debut. She felt that she finally did something that was meaningful. And she was very proud of it.

Outside of the courtroom, everyone 's standing around the attorney, as he speaks about the case. "Matri, ' the attorney says, "This was the sweetest case I've ever had. This case fell under everything the appellate court stood for." He pauseds, "Umm, there was a bullet for the snake too. You guys did an excellent job, by pursuing the case further. The detectives just pushed it under the rug, as usual… Matri you got a lot of love." He smiles.

Matri asks, "I need to ask you something."

"Sure," he says.

"What's going to happen to Antanette? I want to have a redress or represent her, in a small court. I feel indebted to her," says Matri.

He smiles. "As a matter of fact Matri, you can. I hear you're in school for law."

She answers quickly, "Yes- I- am."

"I'll speak to the judge, and get back to you."

"Yes," she says.

Reporters approach Matri, taking pictures. The attorney pulls Matri close to him for a picture. He smiles proudly.

"Matri, tell me how do you feel, now that you're free?" askes a white female reporter.

Matri pauses, staring at the reporter…. "Are you free?" she asks her. The reporter looks baffled.

Matri says emphatically…. "Are you free? Can you look at me without prejudice eyes, and not hold me in contempt, just because of my skin color. Are you free? ….Can you not look at me, like I'm some animal less than a human being. …Are you free? She pauses and smiles, people begin to cheer her on. At that very moment the crowd of people became the jury and she became the prosecutor. "Can you look at me with the willingness to understand that there is one soul... one God, that has no color... but is permeated with love, that we all share equally."

She lookes around at the people. "The soul is our residence, and no matter if we're put it in a maze, locked up in some box, or chained with shackles... we are still free, because you cannot, lock the soul up. You can't you give it, your diseased prejudices... it's a separate entity." Emphatically, she says staring... "Am I free?" She holds her head up high, smiling proudly. "Yes... I'm free.... just like a bird." She starts walking away with her head up high. Stopping she says, looking back at the reporter and smiling compassionately... "You do have the right, to defend yourself."

Isiah and everybody follows her. The reporters and a crowd of people are left standing, silenced by her remarks.

A reporter says, "Yes, that was certainly a dynamic speech, yes indeed. We all occupy the same soul. She certainly gave me something to think about, that's for sure."

Matri Cameron, was accused of murdering two men. One white male, Luther, no last name is known. One black male, named Ramone, supposedly he's a pimp. The white male was his chauffeur. A prostitute by the name of Antanette confessed to the killings of the two males. She said she killed the snake owned by Luther, because it was evil just like the two of them, and why should he live too?"

CHAPTER 22

THE M'NAGHTEN RULES

H ello Mr. Shaw, when can you set up a hearing for me and Antanette?"

Happily he says, "Oh, good news Matri. I have a hearing for next Wednesday."

Matri jumps up, with joy. "Yes-yes!" Mr. Shaw waits for her to calm down.

"Matri, " he pauses, "Are you sure you want to do this?" He asks.

"You know, Mr. Shaw, my very soul bids me to do this. I have a lot invested in this. I feel like this is predestined. Besides, I'm a woman. Therefore, I could feel her emotionally, psychologically, mentally, and physiologically."

"Okay, okay, I'm sold. Now, only a few people will be there, this time-no jurists." says Mr. Shaw, staring at her, in his minds eye.

Excitedly she pants, "So you said Wednesday, but what time?"

He points, "9:00 am sharp… and I mean sharp, don't ever let the judge wait for you. We're not having a trial by jury. We're going on the M'Naghten Rules. It will exclude her from the process of a trial. It's a rationale of compassion; it being morally wrong to treat a person with severe mental illness or intellectual disability; being deprived of the capacity either to choose whether to obey the law, or to distinguish right from wrong," says Mr. Shaw.

Matri says, "So I'll go with the term, "M'Naghten Rules," meaning... rules to establish insanity as an excused potential criminal liability, but the definitional criteria establish insanity in the legal and not the psychological sense."

"Yup," says Mr. Shaw.

Matri uses the Law. "I have to prove, not guilty by reason of insanity. I will be requesting a mandatory and indeterminate period, for treatment in a secure hospital facility. We don't have to worry about the country... the U.S. recognizes, this plea of insanity."

Mr. Shaw puts his left, index finger on his face, "Do you think you could handle this?... If not, I'll do it," says Mr. Shaw.

Folding her arms, she says, "Beyond a reasonable doubt. Now you and I both witnessed the fact that... emotionally, she's in no condition. Yes, she has in fact been deprived, mentally and intellectually; of the capacity to choose to obey or distinguish right from wrong; because of psychological damage. Due to a presumed incapacity, to perform a criminal intent. If she's proven genuinely insane, no law or threat of punishment will be effective," says Matri.

"Didn't you say that she told you that, after she killed the snake she laid it over their bodies, because she felt they both were evil like a snake?" says Mr. Shaw.

"I'm hearing you, Mr. Shaw," says Matri.

"Well Matri, I want you to know, I'm very confident that you could do the job," says Mr. Shaw, smiling with confidence.

Court: Wednesday morning at 9:00 a.m.

Matri sits, looking very professional. She's wearing a two-piece; dark blue suit; white blouse and small white pearl earrings. Checking her watch, Matri patiently waits for them to bring Antanette out. Matri turns around to see whether or not her mother and father is here. Isiah, Robert, Hezikiah, Dawn, Thaddeus,

Gil and Sadie are sitting quietly. The door opens… "Thank God they came. I know it must be very hard on them, not seeing their daughter in years, thinking she's dead… and when they see her, it's in this painful situation." Matri gets up to say a few words.

Hello, how are you two feeling this morning? Mrs. Smith's eyes are glossy from crying… slightly smiling. Her husband just looks straight ahead. Matri holds her hands tightly, and then walks away.

A voice says, "Those seated, at the sound of the gavel, rise and remain standing until the robed justice is seated, following the traditional chant."

The judge, Mrs. Moore; a very stern looking, middle-aged white woman says, "Please be seated."

A door opens bringing out Antanette, dressed like a bag woman, with chains. Matri glances back at her parents. Matri thinks. "Why would they let her come out here like this? I must object to this!"

Antanette walks proudly with a big smile on her face, as she looks at everyone. She could barely walk, because of the chains on her ankles and hands. Matri glances behind her, looking at Antanette's parents. Mrs. Smith has a handkerchief to her mouth, leaning on her husband's shoulders. Matri goes over to the judge to ask him why they would let her come into the courtroom like this. Then he leans over to ask the correction officer, why they would allow that.

"Your Honor, we tried our very best to convince her to dress more appropriately. She said she had no more clothes and she didn't want to wear our clothes. She also said, she loves the clothes she wears," he pauses, "And, she said… she wanted to be chained."

The Judge looks over at her… and says, "I- see."

Matri starts pacing back and forth, cheekbones rising, displaying dimples and a picture perfect set of white teeth; she smiles very pleasantly at Antanette, with compassion. She says, "May it please the court." Swaying her hands towards Antanette, to get the attention of the way, she wants to present herself in court. She glances towards the back of the court, noticing her family and Mr. Shaw"

She thinks of her bird Civil. She says to her self, *Thank you Civil, what better way to start this hearing off. Civil, we know that justice isn't blind, people just don't want to be civil about it.* She paces back and forth smiling, with the eyes of justice... saying, "I want to ask the question...what does the word civil mean? Well, I'll tell you what it means, to me. It means, having to do with the private rights of individuals. Ummm... you... Dr. King, one of our late, Civil rights leaders played a significant part in this movement. But I must admit..." Matri thinks about the shooting and killings of the drug dealers...."That, it's sad to say...that we have come to this black on black crime, when there is such a movement going on."

"Dr. King was a moral humanist. He appealed to the conscience." She turns around, eyes like a radar, passing by the judge intentionally... and to the people in the court, smiling. "Dr. King defined a strategy, of nonviolent resistance, for the American Civil rights movement. He said we should have the Agape love, in which there's nothing sentimental or basically affectionate; but the attack is against the forces of evil, rather than against the person who is caught in those forces. We are seeking to defeat evil, not the persons victimized by evil, such as Ramone and Luther." Hearing the names, Antanette starts whining, rocking back and forth, massaging her bag. Everybody looks at her.

Matri walks over and rubs Antanette on the shoulder, compassionately. She walks away looking back at Antanette. "I 'clare, now here's a perfect example of black on black crime. What we want to know is, what was the real nature of the crime, here? Well, let me tell you about this young lady, sitting before me, people."

"Let's take a look at the back of the court. There you'll find Antanette's parents, who haven't seen her in 10 years....not to mention they thought their daughter was dead. She was taken away from them, by a total stranger… a snake… a charming slickster, who knew all the right words to charm a beautiful young girl." Waving her hands in the air, smiling cunningly, staring at the people. "I 'clare he completely swept her off of her feet. Taking her off into the sunset of no return, from her parents and three brothers." Antanette continue to rock back and forth, whining.

"I 'clare, who was the big bad wolf that captured her?" Pacing back and forth, she says, "His name was Ramone, a.k.a. … a "Pimp." She points her finger out, pacing back and forth. "Now what is a pimp? Well I'll tell you, what a pimp is. A pimp finds and manages clients, for a prostitute. He engages her in prostitution, often street prostitution, in order to profit from her earnings. Typically, a pimp will force or pressure the women to stay with him. He may also protect them from other pimps or abusive clients. Pimping is a sex crime in most jurisdictions. Women cannot be considered pimps, as it is inherently a derivative of the male socialistic dominance over the fox… female dog… better know as 'the bitch'. Umm, by his hands, he brings the worst out of her. Like homeless cats in the streets on a prowl, he takes her dignity, turns her into a prostitute." She smiles cunningly, "Then he has the audacity to call her a bitch (female dog)… that's interesting, I clare." Facing the courts, she says, "Some pimps, present themselves as father-figures and lovers. Most of these relationships are abusive, using psychological intimidation. Keeping them in the, "stable," by manipulation and physical force… okay?" she looks around at everyone.

"Now in 1949, the United Nations adopted a constitution, stating that prostitution is incompatible with human dignity; requiring all signing parties to punish pimps and brothel owners with operators; and to abolish all special treatment of registration of prostitutes. The convention was ratified by 89 countries.

In the United States, urban pimps and prostitutes constitute a colorful and often overly dramatized subculture. American pimps are also known as "Macks" and often refer to their business as "The Game."

Matri walks over to get a picture to give to Judge Moore. "Here we go, Your Honor. This is a picture of a street prostitute." Judge Moore, looks at the picture, giving it back to Matri. "This is an outside prostitute. The prostitute solicits customers while waiting at street corners, usually dressed in skimpy clothing. The act is performed in the customer's car or in a nearby alley or rented room. Motels that service prostitutes, commonly rent rooms by the half or full hour.

"Your Honor, this young woman's life has been destroyed by Ramone. He took her at the age of fifteen. Your Honor, I would like to bring Antanette to the stand, please."

Judge Moore looks at Antanette. "Please enter the stand, Miss Smith". Antanette comes to the stand, whining.

The officer brings the Bible to her. "Put your hand on the Bible please, and just say 'I do'."

She stares at the Judge … then she stares at Matri… finally, she says …"I do."

Matri walks up to her and smiles. "Miss Smith, in your own words, tell us why you didn't want to change your clothes."

She yells… "I'm a bag lady, and this is what we wear!"

Compassionately, Matri says, "Oh, I'm so sorry... I 'clare."

She begins to whine, rocking back and fourth. Matri begins to walk away, facing the people, pacing from side to side. "Ummm… There are certain diagnostic tools, a psychiatrist uses to make an accurate diagnosis of patients. Some of them are determined by it, the moment the patient enters the office. They are identified by the presentation; the personal appearance; social interaction; talking to themselves, and how many layers of clothing they might be wearing."

Matri turns around, facing Antanette. Gently she asks, "Miss Smith, who is Ramone?"

She starts whining, rocking back and fourth. "Ms. Smith?" says Matri.

Antanette freezes. "Ramone… I love Ramone. He's my Mack daddy."

Matri asks, "What is that?"

She smiles, bubbly. "He's my pimp… I work for him," she stares, seductively.

"Where?" asks Matri.

"I work on the street corner, and sometimes I work in ugly motels". She frowns.

Matri tilts her head. "I see," says Matri. Matri turns around, noticing Antanette's expression has changed, in a matter of seconds. She walks up to Antanette, very caringly she asks, "What's wrong Antanette?" She starts rocking back and fourth, shaking her head. Looking into her eyes, she asks again, "Honey, what's wrong?" Matri pleads.

She finally stops rocking. In a little girlish voice, she says, "He beat me…he lied to me," she blushes with a big smile, "He told me he would marry me," angrily, she says, " I got pregnant… always called me a bitch." She pauses, "I had gonorrhea and syphilis, five times."

Matri moves closer, in a nurturing way. "You got pregnant and what happened?"

"He beat me up, kicking me in the stomach and giving me black eyes and he busted my lips… he even broke my jaw too. Every time I got pregnant he beat me up. He told me he didn't want no baby." She whines.

Matri slowly turns away from Antanette. Her eyes continues to move like a radar, meeting with the judge's eyes, then turning towards the people. " She reads, with pungent wit: 'Whosoever shall unlawfully and maliciously by any means whatsoever, wound or cause any grievous bodily harm to any person, with intent to do some grievous bodily harm to any person, or with intent to resist or prevent the lawful apprehension or detainment of any person, shall be guilty of an offence and, being convicted thereof, shall be liable to imprisonment of life. Also known as ABH (actual body harm), providing evidence of the intent to harm, could result from repeated attacks."

"Miss Smith said out of her very own mouth, that Ramone beat her during three pregnancies, to be exact. Causing her to loose her unborn children. Now there's an "Unborn Victim of Violence Act... 2604. ... 'First degree murder of unborn child." Matri looks stone faced. "Why- that's, a criminal homicide of an unborn child, which should constitute a degree of murder, whether it's 1st degree, or 2nd degree... let the judge decide, but there have been murders of unborn children, committed by an intentional killing. And it should go under the guidelines of 1st degree murder," turns towards the people, nodding her head.

"Your Honor, can we recess?" asks Matri

"Yes, recess until 12:00 noon."

⪛ ⪜

Half an hour later:

Matri walks around like a professor. "Your Honor, the rules in the English law states: the jurors should be told in all cases, that every man/woman is presumed to be sane; and to possess a sufficient degree of reason, to be responsible for his crimes; until the contrary be proved to their satisfaction; and to establish a defense on the grounds of insanity. A person with a disease of the mind, not capable or qualified to determine his/her state of mind; to distinguish whether he/she is, in fact; fully able to discern right from wrong, or committing a crime."

Turning towards the people of the court, looking compassionately into the eyes of the people, she says, "We could all see that Miss Smith is not operating out of a sound mind. She's been subjected to diseases, and taken out of her rightful environment, by someone who was much older than her. Never seeing her parents again. Causing her parents nothing but grief. Not to mention her mom, going to a mental institution because of her disappearance." Matri stands firmly, "Asking Antanette, "Can we take a look at a few of your bruises. "Her jaws is twisted, four teeths are knocked out; some of her fingers have been broken; and she shows a big bald spot, where stitches were sewn in her head, after being hit in the head with a pipe. "He is in fact, guilty of mental abuse; deceiving her; maliciously beating her and prostituting her. Along with venereal diseases, and killing her babies… all causing her bodily and mental harm. "Matri looks at the people with contempt! She yells, "And he cheated her out of her life!" she freezes looking around the court.

Matri turns towards the judge… "Your Honor, I'd like to make an appeal. Look at her, your Honor…" Antanette rocks back and forth. "She's been victimized by a diseased brute. He took a precious tool away from her, that we need to be able to function with, as human beings. That is… her mind." Matri stills herself. It's hard for her to go on… she regroups quickly…pacing back and forth…. "Yes, we're only given one life to live… and by God, he took that away from her, and sold her like cattle. He took the one thing that's so very precious to a woman," Stares into the judges eyes… "That's her virginity, representing her innocence… life... her purity... and sold it for a very measly price." She steps back, facing Judge Moore, and the people. She says with veneration, "And she wants me to intercede for her, with God… because she feels... that she's too dirty to talk to God."

The Judge Moore, is made motionless, by Matri's comments. You could hear a pin drop, silence permeates the room. Matri turns towards the people, then slowly turns towards the judge again. Standing firmly, she says to the judge with a bright smile, "Your Honor, one of our great Black Martyrs, El-Hajj Malik El-Shabazz says, "We as a people need, Human rights…how can we get Civil Rights, if no one acknowledges the fact, that we're human beings, first and foremost."

"Well, I conclude that, El-Hajj Malik Shabazz also said, the truth is not always pretty. Sometimes it's ugly, but it's the truth." Adamantly she says, "The truth is… she is not just a color, nor is she an animal… but in fact, a human being above all else," Matri says very compassionately, trying not to show emotions… "He took her life from her. He broke the finest of crystal… into pieces…" Matri steps back, with a grimaced facial expression, facing the judge and the people. Finally she breaks, speaking with ardor, "Humpty Dumpty sat on the wall, Humpty Dumpty had a great fall; all the Kings men and all the Kings horses, could not put Humpty Dumpty back together again." Matri places her hand across her heart gently, turning away quickly…she says looking back at the judge, with firmness, "Can she be put back together again…? Looking towards the people she says, smiling cunningly, "Can she be put back together again?" She looks at the judge and the people, silently. Fighting her emotions, anger and hurtful feelings. She smiles, "I rest my case."

Antanette's mother bursts out crying. "My baby, she don't even recognize me… oh my baby. Why did he do that to her… somebody, please tell me why? With pleading eyes, she asks, "How could he?…Oh God… help me," she shrivels down, holding her heart.

Matri walks away looking at Mrs. Smith smiling, with teary eyes. Antanette is rocking back and fourth whining, looking straight ahead at Mrs. Smith. Matri brings her off of the stand. "You're going to be just fine. I'll see to it, Antanette… you've got love," says Matri.

All of a sudden, Antanette starts walking towards Mrs. Smith. She stops by her, staring at her. Putting her hand across her mother's face, grabbing the tissue, she begin to rub her face, whining….

Mrs. Smith stares into her eyes, slowly touching Antanette's hands. All of a sudden Antanette stops, backs up slowly, and starts whining... looking back at her.

Matri wants to explode, but she can't... she places her hands on her heart, looking at Mrs. Smith and smiles. "Counselor please approach the bench," says Judge Moore.

Matri's attorney says, "I'm proud of you, you were great!"

"Matri, when you're good—you're good," says Thaddeus.

"Matri, if mama waz' here, she would be proud of ya'," says Isiah.

"Yeah, too bad Claudia and Osmon couldn't be here," says Dawn

"Where is she?" asks Sadie.

"Oh they went to that Rehabilitation place, in South Jersey," says Dawn.

Robert says, "Matri, Sadie and I want to take you, and treat everybody to dinner, when you're done here."

"Sure will," says Matri.

⟫⟩ ⟨⟪

Two months later... Matri is talking to herself. "Oh I have to go to the bathroom." She starts shaking her legs. "Oh come on now! I have to go to the bathroom...will ya." She continues to twist the key around. *Doesn't seem like it wants to fit anymore.* The phone rings. "Wait." She pauses, "Is that the phone I hear?" The phone rings...She twists the key again. "Ooops, here we go, I got it." She runs to the phone. "Wait—wait a minute I have to go to the bathroom." She drops the phone running to the bathroom.

Five minutes, later. "Okay, okay, I'm so sorry... had to go to the bathroom. I just got in from the Rehabilitation Center in South Jersey."

"Hello, Matri."

"My apology, I'm just talking and I don't even know who I'm talking too." Matri chuckles.

"Matri, this is Mrs. Smith. I need to talk to you."

"Sure hon."

"Guess who's here with me?"

Excitedly, Matri jumps off the couch. "Don't tell me… don't tell me… Antanette!"

"Yes, Matri they let 'er come home for two weeks. She'll go back, but this is just a trial basis, she was doing so well." She cries.

"Where is she now?"

"She's watching a movie with her father."

Matri jumps up with joy. "Great!"

"'Matri, my husband and I are so indebted to you. You've been our bridge over troubled waters."

"I 'clare…you bring so much joy to my heart." Matri looks over at Civil.

"Mine too, Matri."

"Mrs. Smith, when you do good by people, I believe it's a cleansing for the heart."

"We would like to invite you over for dinner, with Antanette when she comes home again… hopefully it's for good. She's making such great progress."

"Mrs. Smith, give her a bath. And when you do that, sing to her. Brush her hair gently. She needs that. It touches the heart."

I'll do everything I need to do."

"Just call me when you want me come over for dinner, I'll be there with bells on."

"Okay-bye, hon," Mrs. Smiles, with teary eyes.

Two weeks later, on a Friday night, at 10:00 p.m.

There's one small night light, on in Matri's room. Civil is watching Matri as she sleeps. Matri is tossing and turning, talking in her sleep. "Oh where am I, Civil?" She walks up to this white framed window, and the closer she gets to the window, the bigger the window gets. She's drawn into the window. Looking through this window, the sun is luminous. "Who is that with their back turned, holding a big straw hat... standing in a bed of beautiful flowers. The wind is blowing, giving off the fragrance of the flowers. Yellow, white, purple, red and pink..."Ohh, that's Sadie picking those flowers."

She rushes over to Sadie... but when she gets close to her and touches her on her shoulder... she discovers, it's not Sadie... "It's... Antanette." She turns around with the most beautiful white dress on. Her hair is parted in the middle, hanging down to her shoulders... her teeth are pearly white, and perfectly even. Matri's ecstatic. She says, "Antanette, you seem so happy." Antanette's eyes are glittering, her face is glowing. She's smiling brightly, like the sun, staring into Matri's eyes. Matri laughs with joy, "I've never seen you so blissful like this. I'm so happy to see you, so happy Antanette." Their eyes meet. "Yes, the eyes are the windows to the soul." Antanette picks a white flower, giving it to Matri. Matri reaches for the flower, smiling with joy in her eyes. Matri starts backing out of the window, then everything disappears. Matri jumps up smiling, feeling exhilarated. She gets out of bed, turning the light on, looking at Civil. "Civil are you asleep? I'll get a glass of water, then I'm going back to bed."

While laying there, thinking about the dream she just had, the phone rings. "Hello."

"Matri, this is Gilbert."

"Yes, Gilbert."

"Matri, I think you better come down to the hospital."

Matri sits straight up in the bed. She pants, "What happened?"

"It's Antanette."

"It's Antanette!" She says frantically.

"I can't tell you over the phone."

"Okay, I'll be there in a minute."

Matri jumps into her car, throwing her pocketbook on the flowers, laying on the seat. She notices the flowers. "Ooops, I forgot to give, oh... never mind. I'll give them to Antanette..." She thinks... "Oh God, what happened? I have to be patient... turn the radio on, it might calm me down. This is that new song "Wild Flower," by New Birth, everybody's talking about."

She listens attentively. "She faced the hardest time you could imagine. Many times her eyes fall back with tears, Lord, Lord. When her youthful world was about to fall in. Each time her slender shoulders brought the weight of all her fears. And the silence none hears, still rings in midnight silence... in her ears. That's a cry, she's a lady. For she's a lady. ... Let the rain fall down upon her, She's a sweet and gentle flower growing wild.

⇌ ⇋

Matri starts thinking about Antanette. "Yes, "New Birth"... she's a lady, just like a wild flower. Let the rain fall down upon her." Matri stops in front of Maryland Hospital, on Bergen Street. Thinking about the dream she had of Antanette, while listening to the song. With the flowers in her hands, Matri runs down the hall of the hospital to the visiting room. Gilbert is there waiting for her. "Gilbert what happened?" She pants.

"I looked out of the window, seeing this bag woman, leaning on Ramone's office door, crying. Noticing it was her, I ran downstairs," he pauses. ..."When I got to her," he pauses, shaking his head, holding it down.... "Umm...huh."

Looking at Gilbert with frightened eyes, Matri becomes anxious waiting for him to tell her what happened. He finally got the strength to tell Matri... looking up at her.

"When I got to her, I couldn't move Matri... there was a puddle of blood. She kept calling for Ramone, cutting her wrists and arms, on both sides. My God Matri, blood was coming from the side of her neck, where she... cut, it too." water in Matr's eyes, risies like the ocans tide. Matri is furious," Her neck was cut, too!" They both become silent, staring into each other's eyes.

Finally the silence brakes. In a very low voice, Matri asks, "Did you call her parents?" In a daze, he wispers, "I... I... don't know, their number," he looks at Matri.

Matri goes through her pocketbook, nervously. "Here, call them now, Gilbert.

The doctor comes into the waiting room. "Are you....?

Matri answers abruptly, "Yes, where is she?" asks Matri.

Matri slowly opens the door. Antanette has an intravenous bottle. Her arms are bandaged and her neck is bandaged. Her hair is matted down on her head. Matri goes closer to talk to her.

Matri speaks with, undying compassion, "Antanette honey... it's Matri." Sitting on the side of the bed, she asks, "Antanette honey, can you hear me? I love you." Matri starts rubbing her head. Antanette opens her eyes. She starts whining. Matri gulps, feeling very hurt. She asks, looking into her eyes, "Oh honey, what's wrong?"

Antanette continues to whine... quietly she says, "I ... I... love him."

Matri is veryhurt and baffled, by what she says.

Antanette smiles, as if she sees someone. Speaking like a happy little girl...."Ramone, it's a girl..." She moves her eyes, staring at Matri. "Where is my baby?"

Matri's eyes start tearing. Wearily she says, "Honey..." Matri starts shaking her head... "Oh- honey..."

Antanette starts whining, rocking from side to side in the bed. Dr. Johnson, comes in.

"Doctor?...." whispers Matri.

He stands at the end of Antanette's bed, with his right index finger, holding his chin. Looking at Antanette. He says, with his eyes fixated on Antanette, "She tried to commit suicide, by slashing her neck, and she cut both of her wrists, terribly. She's lost a great amount of blood." Matri places her hands on her heart. The Dr. Johnson stares at Antanette, observing her. "Whoever the guy is, that destroyed this young woman, needs to be put behind bars for life. Whatever he did to her," he pauses, "Destroyed her. I doubt if she's capable of coming back. She's oblivious to her surrounding... in another world, virtually."

Straining to speak, Matri whispers, nodding her head. "No, I.... I thought she was going to be okay," Matri stares at the doctor, with innocent eyes.

"I've seen schizophrenic cases like this before. One minute, they appear to be coming back, then all of sudden, out of nowhere they go back. Almost, like it's too painful to cross over that line. Don't think they can handle, knowing the other person they used to be... it's too painful to see who they once were, comparing to who they've become now. Tthe psyche is a very tricky thing," says the Dr. Johnson.

Antanette continues to whine. All of a sudden, she starts screaming, yelling and wailing. Now, sounding like a very sad little girl, calling Ramone. "Ramone I love you... Ramone," she screams. "Please don't leave me... I didn't mean to kill you, I love you." She startes wailing.

Matri grabs her, brushing her hair back with her hands, thinking back to seeing her in her dream. How beautiful and happy she was. Envisioning her in her mind, she says kissing Antanette on the forehead, giving her poetic justice. "Oh Antanette, you're just like a flower, growing wild in the garden... surrounded by all sorts of colorful flowers, sharing the garden with each other." Matri gets the white flower she laid on the table. "Here, hold this in your hand honey. You're a beautiful flower ... white is for purity. The soul is pure Antanette, no one can make it dirty." Matri looks at Antanette, eyes teary, with the biggest smile and compassion.

Charmingly she says, "Antanette, you're not too dirty for God. You're a lady Antanette, no one could take that away from you," she says sweetly. "What happened in my dream with you, tells me you're special, a prodigy... of something to come. Antanette I know now, why I'm here with you… you looked through the windows of your soul…and you called me. You called me in my dream, you wanted me to see how beautiful you looked."

Matri says with exhilaration, smiling brightly at her, "And yes, you were so beautiful… with that white dress on. The wind that blew, had a sweetness coming from the smell of the flowers." Antanette whines. "Yes, I looked through the window of your new world, and you no longer suffered... you were peaceful and happy." Antanette drops the flowers, jumping up, snatching the intravenous bottle out of her arms. Just hollering, screaming and wailing…sounding helpless, "Ramone, I love you... .Ramone… Ramone." Matri held on tightly to her, rocking her like a baby. "Yes," she kept repeating, holding onto the white rose. "You're a beautiful flower… growing wild…you're a lady."

Antanette cries out, and screams to the top of her voice, then she falls back onto the bed. Her mother comes busting into the door, screaming and yelling. Her husband stands outside the door listening. It's is too painful for him. Gil comes in, grabbing Mrs. Smith.

Ten minutes later... the doctor comes over to them in the waiting room. "You know she could've made it but…I hope you don't think this is unprofessional of me, for what I'm about to say… this may help from a religious point of view… I don't think God will charge her for suicide… she didn't die because of what she did to herself. "He pauses, looking at everyone. "She died of a broken heart. I believe in this…I'm so sorry." He walks away, touched by this untimely death.

At the gravesite, people throw dirt on Antanette's coffin and walks away. It starts getting cloudy, sprinkles of rain starts to trickle down. Matri and Mrs. Smith are the last two, standing at the coffin. Mrs. Smith and Matri holds each others hands tightly, looking at Antanette's coffin.

Mrs. Smith listens as Matri speaks. "Oh Antanette, at least I got a chance to see you as beautiful as you are. But Antanette, you've never lost that beauty, because real beauty is within… that's a beauty that no man could take from you. …. You are a real lady in my book… God has picked you, to return to the garden, Antanette. Be happy to meet your Lord. A being that's, so compassionate, and his mercy is his law. He says, 'His mercy precedes Him'.' " I 'clare, we all should be happy to meet him. Antanette, I may not get there with you… but I hope to see you again," says Matri. She throws the dirt on her grave.

"Matri, you've been my bridge over troubled waters, and I'll never forget that."

Matri looks into Mrs. Smith eyes. "We all have a destiny and a purpose—I had to be here for you, Mrs. Smith."

"You know Matri, she's my last child to die. I lost two, one to drugs… one to the Black Panthers… and now, one to the world of prostitution." She looks into Matri's eyes. Her eyes are red from crying. Looks around, for her husband. "Where's my husband, Don't tell me he's gone too?"

Sometimes, emotionally, men can't take as much as we can," says Matri.

"Matri, I don't feel like saying anything… there's nothing to say. Just give me a minute of silence, with her."

Matri walks away, thinking, "God, I don't have all of the answers, but I know that you do. But can I just ask you, to cushion her pain… of course" Matri smiles. "Just like the birds, you will hold her up, by your leave."

Turning towards Matri, Mrs. Smith says, "Matri… please come."

"Yes ma'am," Matri says.

"Look with me for a minute." Matri gives Mrs. Smith a white rose to put on Antanette's coffin, along with hers. They walk away holding each other's arms, smiling.

New Birth sings:

She' faced the hardest times you can imagine, many times her eyes fall back with tears. When her youthful world was about to fall in. Each time her slender shoulders, brought the weight of all her fears. And a siren no one hears, still rings in midnight silence, in her ears. That a cry, oh she's a lady. Let her dream for she is a dreamer... she is a child. Let the rain fall down upon her. She's a free and gentle flower growing wild. If a chance I should hold her. Let me hold her for all times. If I'm allowed just one possession, I would pick her from the garden to be mine.

Be careful how you touch her. Sleeps the only freedom, all that she knows. Lord, Lord. When you look into here eyes, you won't believe she's paying for a debt she never owed. She's a sweet and gentle flower growing wild.

CHAPTER 23

THE WILL

Saturday evening, Matri is laying across the bed.

"This is going to be a beautiful wedding, Claudia. After all that's happened, I guess with some rain, some sun must shine." Matri exhales, "It sure feels good to relax." Someone knocks on the door. "I guess I spoke too soon," says Matri.

"Thaddeus, what brings you here tonight, in all this rain?" asks Matri.

"Matri, I needed to touch base with you before tomorrow."

"Okay," says Matri.

"Matri, are you prepared for the lecture tomorrow?" asks Thaddeus.

Matri looks over at Civil. "We're ready."

"Matri, my beloved sister, as I told you before. We're going to re-educate and redefine the pages of history, with it's subtleties of misguidance."

Quietly, Matri says, "Yes, I know we have work to do. Thaddeus, if anything ever happens to me, before I get a chance to take part in this new birth... I want you to get your portion from Isiah.

"Money?" He asks.

Matri pauses. "'I didn't tell you, Mrs. Watenburg, left me an inheritance… I have five million dollars. She was loaded… the money is undisputable … leaving me her limousine. She said it, was fit for a lady. Her chauffer Roosevelt and I, witnessed the money transaction together with her lawyer before she died. So that no one, because of my color, could dispute it. She came from a long line of wealth. Her family discovered oil. And from that, they invested the money in foreign policies, architecture and land. Of course, land is wealth in itself. Plus, she was an excellent business-woman. She and Mr. Krutz were in the stock market, and when Mr. Krutz died, he willed me thre million. He didn't have any family but his father, and he died. The rest of his family got wiped out during the Holocaust… Hitler's time."

"Thaddeus, Elijah Muhammad said, 'I appeal to all the Muslims and to all the members of the original Black Nation in America, to sacrifice at least five cents from each day's pay to create an "Economic Savings Program" to help fight unemployment, abominable housing, hunger, and nakedness of the 22 million black people here in America who continue to face these problems.' "He's trying to empower us, economically… Thaddeus. My purpose is to try and empower people just like Elijah Muhammad is doing. I refuse to let him or anyone for that matter, walk alone… I'm about the "Cause."

If I was sentenced to death, Isiah would've handled my money for me."

"Wow, Matri! That's a lot of money! What are you going to do with it?" asks Thaddeus.

"Thaddeus, the money doesn't belong to me—it belongs to God. He just entrusted it to me for a "Cause'. He had to give it to somebody, because he couldn't come and do it Himself. He leaves his custodians in the world, to take care of it for Him."

"I spoke with Isiah, Hezikiah and Robert, and told them I want them to open a program for Veterans. A program that will be sensitized to their plight, and help them when they come out of the service. A program that will help them emotionally, mentally and physically. Also, from this program, Osmon will play a part in giving them jobs. I want Osmon to have one of the biggest construction businesses, catering to Veterans first. He must have a strong union. I'll take care of the legal aspects in my will. He will create other jobs for them. I want this program to let the world know that these men should be respected with honor and dignity. And please, please take my friend Civil back home to his people."

"Mama used to say, before we came to the city, she never wanted to lose her home in the south. I will have reconstructions done to it. She wants to go back home. The cemetery… I'm going to have Osmon construct a new cemetery, with our last name, called… 'Cameron's Cemetery'. I want Isiah to buy up as much property as he can, buying people out if necessary. Somebody has to become the farmer, even if you have to employ some people to do it. Money makes money. We will take the money from that and build trailer homes at a reasonable price. Monies from that will also go towards Claudia's two sons… Hattie gets money also. Taresa's two children and Antanette's daughter for their education. We will have a little farmers market, from the vegetables and fruits we grow. I told Osmon to get together with the Muslim women and get the factories for Muslim women's attire. Also, I told him to get two Steak and Takes—it will be in his and Claudia's name. I want Osmon also, to find out, if we can set up a food pantry at the Mosque, and a church feeding the poor—that's a must."

"I'm going to make sure every month Antanette's baby receives a check from me. I want Claudia to keep a special eye on her. Take turns with her grandmother, helping her to take care of her. She will not become a victim of circumstances, not if we could help it. Ask her grandmother, if she could start going to the Mosque, when she turns eight. Keep her dressed Islamically… covered up, or culturally. I've named her…Fajr1X."A dawning of a new day," representing the light, and a new way of thinking… "A New Woman" …My little precious friend. That's my wishes for taking care of her financially. If I'm alive, I'll ask for shared custody, I'm sure her grandmother wouldn't mind. Thaddeus, dear heart, your share is included also."

"Last but not least, I want you to write my story. On the cover, I want to be standing holding Civil. Mrs. Watenburg has a great library. We'll have a picture of her painted with Mr. Krutz, beside her. We will have our family drawn by Dawn, meaning all of us: Mama, Thaddeus, Robert. Claudia, Isiah, Hezikiah, Dawn, Osmon, Fajr, Theodore, Hezikiah, Taresa and her husband. We're going to make history because," she adamantly says, " We should. It will be ours, displaying not just African history, but all history… correct history, that is." She exhales. … "I told Isiah if I forgot anything, they could handle the rest. Oh, make sure you befriend Theodore… and my limousine…you can use that for business… let me see . … Somebody will get the paper and look up rich Caucasians or business people, who need chauffeurs, there's money in that. That will offset money for Antanette's daughter… okay that's it," she says, tediously," I'm very tired. "

"Matri, I'd like to make a contribution, from the money I get from my books. I'll send extra money for Antanette's daughter, and money for the new trailer homes. We are family and unity is the key. Plus we have the greatest thing going, we all trust one another." Thaddeus raises up his thumb, with a closed fist.

"Robert says, he's going to contribute to the Veterans, and Hezikiah says, he'll be getting two million dollars from Uncle Sam," says Matri.

"You mean to say, he got what he wanted?" asks Thaddeus.

"Yup… but I don't know where Robert got all that money he has." Matri asks.

"Matri, can you keep a secret?" asks Thaddeus.

"What's that?" asks Matri, tiredly.

"You remember the Black Panther Cat, robbing the banks. Well, you notice they stopped talking about that?" says Thaddeus.

"Ah- ha" says Matri.

"Well, I think it was Robert," says Thaddeus.

Matri is shocked, "Why do you say that?" eyes juts out.

"Well, I went to his house one day…went to the bathroom, and saw the weirdest piece of clothing on the floor. He must've forgotten that he left it there. One night at Town Café, he said something that led me to believe, the Black Panther Cat was him… as a matter of fact, he hinted to me that it was him. He played a psychological game of telling me, but not telling me… and I caught it."

"Let me share this with you too. I found grenades underneath Isiah's bed."

Thaddeus's mouth drops. He nods, "Yes-ah-ha... the "Chess player."

Matri says, "Well, I was and still am devastated, but we have to keep their secret... a secret."

"I'm speechless," Thaddeus just shakes his head.

Matri pauses, pondering.…"But if I should live, I will also live to enjoy the money, God has entrusted to me. Now, I know my purpose."

CHAPTER 24

LOOKING OVER YONDER

It's June 9th, a Sunday afternoon. It's so quiet, you would think the Marshal of the court, is telling everyone that the judge, is entering the courtroom. The only thing different from the courtroom is, this hall is decorated in light green, mint green and brown. People are wearing their Sunday best, but there are men and women wearing uniforms: Panthers, Muslim women, MGT uniforms, Muslim men, FOI uniforms, Men in military uniforms and Matri's chauffeur, in uniform. The air smells fresh with perfume and after shave cologne. Air conditioners are keeping the room comfortable. Every now and then, there's the sound of a child playing and giggling.

There's someone walking up the aisle with a big bright smile, walking tall. Holding her head up high, like an African Queen; with a glow, personifying her spirituality. She wears a colorful dashiki, with some of the most radiant colors, of a peacock. The dominant color purple is the color of her head-wrap, representing royalty. Her jewelry sparkles, adding luster to her attire. When she passes by…ahhh… the aromatic smell, of her costly perfume, awakens the senses; lifting the spirits high, bringing a smile to all faces. She carries a gold cage with a big beautiful white bird, to the podium. Four pictures were hanging behind her placed across the stage: Honorable Elijah Muhummad, El-Hajj Malik Shaabazz (MalcolmX), Dr. Martin Luther King, and Beloved Empress, Professor, Angela Davis.

Matri pauses, slowly looking around the room, smiling. She sees Charlotte smiling, waiving her hands. Matri portrays a very nurturing expression, with great compassion to the audience. The audience is captivated by her beauty, and facial expressions.

She starts looking around the room again, "Charlotte, stand up please." Charlotte stands proudly. "This is another endearing friend of mine. We worked together." Looking around again, she says, "Is Theodore here, did he leave?"

He stands up smiling; husky broad shoulders, handsome smile, with militancy. "I'm here Matri, I wouldn't miss this for anything in the world...after all, I'm your chauffeur."

"Everybody meet Theodore, he is truly a remarkable person. We realize that it was destiny for us to meet. We served a unique experience with a unique person, that's no longer here." Matri looks around smiling. "That is, in the flesh. But she's very much alive, in spirit...I could feel her presence. Mrs. Watenburg, a unique, awesome Caucasian lady, who endeared me to her... for the rest of my life. She was a freedom fighter for blacks, and boldly challenging her race, trying to change the disease of prejudice amongst her people, as well. Having great love and understanding for our leaders, she left behind a handsome amount of charity for the "Cause" and a library for us all to marvel and ponder upon. Mrs. Watenburg was a dear friend of my boss. Mr. Krutz, who was a very charitable, kind generous Jew, leaving me another large amount of charity. He's no longer with us, unfortunately... he was murdered. Nevertheless, I can sense his spirit also, with us. "As a man/woman thinketh in his/her heart, so is he/she.

Matri is experiencing a spiritual high, smiling blissfully, with glossy eyes. "When I first came here from the south... I saw men in uniforms. The Muslims were the first one's I saw. Oh, I was certainly impressed with them. The Black Panthers, left an impression on my heart. Then, I saw the policemen and firemen too." She smiles, "I cannot forget, the Soldiers in uniforms. What really got me was, Muslim sisters in uniforms, I 'clare."

"After I begin to think about it... I saw something so meaningful about uniforms... there's a bigger picture here. It's said, 'A picture is worth a thousand words'." She nods her head, "Well, I—saw a Cause, with our people particularly, in uniforms. There's a coherence, a consciousness, a submission; a crying out for something that was missing. I saw militancy, gallantry, representation, unity, respect, trust... and certainly diehards."

"You know, uniforms have a way of getting your attention." She smiles pleasantly.

"Uniforms tell a story that must be told…and not only told, but they must be addressed and understood. I salute you, my brothers and sisters in uniforms, not with the traditional saluting… I must bow to you." She bows to them.

She stares off into the eyes of the audience, for about 15 seconds, not saying a word. Finally she says, "The eyes are the windows to the soul. My beloved brothers and sisters, Mahalia Jackson said, "Go tell It On The Mountains". Dr. King said that, he's been to the mountain-top, and he was not afraid. His eyes have seen, the glory of the coming of his Lord. El-Hajj Malik Shabazz (MalcolmX) went to Hajj and he prayed on Mount Arafat, and connected himself to his Lord, bringing back the light of truth. Moses went to the mountain, and saw his Lord, bringing back a tablet of commandments. Dr. King and El-Hajj Malik were fearless men. They must've known that, after they looked on the other side…." Matri pauses, holding her heart.…

"Sister you want some water?" asks Osmon

Matri smiles pleasantly, holding her head up firmly.… she softly says, "No," and smiles…her eyes flutters.

Assuredly she says, "After looking on the other side... they knew they would not be here too much longer." Her face glows... eyes gleams and roams around at the audience.

She pauses, never ceasing from smiling. "So, I too, "looked over yonder," and what did I —see?....Well, right now I would love you to trade places with me... to see what I'm seeing...." Seeming a little startled, looking at everyone, she says, "I 'clare... God tells us to look at his creation... and there you will find Him." She wipes her eyes, smiling brightly. "And what I'm seeing now, is the unity of a beautiful creation of His... the children of Adam and Eve... in unison." She pauses, "I see freedom." She holds the bird cage up. "This is another one of God's creations. We both had a destiny together. I felt that I selfishly took away his freedom, and learned that it was wrong for me to do that. But on the other hand, he was put in my path, because I could never have caught him... if God didn't allow me to. He was a part of my destiny. I 'clare, he taught me a very significant lesson. That is... everyone has a purpose... including a bird. It's always been miraculous to me, how birds stayed up in the air without falling. He showed me that, when we are at our lowest in this life, and can't go on...God will hold us up, just like He does the bird in the air...by His mercy... by His leave."

With a sudden burst of energy, she paces back and forth, just like an attorney. Trying to convince the jury for the verdict, with exhilaration. " Well, I looked over yonder and I've seen through the eyes of all, our souls. I no longer see with the physical eye, I'm seeing with the spiritual eye, that sees the soul of man/woman . ... My beloved Brothers and Sisters." Quietly, with teary eyes, she says, "I love you dearly. We must learn and take heed from those who carried the light. We must go to the mountain top. Go tell it on the mountain, go make Pilgrimage, take the journey that leads you to, yourself and your Lord."

"Yes, brothers and sisters I know, we are in a lot of pain." Shaking her head up and down, she whispers, smiling, "I know you are." Firmly, she says, "But Mama always told us that, when you're tired, God says. …. "Be still and know that I am God." What that means to me is that, if you could be still, you can hear the voice within. It wants to talk to you. It wants you to know, that there's a higher power greater than those who've oppressed you… and with that, it knows and sees all things."

"We must understand, that there's a purpose for everything. And yes, there's a reason why we were treated less than human… there's a reason why we had to endure the atrocities of massa… mentally, physically and physiologically…" With tenacity, she says nodding her head. "Yes, there is a reason." Noticing the silence, she looks around the room. "Everything has a season… and everything has a reason. …. It's called, trials and tribulations."

"Perhaps God has something so great for us, but he wants to see if we're going to come to know Him, and depend on Him and to be worthy of Him. I came to know Him better through my trials and tribulations. People, we all do things in life that we're not too proud of, some things you can tell, and some you shouldn't tell to anyone but God. He says, "Let anyone without sin cast the first stone," "Are there any stones in here?" She looks around at the audience.

"I went to jail for a crime I didn't commit… was accused of murdering two men and a snake. Yes, a snake, would you believe that? The devil is busy, he's out to destroy. Some of our greatest leaders were locked up. Our beloved Dr. King, and El-Hajj Malik (Malcolm), and Elijah Muhammad." Tilts her head, "Ummm… our beloved El-Hajj Malik says, "We're all locked up." You don't think you're in prison? Brothers and sisters, Willie Lynch, (slave master) said, " He has done all he needed to do to you, and he didn't need to do anything else. He threw away the key because, he thought you would never be acquitted. You had no right to think, the only crime is your skin color. Now, you're not in prison? I totally agree with El-Hajj Malik. These men came out of prison free, carrying a light that illuminated the world. The beloved Dr. King and El-Hajj Malik loved us so much, they died for us." She seems mesmerized by this.

"Being in prison was a struggle for me. Life is about struggling, and it makes things come to life. In our mother's womb that bore us, there was great struggle for her to carry you." She smiles pleasantly. "In the womb she carried you - you were in darkness, she had to see for you. No matter how tired she became. She had to take you everywhere with her, in the womb. As an infant... an adolescent... throughout life... her role is awesome. Did you know I thought that I was carrying Mama? But I've come to see that, not only did she carry me for nine months... but in my darkest of moments again, just like in the womb, my mama was carrying me, through her prayers. She called on God so much, telling Him that she would be patient, because she understood that, if she lost patience... He would leave her. She tried so hard to continue to be patient," she pauses, she cries. "She pulled out, everything in her soul and spirit, begging God not to leave her. .She became melancholy, because of her pain... she thought I was going to get the electric chair." She cries, looking into the eyes of the people. "My mama went blind, because of her love for me. The doctor said, there was no reason that he could find, to justify her blindness. He said sometimes trauma could bring on so many physical things...The loss of a loved one and a broken heart could even cause death." She pause, "So, an old woman told me that Heaven (Paradise), lies at the feet of the mother. She's the first leader...for man and woman. Respect the womb that bore you."

My beloved brothers and sisters, we have to stand for something. Brothers, women experienced the type of pain bringing a child into the world that you can never imagine...." Looking around at the men. "Brothers, she felt pain before you, and she struggled before you. She could feel your pain, come closer to the woman. We must stand up and look above our hurt and pain, so that when we look over yonder, we will all see something different, with our own light... I rest my case." The audience applause sounds like heavy rainfall. Eyes are teary, tissues are passed around... men are crying... women are crying.

Part 2 of lecture:

Joyfully Matri asks, "Osmon, are you ready?" Osmon's uniform is immaculate and uniquely tailored. Wearing a dark blue uniform and bowtie, fez with the emblem of a star and crescent on both of his shoulders, he stands like a proud soldier. "Thank you my sister," says Osmon.

"Thank you my brother," says Matri, walking away in a very stately manner.

"As-salaamu 'alaykum. May peace and blessings be upon you. First, I need my wife, my Queen to stand up. She looks so beautiful in her uniform. Stand up baby." Claudia stands up proudly, with a white MGT uniform on. "Okay, thank you... he chuckles."

"My beloved brothers and sisters, "The honorable Elijah Muhammad says, "You cannot love anybody until you love yourselves. We must understand self and learn the true knowledge of self. We're not Negroes, we are not colored... you can discard the name Negro. We must stop representing ourselves by the slave master's name. A good name is better than gold. One is able to associate an entire order of a particular civilization, simply by name alone.

"It is knowledge of self, that the so-called Negroes lack, which keeps them from enjoying freedom, justice and equality. And you must want for your brother and sister what you want for yourself. Allah (God) says, "To each is a goal. To which Allah turns to him. Then they strive together as in a race towards all that is good. Wheresoever ye are, Allah (God) will bring you together. For Allah (God) Hath Power over all things."

He hits the podium. "We must! Respect our women—respect the womb that bore you. When the woman is sacred in her obedience to God, guarding and protecting her relationship with God, guarding in your absence, what God wants her to guard.

Brothers and sisters…when a woman understands these things and practice it, there's nothing that energizes, motivates and secures him, more than a chaste woman. She has to make him feel like he's the apple of her eye. He should respect her highly for this."

Because if our enemies see us disrespecting our women, they will never respect us as men. Brother El- Hajj Malik Shabazz (MalcolmX) says, "There is no fair exchange between us. We are their maintainers and protectors. When the sisters want to help you brothers, then know you've been blessed. Sisters I love you all, but you too must respect yourselves…" He pauses. "Stop wearing massa's disrespectful clothes, they may be good enough for his women, but…" He hits the podium again. "But they're not good enough for our women! You are the cream of the crop…a diamond in the rough, Matri…" He looks at her and says emphatically, "Matri, the woman is man's field, to "Paradise (Heaven) and his nation. He must be careful how he plants his seed. … As-salaamu 'alaykum, may peace be upon you." Everyone applauds him.

"Thank you again my brother," says Matri. Taresa gets up from the audience with a glow, not a blemish anywhere. She is wearing white pearls and a necklace, white MGT uniform, white headpiece, gloves, and white shoes. Taresa walks up to the podium. "It's yours," says Matri, smiling.

"I greet you with the greetings of As- salaamu 'alaykum…. may peace and blessings be upon you." She stands tall, looking at Matri, smiling. "First, I have to let you know that, this lady to the right of me… Matri was my bridge over troubled waters, for my children and myself. She came to me and gave me the kind of love, that you don't find every day. She made me see, that I deserved the best that life has to offer. She let me know that, I too am a "Lady," and that I too, am one of those beautiful flowers, that deserve to be picked… and I was. Her love wants nothing in return. My children and I thank you with all of our hearts-oh, including my husband, he thanks you too."

Taresa pulls out a book. "I'm going to read you something from the Quran. It says, "What can be a holier cement to Society than that woman should be chaste and Pure. And crimes against sex be rooted out? Let decency, kindness, and justice prevail in all sex relationships. Let marriage be cherished, and carefully guarded. Women's rights secured; family jars adjusted; and life lived In faith, charity, and kindness and sincerity. To all our fellow-creatures. As--salaamu 'alaykum." Everyone applauds her.

With a cool poze, Isiah walks up the aisle smiling. identically dressed like Osmon, wearing a Muslim uniform. He kisses Matri on the forehead. Matri stumbles, pressing her hands against her heart. "Ya' okay?"

She whispers, "Oooh, I feel a little chest pain… it must be indigestion. Oooh, I feel a little dizzy," she places her hand on her forehead.

"Just sit b'hind me, there's a chair behind us," says Isiah.

He stands up like a soldier, looking around at the audience. "As-salaamu 'alaykum. I greet you with the greetings of peace. Well … I'm not too good with words… I guess I'll let ma' heart speak fa' me… that should work. Can I git a Amen ta' that?" Everyone says Amen. "Alright now, I could do this. I need ta' be a little charged up. I guess that comes from bein' in Nam. I alwaze had ta' be charged up, ta' fight."

"Like Matri said, "We've all done things we ain't too proud of. Well, I ain't proud of what I did in Nam… and never will be. When I came back, I waz' in turmoil. I waz' in so much pain… still felt like killin'… felt like I had been duped. like I been had, as ma' beloved brother El-Hajj Malik said. Ya' kno,' pain makes ya' do things that, cha' ain't too proud of. I felt guilty fa' things I had done, when I come home… but then, I met this man on a train,"he pauses,

"He waz' like an angel, a wonderful intelligent man. I never met nobody as smart as this cat." He starts looking around. "Where is he?...Oh, there he is. Stand up ma' man, Wallace Friedmen." He stands up... shyly, blushing.

"Y'all wanna' kno' what this man told me, in the twilight of ma' life? He said, he was studyin' a book written by a Scholar, Warith Deen Mohammed. He said he was from a different school of thought. In his own words he says, 'Man's errors is only in pursuit of his perfection.' He pauses. "Now y'all kno', I told 'em I didn't kno' what he mean... I told 'em I waz' dumb ta' the fact... b'leeve me... I wazn't the only one that didn't kno'," he chuckles. "I told him I needed ta' write it down, so that I could study it. I needed ta' be able ta' say it here... It really gave me somethin' ta' think 'bout."

"Okay, what he said mean this: "Man never intends ta' do wrong. Adam slipped into sin. He didn't do it intentionally. He waz' deceived by Satan. His nature bids him ta' the right thang, but sometimes circumstances gets him out of control, causin' him ta' fall. But his direction or his path is ta' find perfection. So he continues ta' strive fa' perfection. So, man never intended ta' do wrong, he slips into it."

"Now I have the understandin', the circumstances of slavery and Nam, made me slip inta' a person, that I didn't wanna ta' kno' anythang 'bout. So I realize, there waz' two thangs workin' against me... being Black and 'Nam.." He pauses, teary-eyed. "Ya' kno' Matri saw me lookin' up inta' the sky— started doin' it alot—so she asked me, what waz' wrong? I asked, where waz' God, cause I just couldn't understand, why He allowed me ta' go ta' that horrible war, and see the thangs I saw, and killing people. But now I understand, " he pauses again...and asks, "Where is God?... He looks around at the audience . …. He finally says, "He's everywhere." He says with passion, "And, I don't need nobody ta' tell me that. Before, I couldn't help ma' self, but now I can do better fa'; ma' self... Adam made amends. I'm brother Isiah2X now."

"I don't wanna' to slip inta' talkin' a long time, but I'd like ta' say that I'm goin' ta' marry ma' Queen, Dawn… and I didn't slip inta' it, I'm intended ta' do it. I love ya' all—" He smiles, "Really. As-- salaamu 'alaykum." Everyone applauds him.

Hezikiah walks like a dignified militant… husky chest, protruding. Uniform identical to Osmon's. "As- salaamu 'alaykum, I greet cha' with the greetins of peace. Well I just wanna' ta' say, that I love ya' all. I want everybody ta' kno,' that I had a very serious problem with ma' health. Thought I would never have the chance, ta' love again or have a family. When a man loses all hope of ever bein' a man, that does a lotta damage ta' 'em. Boy waz' I doin' crazy thangs." He chuckles… "Like Matri say, some thangs ya' shouldn't tell… can't tell ya' what I did. But, thangs have changed. I had a case with Uncle Sam and I won. God says, 'seek and you shall find. I found a specialist in Europe, that's goin' ta' do surgery on me. He said thangs ain't as fatal as I thought it waz'." He pauses… "And now, I can have, and do have one of those Muslim sisters, that I so desired. Stand up ma beloved Queen." She stands up proudly. "We'll be gettin' married within a month, and we have ta' go ta' Europe for ma' surgery." He cries… "Oh by the way, I'm brother Hezikiah1X. As-salaamu 'alaykum." Everybody applauds him.

Robert comes up, dressed in his Muslim uniform, identical to the others. He starts laughing, waving his hands, looking around at the audience, like he's a President.. "I feel like a President….actually I'm a mathematician. I guess you're wondering why I'm laughing. I have to admit, I do laugh a lot anyway. Laughing kept me going in 'Nam. If I didn't laugh, I probably would've cracked up." His shoulders starts jumping, his mouth twists as he laughs. "You know, there are so many stories to tell," he nods, slightly closing his eyes, "And some of them, are really unbelievable. You know, I never thought that I would be wearing another uniform, and a bowtie to match." He starts looking up and down at himself, chuckling. "But that just goes to show you… never, say never," with seriousnesss in his eyes, " Listen, I want my Queen to stand up for me… stand up baby."

Squinting her eyes, she says, "Oh Lord now, what chu' go and do that fa'?" Sadie stands up, dressed identical to Taresa's attire, all white MGT uniform..

"To make a long story short, I would like to read this verse from the Quran…. Anyway, here's what I got for you… listen up," he winks his eye, "It goes like this: "To the Glory of God, and men of fraud and hypocrisy are but rebels in the kingdom of God. God is the light of the heavens and the earth. High above our petty effervescent lives, He illuminates our souls with means that reach our innermost being. Universal is His light, so pure and so intense, that grosser beings need a veil to take His rays. His elect are absorbed in prayer and praise and deeds of love, unlike the children of darkness. Struggling in depths of profound vanities… false. Hey, I love you all. My name is Robert 5X. As-salaamu-'alaykum." He walks off stage in a dignified matter, waiving like the President.

Wallace walks up to the podium, wearing a blue suit with a blue tie and a blue fez, with a star and crescent, trimmed in gold. I must also greet you with the greetings, As-salaamu'alaykum. I'm not going to take too long." He smiles, meekly. "I'm a conductor… I've traveled quite a bit, around the world, that is. I've been around many Muslims with many different schools of thought, different perceptions of Islam, that is. There's one that really hit home with me, as a black man. His name is W. Deen Mohammed. Now I want you to know that, people often tell me that I have a photographic memory… so I have no problem memorizing what he wrote, without reading it to you. I have to say that, normally I don't reveal this because, I don't want to be used as a guinea pig or some experimental specimen for the laboratory." He chuckles." But anyway, this is what Mr. Mohammed says about the original man:

"Everything is created good, excellent. When you stray from the natural way, we can slip into sin. Adam slipped into sin… it wasn't intentionally. He didn't follow the devil willingly or know-ingly, he was deceived.

"When God said He made us from one single soul... that is Adam. This does not allow for racism. It says also, that our dignity is to be traced back to our originality. Your real dignity shouldn't be traced back to a land that you come from, for Muslims that is.

You're looking for your dignity in Ancient Africa or some Ancient black civilization... that's wrong for, Muslims. We are to look for our dignity in our original essence. We are noble by the act of creation. We are noble esteemed creatures, so says "God," He says that, "He made all the children of Adam honorable and noble. With great esteem and great values." He pauses, "I love you all. Thank you. As-salaamu 'alaykum."

He walks away. Everybody stands up and applauds him. All of a sudden, he turns around and starts walking back to the podium saying, with great vitality, "Never...." He continues with vitality, "Never...." He reaches the podium, staring off at the audience like a man on the battlefield, knowing that he's being outnumbered by the enemy, but he's not going to give up... he stands, galvanized by what he sees...He says with an electrifying voice, "Never! " He stands still... Points his fingers out, shaking..."Give up!" Turns around walking away meekly. The audience was left speechless, watching him walk off the stage.

Ruth walks with grace, holding her head up high. Dressed like an African Queen, in a white and gold dashiki. Wearing a white head-wrap on her head, with gold accessories. Matri reaches out for her hands. "The funniest things, brothers and sisters, all the time, I thought I was carrying Mama because of her heart. But I was only walking out of the strength she instilled in me. I knew nothing until she taught me, from a baby..." Matri points to Ruth..... "This is the "Matriarch" that carried me three times... nine months; when I was an infant; and when I was at my lowest, facing death." Ruth kisses Matri.

Ruth says, "God is good, ain't He?"

The audience responds. "Yes—maam."

"Yes!" She exhales.…"Well, I need ta' tell you a very short story. I won't hold ya' long."

"That's alright," the audience says.

"I do, as Matri said, suffer with a very weak heart. Recently, I become blind, but thank God, it wasn't perr--ma--nent. But I told the Lawd if it waz', I don' need ta' see what this world got fa' me ta' see no moe. I clare, don' seen enuff."

"It waz' wanna them hot days. I fainted, and when I start ta' come to, I notice Matri…she was just a toddler. I waz' on ma' back, and when I start ta' come to…I feel somin' on ma' face…" She laughs… "I notice it had a smell to it. It smell like urine. Matri waz' dippin' a rag in the urine bucket, we used fa' night time. Lawd the child waz' puttin' it on ma' face, ta' bring me too... I look at 'er. When she noticed me wakin' up… she went ta' the bottom of the bed, and put 'erself right at ma' feet…" Ruth and everybody laughs. "So I know'd then, that Matri would be the one, that would look after me. Even now, she don' think she looked after me, but in so many ways... she's one of them words she call me, ah... ah... Ma... tri... arch... to come."

Matri comes over, hugging Ruth. Everybody hears a baby laughing and rattling a toy. Thaddeus comes towards the podium with an eight month old baby, dressed in white with two reddish long pony tails. He steps up the stairs, holding the baby in his arms.

Thaddeus walks towards the podium dressed in a multicolored dashiki. His hair is grown out into an afro with a beard. The grey spot in his hair glistens. He kisses Ruth and Matri, giving the baby to Matri.

He holds onto the podium tightly. "Recently, I just found out that Matri, is my fraternal twin. The way we found out, was devastating for both of us." Feeling constrained, he turns towards Ruth…waiting for permission to tell the story.

Ruth nods her head, "Yes."

"To our surprise, Mama didn't know I was her son, either. Matri and I…" He looks at Matri lovingly…"Matri and I have a very special love for one another. We decided to forgive the person that withheld this from us, because… it is said that, man's/woman's errors, are only in pursuit of his/her perfection."

Looking at the audience he holds tightly onto the podium with fervor. He tries to make sure that, what he's about to say, will be imbedded into the audience's mind. "We've been unjustifiably taken out of our Garden… losing our bodily prowess. The people that died for us, left us the tools of courage, faith, and a strong will. If we will only reach out and embrace them, becoming its rightful gardeners, through cultivation. It is said that, "Each day we start out as the vendor of our own soul. Either freeing it, or bringing about its own ruin." We must learn the tools of forgiveness and trust. After all, isn't the Garden where it all started originally? We're all trying to make it back to that Paradise (Heaven)… don't go looking around for it… it starts here."

Thaddeus holds Fajr, high up in the air. "This is our future Matriarch. I wrote a book entitled, "The Birth of a Fetus." Because this little girl, had a very unfortunate life… put in a dumpster, at only five days old. I began to think what will my book be about… bam!… it came to me…"The Birth Of A Fetus."

Elijah Muhammad said, "A good name is better than gold." Matri wanted to give her a special name, "Fajr." Now Matri will tell you briefly, what it represents.

She reaches for Fajr. "Fajr means the dawning of a new light… a new day… the break of day. Fajr is when the blanket of the night is slowly pulled back by a powerful rising. A luminous morning light; giving a sign to the sleepers; that it is time to start another day, to work in their, "Garden." Perhaps when she understands the name Fajr, she won't be taken out of the garden, by evil suggestions, like her beloved mother… who is no longer with us."

"Everything happens for a reason. Moses was found in the water. But I 'clare, look at what was down the road for him. Joseph was found in the well, became a wealthy intelligent man. She was found in the dumpster…so what will be ahead of her…a, " Matriarch?"

Taresa's daughter wearing an MGT uniform, breaks away from her mother, continuously calling Matri. She runs up the steps, with her headpiece flying in the wind, pleading with Matri to let her say something.

Matri laughs. "Now I 'clare, you could say whatever you want. Go ahead, my angel."

She faces the audience. "I just want everybody to know that I love Matri very much. She helped my mommy out so much, when we didn't have nobody else to help us. She bought us food, toys, and she let us stay with her and her mom. I was so happy when she did that." She turns around hugging Matri. "I love you so much Matri, and Mama, I love you too."

Ruth says, teary-eyed, "I love you very much, kissing Taresa's daughter.

Matri says abruptly, "Oh, before I forget. Isiah and Dawn will be getting married here tomorrow, Sunday at 1:00. I need to say one more thing." Matri stands proudly with tears of joy. She says firmly, "Donny Hathaway says, *Brighter days will soon be here. Take it from me, someday we're gonna be free… just wait and see*" The audience stands up applauding, clapping, cheering and crying, chanting "*We're going to be free, someday.*" They kept repeating it over and over.

CHAPTER 25

DAWN'S WEDDING

The hall is beautifully decorated in pink and white. There are about 200 people. Dawn is dressed in an all-white headpiece, white gloves and white MGT uniform. Isiah is in his dark blue FOI uniform, and a blue fez, with a crescent on the side. "Come on everybody, they're going to cut the cake," says Thaddeus. There are cameras from all across the room.

Theodore says, "Matri, you truly have a beautiful family."

Anthony comes up to Matri. "Sister, you look beautiful."

Matri turns towards him, as the deepness of his voice echoes in her ears. She's surprised to hear him talking to her. "Thank you, thank you. Anthony, meet Theodore and Gabriel."

"Pleased to meet both of you," says Anthony.

"Matri, do you intend to get married some day?" asks Anthony.

Matri stares at him, with her eyes fluttering. "Well I 'clare... I sure hope so."

He imitates her, "Well I 'clare, would you go out with me? Of course, we have to be escorted by Osmon and Claudia."

Matri pauses. He stares back at her. She exhales..."Well I 'clare, Anthony..."

Anthony is baffled, "You 'clare... does that mean yes?"

Osmon and Thaddeus listens. "Well I 'clare, this calls for a piece of gum. I'm gettin' nervous," says Osmon.

Matri looks at Osmon. "Maybe you better give me a stick of gum too," says Matri.

Anthony, is not taking his eyes off of Matri.

Thaddeus overhears the conversation. He coughs, clearing his throat. "I think you better give me a piece of gum, too." Matri, Thaddeus, and Osmon, starts chewing gum, smiling at each other.

"Well I guess I better ask for a piece too," says Anthony. They all are, chewing gum, watching Matri.

Matri bursts out laughing. "I 'clare, Anthony, I'll go out with you." They all laugh.

"Matri, hi," says Mrs. Smith. Her husband is holding Fajr.

"Oh hi, Fajr. Let me hold her," says Matri.

"Mr. and Mrs. Smith…you too… Matri with Fajr. I want to take a couple of pictures," says Thaddeus.

"Hey everybody, let me git cho' attention for a minute," says Isiah. Dawn stands beside this big white sheet, wrapped around, what appears to be a big picture frame. "Now I want everybody ta' close ya' eyes, and when I count ta' three, open ya' eyes."

"No cheating," says Dawn

Isiah counts, "One, two, three… open yo' eyes." Everybody is shocked.

Thaddeus is in awe, "That's a beautiful portrait of Claf, Isiah, Thaddeus, Claudia, Matri, and Mama," says Osmon.

Everybody agreed that it's beautiful art. "Who did it?" asks, Theodore.

Isiah looks at Dawn, proudly. "Well, I not only married a wife, but I have a very talented woman. She's a artist, and she could sing too."

Dawn says, "I just want everybody to know, that I put my heart and soul into this picture. It's yours, Mama."

"Hey, will all of you on the portrait, stand behind the portrait. I'd like to capture this memorable day," says Theodore.

"Hey, I need one for myself, and one with just me and Fajr. I'll hold my book in front of us. "*The Birth of a Fetus*," says Thaddeus. Flashes from cameras comes from everywhere.

⊨⊨ ⊨⊨

Hour later, a conversation ensues:

"I'm telling you, these last two days, were days I'll never forget," says Matri.

"Yeah, it was one momentous day," says Thaddeus.

"Well, we better go home now, and git ready fa' that long ride, south tomorrow," says Ruth.

The next day, Ruth, Dawn, Isiah, Matri and Thaddeus get into the limousine, driven by Theodore.

CHAPTER 26
THE GARDEN

Wearing his leather cap, Theodore pulls the limousine in front of the house. "Here we go."

"Wake up Matri, we here," says Ruth.

"Oooh… I feel dizzy," says Matri.

"Maybe ya' just need ta' git outta this limousine and stretch," says Isiah.

"You didn't get out along the way, because you were asleep," says Dawn.

Everybody notices, Ruth standing in front of the car, staring at the house, teary-eyed. Dawn puts her arm around Ruth's shoulder, staring at the house with her. Everybody stands with Ruth, not moving, just staring at the house.

Osmon, Claudia, her boys and Anthony pulls up into the yard, noticing everybody looking at the house.

"Why is everybody just starin' at the house?" asks Claudia.

"Oooh, look at grandmama's house, it is so pretty," says Roy.

"You right bout' that, Roy. Who did the house over like that?" asks Claudia.

"When Isiah, Hezikiah and Robert came down, they worked on the house," says Osmon.

Ruth starts going into the house. Everybody follows behind her. Osmon turns around and says, "Here comes Robert, Sadie, Hezikiah and his intended."

"Mama got a big house, but it ain't big as Hattie's house. Some of us will have to stay with Hattie," says Claudia.

⚊⧾ ⧾⚊

The next day, everyone gathers at Ruth's house.

"Now, we can't all have breakfast at the same time. But we all gon' eat just the same," says Ruth.

Claudia comes in the house. "Here comes Hattie, Mama."

Abruptly, Ruth pauses. Her eyes are getting teary. Matri and Thaddeus stares at Ruth. "Mama, let me help you with the breakfast," says Matri.

"Let me help, I used to cook for Mrs. Watenburg," says Theodore.

Hattie and Nosa walks up, the steps with food in their hands. Everybody stares.

Forehead wrinkles up, "Well, don't just look at me like that," says Hattie.

"Hi Miss Hattie, you and Nosa, come meet ma' husband, Osmon1X," says Claudia.

Hattie looks baffled, looking at Nosa. "Osmon1X?" eyes moving from side to side.

"Never mind that, his name is Osmon," says Claudia.

Nodding, her forehead crinkles, "Pleased ta meet chu' Osmon1X," says Hattie.

"Pleased to meet you too," says Nosa, nodding with a big smile.

Isiah blushes, "Miss Hattie, you and Nosa meet ma wife, Dawn," he says.

"Lawd' everybody don' got married on me, she smiles, "Well, I don' got married too."

"To who" Claudia asks, with suspicious eyes.

Eyes juts out, looking at Nosa."Who else but Nosa... ain't nobody else love me like him."

Everyone says congratulations, to Nosa and Hattie.

Hattie is looking around. Finally she goes back to the kitchen. "Well I waz' just sayin' ta' ma'self, where iz'..."

"Hi, Miss Hattie," says Matri.

"Well Thaddeus, don' chu' see ya' mama standin' here?" asks Hattie.

He walks over, kissing her on the forehead. "Hi, mama," says Thaddeus.

'Hattie goes over and hugs Ruth. "Child, ya' back fa' good?" she asks.

Ruth doesn't look at Hattie. Biting down on her jaw, "Yup, I'm back fa' good," says Ruth.

"Hello, my name is Theodore, Miss Hattie."

Hattie stares at Theodore's complexion. "Well, pleased ta' meet chu' too," says Hattie.

"Okay," yells Ruth. "The first group, let's eat. I'm comin' in ta' put the food on the table, now."

Two hours later... Ruth stares at Hattie, biting down on her lips. "Hattie let's take a ride ta' ya' house. Matri, Thaddeus and me, we need ta' talk ta' ya'. I got ta' git' this off ma' chest, fore' it kill me," says Ruth.

Hattie's eyes look myserious, troubled by Ruth's remark. "Okay Ruth."

"Theodore," yells Matri. "I need you to take us to Miss Hattie's house."

Half hour later:

Theodore, looks at Miss Hattie's house from the car. "This is some house here, Miss Hattie got."

"It sure is," says Thaddeus.

"It used to belong to a rich doctor, named Dr. Rodgers. Mama ran across it, when her sister went into labor on their way home. Nobody claimed the house, so she claimed it. That was the beginning, of Mama becoming a midwife."

"Okay, what time do you want me to pick y'all up?" asks Theodore.

"Give us about two hours," says Matri.

"Y'all come on in son, let's git the show on the road," says Miss Hattie.

They all sit down in Hattie's huge living room. Ruth holds a handkerchief in her hands, wiping her eyes. Hattie becomes afraid, to ask what's wrong. "Mama, come here, sit down in front of us," says Thaddeus.

Hattie acts nervous, wiping the sweat off of her face. "Lawd' I don' know if I'm gon' like this, Thaddeus." She starts panting.

Thaddeus says firmly, "It's not about 'like', Mama. It's about what's right."

Hattie's breathing hard, her forehead becomes deeply wrinkled. "It's 'bout what's right, Thaddeus?"

Thaddeus holds Hattie's hands gently. Lovingly he says, "Mama, Verna gave me, Ruth and Matri a letter.

Ruth said, "Verna speak ta' me 'bout the letter. She say that Mrs. Annielu give 'er the letter b' fore she died, tellin' her ta' make sure I gits the letter."

Thaddeus looks into Hattie's eyes, "Mama, Mrs. Annielu said, somebody had to tell the truth to us all."

Hattie jumps up, panting, shaking her head frantically. "Lawd boy, what is y'all talkin' 'bout? Now, I don' gave ya' all I had. Even sacrifice ma' love fa' ya'."

"Oh—Lawd Hattie…!" Wearily, Ruth cries out… "Why?… I 'clare now, the Lawd' kno' what chu' did, Hattie," says Ruth.

Hattie starts looking around the room hysterically.

Matri's eyes flutters. " Miss Hattie!" Matri cries out, trembling, "The letter said, Thaddeus and I are fraternal twins."

Hattie screams, falling on the floor humming, rocking back and forth. Thaddeus jumps up to pick her up. With pain in his heart, he gently says, "Mama…" He pauses, with tears in his eyes.… "Please, please…" He's in too much pain to talk.

Hattie falls down on her knees, gazing at Ruth and Matri. Pleading, with her hands stretched up in the air, "Oh Lawd, Ruth… Matri." She looks up into Thaddeus' eyes, crying a river of rears. "I didn't mean ta' hurt nobody," Hattie's voice lowers, "The Lawd' wouldn't give me…"

Ruth frowns, shaking her head. "Lawd Hattie, ya' went over the Lawd,' cause He wouldn't give ya' a baby…so ya' take mine Hattie?" Ruth starts rocking back and forth, biting down on her lips, crying and squeezing the handkerchief in her hands.

Painstakingly, pleading to Ruth, "No, I didn't Ruth…" Sounding like a little wounded girl," I just wanted a baby like everybody else. Ma' husband died… I didn't have nobody, Ruth. I waz' lonely here in this big ole house by ma' self. I had the dog, but that ain't like havin' a child, or somebody ta' love, Ruth. I bring so many babies inta' this here world… and I couldn't have none of ma' own. So when ya' fall out givin' birth to Matri, I didn't kno' there waz' no other baby inside cha' Ruth." Hattie starts reliving that time in her mind. She frowns, with sweat pouring from her face. "All of sudden, I saw ya' stomach movin' round," she pauses. lookingaround, staring, "It scare me at first. Then I say… let me look, and I looked… saw a baby's head hangin' out cha'. I said ta' ma'self," Hattie intensely relives the experience. Looking surprised as she speaks, " Lawd' what iz' this here? So I git' ta' thinkin,' listenin' ta' the devil… I say ta' ma' self, Ruth can't take care all them chillin' ha' self… Jessie dead and gone." She looks at Thaddeus pitifully. His face was wet with sweat; he rubs his face gently. "So… I take ya'

Thaddeus. Ruth didn't kno,' cause she was still pass out like a light. Lawd,' I thought she waz' dead….'' Thaddeus gets on his knees taking his handkerchief out of his pocket, rubbing the sweat and tears off of Hattie's face.

Matri comes over and got on her knees with Hattie, holding her hands, looking Hattie in the eyes. "Miss Hattie… the eyes… are the window to the soul." Hattie holds onto Thaddeus' hands, staring into Matri's eyes. Ruth doesn't stop biting on her lips, rocking back and fourth crying. Thaddeus and Matri holds onto Hattie.

Matri asks, compassionately, "Miss Hattie, did you know that we come from the "Garden." We've been taken out of that Garden. Massa took everything from us that he could possibly take from us." She says wearily, "You know Miss Hattie, he said, "He didn't need to do…." She yells out crying and shivering… "Not another thing to us! Because he did everything he could possibly do to us, to break us down." Tears roll down Thaddeus' cheeks. Matri gulps, "They—broke us. They killed our spirit… taking our light from us, and put us into total darkness… putting us into a wilderness".

Matri yells out wearily, "Oh—Lord… I 'clare… the cruel atrocities of how we've been treated, hurts me beyond what you can ever imagine, Miss Hattie."

"For sometime now, my heart began to feel strange. Thaddeus told me to go to the doctor. The doctor said, he couldn't find anything wrong with my heart… this world breaks my heart…" Matri pauses, looking away as if she sees something, so endearing. Everybody's attention went on her, to see what she was seeing. She starts smiling, her eyes get glossy. She says very eloquently, as if in a trance. "Miss Hattie my beloved, I read that…'In the "Gardens of Eternity," beneath them, Rivers will flow; they will be adorned therein with "bracelets of gold, and they will wear green garments of fine silk and heavy brocade; They will recline therein on raised thrones. How beautiful a couch to recline on!'

"Miss Hattie, I've known to have a way with words, but I 'clare... there are no words that I could find to describe the "Garden," beyond this life. But it is also said that, 'The "Garden" has the type of peace and beauty that, no mind can imagine…. no heart has ever felt, no eyes have ever seen… nor has it ever occurred to man… Oh… what awaits him or her."

She looks away again, saying, "Miss Hattie don't weep for me, please. I forgive you, because if we don't forgive one another, we'll never stop the pain. We, as a people, have been hurt deeply. I'll love you, always." She looks up at Ruth… "And I know that you love Mama with all of your heart… you never intended to hurt Mama, you slipped and fell, just like Adam and Eve... Miss Hattie."

"Mama," Thaddeus says. "Let us get up and come sit down over here with Mama…" He pauses looking at Ruth. "Mama, come on now, sit next to each other. Please do it for me." They both sat together, faces wet with tears. Thaddeus gets on his knees before them. He looks both of them in their eyes. He starts smiling, sounding blissful. "I'm a very blessed man here today. I have two beautiful God-fearing women… that I know, without a shadow of a doubt… love me dearly, with all of their hearts. Whatever happened, you couldn't stop it, the script was already written, by the number one Author, Almighty God. Yes, you took me from Mama. He took Moses from his mother, and put him into the arms of another woman. He knew it was a means to an end, for me too." Adamantly he says, "I 'clare, what more can a man ask for, when he truly understands?"

He looks at Hattie… "Beloved, because of what you did for me, I'm the man that I am today. You gave me the best leadership qualities, first. I have a good education. I'm a writer, and have a very good job. You gave me morals to fall back on. And I respect women because, you respected yourself. A good leader has to respect and have high regard for women first, to be a good leader. " He holds Hattie's cheek with his hands. "Just like Matri said, we've been taken out of the "Garden." Sometimes we listen to the wrong voice, and we never intend to do wrong. So I have to judge you by the good that's in you… the 'you' that intended to do good. I love you very much with all my heart and soul… you're forgiven." He kisses her on the cheek.

Ruth looks at Hattie, feeling for her hands, holding her tightly. Hattie grabs Ruth, holding on to her hands tightly. "Oh Hattie the devil waz' 'bout ta' destroy us, and take the love away from us." Mama abruptly, jumps up talking, as if she sees the devil. "But devil!" She yells out, performing an exorcist on the devil. "Oh devil, ya' ain't nothin' but a liar, and that's all ya' gon,' ever be!" She makes a gesture of, spitting at the devil. "Ya' don' took from us long enuff, now. You ain't nothin' but a thief… go round stealin' people's joy, with all that old evil whisperin', ya' old serpent!" She yells and shakes her head bravely, "But I got news for ya'… yeah," she pants, "Got bad news fa' ya'… ya' don' meet cha' match this time… I got a forgivin' heart." Ardently she says, "Yes I do! It might take me time ta' git used ta' thangs… but all wounds heal in time."

She yells, looking around as if she sees the devil again… pointing to Hattie, buckling in her mouth, shaking her head, "Ya' see this wo'man right here? I say, do ya' see this wo' man right here! I want chu ta' kno;' that I forgive 'er, right-now--this very minute. Cause, God iz' a Mrciful, forgivin' God, and He wants us ta' forgive one another. Cause if we don,' and keep listenin' ta' ya… we ain't never gon' make it back ta the Garden. Come on everybody, let's hug and let the Lawd' kno,' ain't no devil gon' beat us. Understandin' iz' the best thang in the world—and I understand," says Ruth proudly.

They hug each other. "Y'all come on inta the kitchen. I got some apple pie, just baked this mornin'," says Hattie.

"Lawd'… ya' still gon' make me fat Hattie," says Ruth. They sit at the table laughing and rejoicing.

Two hours later... Matri says, "Somebody's at the door."

"It's Theodore," says Thaddeus, answering the door.

Hattie says, "Y'all stay the night with me. Tell Theodore y'all gon' spend the night, please."

Matri asks, "Mama?"

Ruth nods. "Yeah, I don' see no reason we can't stay."

"Theodore, come on in and have some pie, they gon' spend the night."

"Now you're talkin,'" says Theodore.

It's 7:00pm, and Matri walks over to Theodore and Thaddeus on the front porch. "Theodore, take me to the house. I need to get Civil. I made him a promise."

"Sure, let's go," says Theodore

"You're coming, Thaddeus?" asks Matri.

"No, I'm going stay with the ladies," says Thaddeus

After arriving, Theodore says, "Matri when you brought me out here, that was one of the most beautiful experiences I've ever had in my life."

Matri looks up at Theodore smiling; then she looks at Civil and speaks. "Come on, my dearest beloved."

"You want me to come with you?" says Theodore

"Oh no, this is between me and Civil," says Matri.

Matri stands before the cliff, holding Civil in her hands, looking into Civil's jet black piercing eyes. He attentively looks back into her eyes, as if he understands. "Here we go Civil. This is where I saw you in my dream. Flying away, soaring high in the sky... free as a bird." Matri pauses, seeming puzzled. "But then, I saw myself flying off with you, too." Matri backs up, putting her hands on her heart. "I better go, Civil... I just want you to know that, I love you dearly. Our destiny has been a memorable one, that I will cherish for all the days of my life." Matri smiles with compassion. Her eyes sparkling, looking into Civil's eyes, she says, "One day, I hope to see you in the "Garden," she releases Civil. He flies away looking back at Matri, making bird talk at her.

Matri walks back to the limousine, looking back at Civil flying away. "Okay Theodore, lets roll, baby." He looks back at Matri, flattered by her, calling him baby. She chuckles.

"You're beautiful, Matri," says Theodore.

Matri exhales, "Ummm, this air feels so good. I'm gonna keep the window down."

"You're right, it does," says Theodore.

Matri ponders, "You know what Theodore, I've been thinking..."

"About what?" he asks.

"The cemetery. I've always wanted to give us a better cemetery down here. Now I will, thanks to Mrs. Watenburg and Mr. Krutz. I told Osmon to start cleaning it out right away..."

"Why?" He asks.

"I don't want another body to go in that horrible place, like it is now," she says.

"That's admirable," says Theodore.

Matri sits up. "I have another name for it now..." "The Garden Cemetery."

Theodore smiles, "Hey, I like that myself."

"I'll tell you Theodore, never underestimate what awaits you in the future. Along with its uncertainties, there lies the challenging, and the good. When we buried my brother Claf, it hurt me so badly, to see the conditions of our cemetery. I was driven to find purpose for my life, as well as my people."

"Whoever thought that I would meet, such wealthy people like Mrs. Watenburg and Mr. Krutz, leaving me all that money. Now, I could better help my people, to serve a purpose in their lives, opening doors of opportunities. Knowing the law, I could do so much for us."

"Yeah Matri, you give me something to think about too. I realized that, I too have a purpose in this life. I think my purpose has something to do with you Matri…and your family. I feel that there's a great connection here for me… and it won't be long before I find out, exactly what it is," he says, smiling, displaying his dimples.

"Ummm, yeah…" Matri lays back on the seat. "I'm so tired, Theodore."

"Go to sleep baby, I'll wake you up when, we get to Miss Hattie's." Theodore says to himself, *Miss Hattie, feel like I belong here just as much as everybody else. This is my extended family. God knows no prejudice… and neither do I. Wallace said, 'We're one soul' and that's all I know."* He nods his head.

"Okay Matri, we're here," says Theodore.

Tediously Matri says, "Okay Theodore, I heard you. I'm going straight to bed."

Thaddeus sits on the porch. "Hey my man, you want to sit on the porch for awhile? I'm not ready to turn in yet," says Thaddeus.

Thaddeus makes him feel like family. "Sure." He smiles. Theodore stays the night.

It's 2:00 in the morning. Suddenly, Ruth sits up in the bed, noticing Matri laying at the bottom of the bed… holding her feet. Ruth chuckles. "Matri, Matri come on up here with me and git' under this sheet, and lay your head on this pillow. Ya' look so tired." Ruth moves her foot around to wake Matri up. "Matri," she whispers… Matri doesn't move. Ruth stops moving, staring at Matri at the foot of the bed, not moving. "Matri." She calls again, easing out of the bed and turns the light on, looking at Matri laying across the foot of her bed, not moving. Ruth's afraid to move, staring at Matri. Then she moves slowly, shaking Matri, to see if she's breathing. "Matri, oh no, Lawd no, Matri!" Ruth yells and screams. Everybody runs to the room. "Oh Lawd no!…noooo!" Ruth continues to scream.

This is a day of emotional purging. The yard is holding as many cars as possible. The undertaker comes to the porch, asking Ruth is she ready. "Oh Lawd, why not me...why not me Lawd?" Ruth cries out, looking up.

Mrs. Smith comes over to Ruth. She stops Ruth, looking into her eyes, saying, "I understand." Fajr reaches out to Ruth, smiling, rubbing her hands all over Ruth's face, playing with her.

Ruth reaches out for Fajr. "Take her... take her," says Mrs. Smith. Ruth takes her.

Isiah and Osmon hold Ruth's arms, while walking down the steps." Mama, Fajr, Dawn, Claudia, Thaddeus, and I will ride with you," says Claudia.

Claudia points out to a beautiful well-to-do woman, with keen features. The medium framed, fair-skinned women with red hair, is walking towards the house. Everyone watches, her as she walks straight towards Ruth and Fajr. Slightly looking around at everyone, she nods. Then, looking at Fajr, and then Ruth. She speaks, "Hello..." she pauses, looking at Fajr again, "What a beautiful little girl. .... I'm so sorry, my name is Shawn. I've had the pleasure of meeting your lovely daughter, Matri... just want to give my condolences to the family." Shawn gives Ruth a card.

Ruth shakes her head. "Thank you, glad you could come." She turns around and walks back to her limousine. Everyone watches as she walks away.

Osmon exhales, "I'll ride up in the front."

"Now, Sadie, Robert, and Hatie and Nosa, will ride with Theodore. The boys will ride with Anthony." Charlotte comes behind Isiah. He turns towards her, surprised she came. "Why Charlotte, Matri would be glad to have..." He pauses, catching himself.

"That's okay," says Charlotte."

"Charlotte, ya' oughtta be able ta' fit in with Anthony," says Isiah.

The journey to the cemetery, seems like it would never end. Isiah looks up, the sky is getting cloudy. The wind is starting to blow the dust into the air, like a sandstorm.

As the cars trail down the long dirt road, everyone is quiet and preoccupied by their own thoughts. Funerals have a way of doing that.

Isiah thinks, *It's somethin' 'bout these cars, black and meticulous, special."* Isiah looks around at the black leather interior. *Strangely enough, it shows elegance. Something a lady would like ummm."* He smiles. *This puts me in the mind of Matri, acting like a lady.* He pauses, *This waz' so unexpected.* Isiah looks at Ruth. *I'm glad Mrs. Smith gave her Fajr ta' hold. They say, these are the hardest deaths ta' deal with... first Claf... but then Matri been actin' kinda strange, but how waz' I supposed ta' kno'? She waz' so happy... had a expression on 'er face at the lecture, like she saw Heaven with 'er own eyes. I just don' understand how the doctor said, she died from a broken heart. Mama say, why not her. I beg ta' differ with he... why not me. Death waz' all around me in 'Nam, but I escaped it. But as they say, it just wazn't ma' time. He saved me fa' a reason. I'm gonna make sure, I prove ta' God, ma' gratitude.*

Robert thinks, holding onto Sadie's hand tightly, noticing the uncontrollable dust, flying in the air. *The line is so long, you can't see where the cars end. All driving in one straight line, like in the military... a direct order... representation of a Divine command, respectfully.*

All types of people came. They reflect colors of a rainbow, shining in an incredible mirror. Claudia thinks, Matri said, *'That's what a mirror does. It's very kind, and it lets you see everything, without prejudice. Matri iz right, if only we could be like mirrors'.*

Thaddeus thinks, The car lights shine, and it seems like cars are moving in slow motion. This is beautiful... the unison, just like Matri explained. There's somethin' special about it. That one straight line represents the oneness of God, and there is only one soul, one spirit, representing conformity and unity... like uniforms worn. We become submissive to the Creator because, death can make us humble. Death shows an example from that straight line, to keep us straight with each other, respect and have regard for one another, because God is telling us here, we're all one in the same.

Osmon thinks, *Ummm... the lights are on, telling us that God is the illuminating light of the heavens and the earth, and Matri's not dead. She's following the light... that light that takes us straight back, to the first Garden in Paradise, to Heaven.*

Driving through the gates, there are so many people at the cemetery, it's a huge cemetery. There's a beautiful sign at the top of the gate, engraved in gold, that reads, "The Garden Cemetery, founded by Matri Cameron"

There are news reporters that questioned her after her trial. They came to find out the importance of this young lady. Questioning, why she was being remembered as the making of a "Matriarch." And why so many came, from all over to give her farewell. People from the city came: Panthers, Mrs. Brown-the manager; Muslims, college peers, Charlotte, Freddie, Taresa, her husband and children, some of the boys from the projects, Gilbert, the attorney, Mr. Sawyer and Wallace, and all the people that were at the lecture came. The two men, that they met on the train. Some came because they heard so much about her. They even carpooled or caught the bus to get there. Townspeople came along with the teachers from grammar school, and Mount Calvary College.

As the minister speaks, everyone is absorbed into their own thoughts, around Matri's grave. Verna continue to watch Thaddeus and Ruth. "Lord, I can't help but feel hurt for Thaddeus, he fell in love with his own sister. Ruth and Miss Hattie, will they ever be the same again?" Ruth never let go of Fajr. Isiah and Osmon never let Ruth go. Claudia and Dawn never let go of Isiah and Osmon. Sadie is leaning on Robert's shoulder. Hezikiah holds onto his fiancé's hand tightly. Wallace holds his head down, looking at the coffin. Mrs. Smith smiles, remembering the strength Matri gave her.

Anthony thinks, *Oh Allah, this was the most beautiful spiritual woman I've ever seen. You gave her beauty inside, and outside. She was a lady,*

I 'clare. I wanted to make her my Queen. I would've been so proud of her as my wife. It felt like I loved her, and I never touched her... but she touched my soul. But Allah, you take the good too, and you are the best knower. I have to submit to that.

Matri, I love ya' so much. It hurts so much. I never met anybody like ya. I probably never ever will, ma' sister. I kno' ya wouldn't want ta' see me like this, ya' would tell me. 'Now Claudia, ya' have ta' be strong fa' Mama'. I have ta' take some of ya, to git over this hurt I feel fa' ya' leavin' me. It just hurt so bad right now. I promise ya' I'm gon' be strong fa' Mama. Matri, thanks fa' showin' me how ta' be a lady. That cha' waz', I 'clare. I may not git there with ya,' but I hope ta' see ya' again.

Ester whispers, "Oh Leroy, ya' still callin' me. I love ya' too."

Anniemae looks at Ester, shaking her head, thinking. *Oh Lawd, that woman ain't gon' never have good since, I don' kno' what Leroy put on er'. She act like he put some roots on 'er. I'm sure glad I didn't marry 'em. She scare me, from wantin' another man. He might do me like Leroy did her. Nooooo-way.*

Hattie with tears rolling down, thinks hard while looking at Thaddeus, fixated on the coffin, *Matri, thank ya' fa' forgivin' me. I hope God let chu' back in the Garden, with our first father and mother, Adam and Eve. God gave ya' a gift with people. We ain't never gon' forgit' chu' and ya' sure waz' a lady. I can tell ya' that fa' sure. I may not get there with ya,' but I hope ta' see ya' again.*

Thaddeus starts looking baffled, as if he feels a presence. He thinks, *Matri my beloved. I feel your presence, so strongly. I know you can see, each and everyone of us, I can feel it strongly. We're fraternal twins... oh my beloved, I feel like a part of me is going with you. I have an urge to jump in this casket, and go with you.*

He backs up. Robert pulls him, putting his arms around him.

"Beloved you died of a broken heart, from the atrocities you've seen placed on our people, by this world. You will never die... your love and your spirit will always be with me. El-Hajj Malik says, 'The pen is mightier than the sword. ....' Matri, you said, 'The eyes are the windows to the soul'. Well my beloved, I will write your story. Entitled, "The Making of a Matriarch." In my writing, I will look through the windows of the eyes, taking your light forward, touching souls; sharing tools to take them to the Garden, that exists right here too.." He's compelled to speak out. "I will help them, look over yonder, and see what you saw in life and in death. I will let them know that, death is only a beginning, my beloved. Just want you to know that, I may not get there with you, but I hope to see you again."

Thaddeus bursts out crying, causing everyone to let out their cries. Robert grabs Thaddeus and holds him tightly. "I'm sorry Matri, hey I just can't help it," says Thaddeus. The minister stops talking, remaining quiet to allow the emotions to be expressed.

Dawn yells out, Isiah holds her tightly. "Matri, you were a lady. I'll love you and I always will. I will help to take care of Fajr. I will draw the most beautiful portrait of you, just like I'm seeing you right now, in my mind." Dawn pauses. Isiah holds her gently. "I will capture the look you had in your eyes, that you had at your lecture. I've never seen anyone so happy in my entire life. Your eyes will tell your story, letting them see that... yes, the eyes are the windows to the soul." Dawn cries out again and says, " Matri, I may not get there with you, but I hope to see you again."

Ruth starts humming, rocking back and forth with Fajr, thinking. Ruth rebelliously draws back, and says with defiance, "Git back off of me devil! I will not be mad at God, 'cause he gon' carry me through this. Yes, I love ma' baby with all, ma' heart and soul. But I thank ya' Lawd, just gotta keep on thankin' ya'. Yes ya' been good ta' me. Ya' coulda took 'er, and me at birth... but no, ya' let me have 'er fa' a little while, and I'm grateful fa' that Lawd. Lawd, just like Mary the mother of Jesus... ya' use 'er ta' bring Jesus inta' the world. Well Lawd, that's how I see ma' Matri. Ya' use me ta' bring 'er inta' this world, fa' yo' purpose, a reason, and everythang got a season. Thank ya' Lawd... Matri baby, yes ya' waz a lady. I love ya'.

and I may not git' there with ya,' but I hope ta' see ya' again." Ruth kisses Fajr, and manages a smile after the emotional release.

The minister resumes. "You may throw your dirt on the coffin now." Thaddeus puts a white rose on her coffin. Everybody throws their dirt on the coffin and walks away.

"Matri was a real lady," says Theodore, smiling pleasantly.

Thaddeus smiles, "Yeah, she used to walk with books on top of her head. She wanted to walk like a lady, she would say."

Suddenly Theodore turn around, noticing a white bird on Matri's coffin. "Hey Thaddeus" says Theodore, "Look, there's Civil on Matri's coffin."

Thaddeus looks, staring at the bird.

"Matri took me to her special place, and took her bird, letting him go. She said she promised to free it," says Theodore.

Thaddeus just keeps looking at the bird. He exhales, "They are both free." Everybody leaves the cemetery, except the bird.

The men left to go to Matri's safe haven. Osmon, Isiah, Thaddeus, Nosa, Robert, Anthony, Wallace and Hezikiah, are together. All standing at the cliff, where Matri would always seek refuge, in her darkest moments. This is where the cosmos is, with its luster, displaying beauty. Possessing a silence, and tranquility that eases its way through the depths of souls. Matri's place continues to speak to hearts, with unspoken words. There is no need to talk, no need to question life or death.

The family men turned Matri's safe haven, into a beautiful Garden, with an array of roses. They cleaned and expanded the area, constructing a white huge gazebo, facing the cliff, with a view of the stars. They added two steps on both sides and two decorative chairs inside. On the front of the gazebo, Dawn engraved a bronze plate that said, "I looked over yonder and what did I see?... Matri Cameron."

Inside the cave, they put chairs and used that, for a place for lectures.

The walls had one big portrait with the faces of Dr. King, El-Hajj Malik, Elijah Muhammad and Angela Davis. Dawn painted a portrait of Matri and Fajr, Mr. Krutz, and Mrs. Watenburg, for the collection.

Everybody in town came to see this momentous view. Matri's safe haven was the talk of the town. Couples chose the area to take their vows, because Matri would be there too. They just couldn't see 'er. People took turns going there, for romantic picnics with their new brides, or just talking out their problems. Because Matri would be there, listening to help them... somehow.

—≺+ +≻—

Some people say, that they see Matri running down the road, fast as lightening. Some even run to catch 'er, to talk to 'er, cause they say she had a lot a wisdom. Some say, they see Matri sitting right there, in that chair watchin' the stars with Civil. People say, she sho' waz' a lady too. I 'clare.

CHAPTER 27

THE SNOW

Seven years later, on July 10,[th] at two in the morning... it looks like snow, in a beautiful crystal ball. The wind is whistling, and snow is falling down like giant tear drops. When it reaches the ground, it piles up like cotton. It covers the earth like a huge blanket, and provides peace, comfort, and tranquility.

Two men stand in front of a beautiful glass coffin. They prepare to place it into the ground. Suddenly a woman appears in the coffin, wearing a beautiful sky blue silk gown and matching head wrap. A white rose, lays across her, in the coffin.

Thaddeus jumps up in the bed shivering. Tears and sweat glides down his face. He looks around the room for falling snow, but only hears the air conditioner. Setting his eyes on the cover of his new book, Matri standing with Civil, entitled, "*The Making of a Matriarch.*" He starts shaking his head from side to side, with humbleness, and says, "Yes beloved, it's time for me to let you go, now." He holds his hands, high up in the air, and he pleads, "Yaa Rabb! Yaa Rabb! (Oh Lord!)."

"Oh God, forgive and have mercy upon her, excuse her and pardon her, and make honorable her reception.
Expand her entry, and cleanse her with water, snow, and ice.
Purify her of sin as a white robe is purified
from filth. Admit her into the Garden. Amen."
"Don't think of them as dead; but nay they are alive."

The End

ABOUT THE AUTHOR

Wajeedah Mohammad, the mother of four, is a Muslim. She was born in Hemingway South Carolina, raised in Newark New Jersey, and is currently residing in Allentown Pennsylvania. Ms. Mohammad is a student of the Institute of Children's Literature, she has written the play "Uncertainties Of Life", and several poetic short stories. One of them, "The Captain Of The Ship", is dedicated to Imam W. D.Mohammed.

Being a Muslim woman, Ms. Mohammad was taught that women should reverence the womb that bore you. Her beloved late leader and teacher Imam, W.D. Mohammed had high regard and respect for women. He said, "Her role is significant, starting with her shaping and molding the society in the home, with the children."

Ms. Mohammad dreamt about her first novel, *Matriarch*, for many years. At age eighteen, before she became Muslim, she had always wanted for women, particularly African American women, to depict a picture in words, of who they are. First and foremost, she began with "A Lady" - a lady is someone with G'd consciousness, morals, and self respect. A lady trudges the path in her journey...but in a dignified manner, adhering to the role of a "Matriarch. "

Matriarch – A Journey to Purpose, is Wajeedah Mohammad's second novel.